STUFF

Poems and Prose by

Dave Gregory

Littlebit Press
Milford CT

Stuff
Copyright © 2018 by David Gregory

Other books by Dave Gregory:
On the Cellar Door, and all that Goes with Winter, Emerald Lake Books, 2015

Notice of Rights
All rights reserved. No part of this book may be reproduced, stored in a retrieval system or transmitted by any means, electronic, mechanical, photocopying, scanning, recording or otherwise, without permission, excepting brief quotes used in critical articles and reviews.

Disclaimer
This is a work of fiction. Names, characters, corporations, institutions, organizations, places and incidents are the products of the author's imagination or if real, are used fictitiously without any intent to describe their actual conduct. Any resemblance to actual events, locales, persons or groups, living or dead, is entirely coincidental.

ISBN - 13: 978-0-692- 17289-6

For information:
Littlebit Press
74 Point Beach Drive
Milford, CT 06460

nojokedlg@att.net

Dedication

To those who love to write
To those who have to read
To those I love

Table of Contents

Chapter 1
Nature..19

Is Your Garden Well Tended?..21
The Race..21
King... 22
March Winter Day...23
The Little Garden..24
The Last Bird's Song...26
Water to the Shore..27
Spring/Summer Day..28
It Is Summertime..29
A Day in the Clouds..30
In Praise of a Summer Day..32
Dandelion..33
Rain Dancers..34
Night of Whispers...34
Mist and Rain...36
Tears From the Sky...36
Tonight..37
Leaf on a Blossom...38
Clinging...39
 A String of Woven Threads..40
Struggle...40
Grumpy Day...41
Jackets and Sweaters..42
Invasion...43
Falling..45
Snow: Morning Arrival..46
Snow: Afternoon Arrival...46
Snow: Evening Arrival...47
As the Snow Melts..48

Chapter 2
Questions & Answers..51

If I were..53
Age...54

Twenty Shadows..54
It's About What We Become..56
The Time Will Come..57
The Robber - The Thief..58
To Watch A Child's Face..59
Two Drink Courage...60
Wren or a Sparrow...61
The Road Knows No Direction...62
Bruised Fruit..63
If I Were a Wonder...66
I've Been To..67
Infomercial 1..68
Ice Cream..69
All Saints Day..72
Babble...74
I Am Older Than the Super Bowl..76
My Son is the Sun..77
Why Do I Sit in the Balcony at Church?..78
Little Girl Walk...79
A Summer Dress...80
Old Dog...82
A Story for Henrietta..83

CHAPTER 3
Poitics - Patriots - Parades..87

Lawn Signs..89
"I Promise"..90
It's all red, white and blue..91
"The Pledge"..92
July 4, 2016...94
The Politician..96
Am I Free?...98
Stripes and Stars and Bunting..101
When Johnny Came Home...103
Politics...106
Johnny, Billy & Muffy Too...108
Politics Jingle...110

CHAPTER 4
Silly Stuff...113

Eggs......115
Doodle Dumb......116
I Should Be Eating Salad......116
RING......117
Oh, Dear Mr. Gardener......118
Padoodle......119
Wiggle Witch......121
I'm Your Fish......122
Rhyming Story – I......123
Composer......125
"Drip, Drip"......126
A (Abner) Meets B (Bob)......127
Mesquite, Mosquito......130
Would You Help?......131
Choices......132
You Are My Creation 1......133
You Are My Creation 2......133
A Day of Celebration......135
Jack......136
Sillies......138
What's in That Drawer......140
Birdfeeder......141
Dust......142
Who invented......143
My Sister......144
I Tasted Yogurt and I Didn't Die......145
A Gerbuttal Fish......146
Flipity, Flopity, Gizmo Delight......147
Whatever Comes Out......148

Chapter 5
People - Stories - Things......153

My World......155
Deep Night......159
Oliver......162
Morning......164
Mrs. Madison was Too Busy to Die......165
Time with Ann and Al Malt (z)......169
Just Before Bed......174
Picasso Lady......175
Raindrop - 2......176
The Race......177

The Point..179
Lonely Rd..185
Sit Down...186
Mrs. Diana Savannah at Planter's Tavern.......................................188
Disconnected..189
When I See..192
Whistlin Willie..195
The Man and His Land..200
The Couple at DQ...201
Wrinkles...203
Diner...211
Cemetary...216
Country Song (Beans, Corn & Alfalfa)..218
The Field..220
Everybody Wants a Laugh..221
Agnes the Angry Raindrop...225

Chapter 6
A Town and Its People..229

Lt. Page..231
First Friend...233
Now When I was a Boy...234
Booths..236
Or Is that the Whiskey Talking...238
Thunderbolt...240
Are We There Yet..242
Mr. Crawford...243
Sammy B...245
City Sounds..246
Rufus..247
The Early Bird Special...253
Billy Buster Bean...256
The Party..257
Joe Pepe...259
Whisper at the Window..262
Joe...264
T.T...267
Noah...270
The Last Train...272
Billy's Place..274
William's Window..279
Bill..279

Frank	281
I Was There at the Beginning	283
Click-a-Mile	284
In the car heading somewhere	284
Nelly	285
3:30 PM	286
Ring-a-leave-e-o	289
Nellie's Kitchen	290
Miss Emma Flag	299
I Step Away and Around and Move on	300

Chapter 7
Other Stuff 303

This Silence Is So Loud	305
Long Night	306
Driving	309
Quiet, Laughing You	309
Travelin' To the Cape	310
Church Bells	311
Winter's End	312
My Song	313
Whiskers	315
Rose it up!	316
Water and Me	317
Willows and Wishes	318
"Kite"	319
I Lost My Hat	320
He Left Her Seven Pounds	321
Apples	322
So I Said	323
Phineous and Benjamin	324
The Lady and the Moon	327
Gas Station Rose	328
Davy Crockett	329
Pedestrian Travel	332
70's Scraps	333
Squares	333
7/26/11	334
When I See You	335
Dewdrop, Raindrop – Little Tear Instead	335
You Are My Friend	336
Quiet Time of Night	338

First Steps..339
Tarnished..340
The Last Seat in the Last Car of the Train..342
The Night...343
The Shortest Day..344
Confusion Time..345
They All Tumble Out...346
"Snap — Snap"..348
Pets...348
The Light...350
Dreamin' Road...353
Rust and Residue..354
Your Eyes Open..356
This Page Is Empty..357
A Night Out..360

About the Author..363

Introduction

Stuff is just that, a whole bunch of stuff: poems, prose poems, and stories that came from my head and found their way to paper. I write to clear my head and make room for more stuff. I don't like to let things fester up there, so as soon as I have it straight, out it comes. I write to express my thoughts and ideas, to vent my anger and frustration, or just to have fun. It is a joy to write, to express my opinion, create a character, tell a story, reminisce, or just be silly.

I started writing in high school; little of that survived. I continued writing in college and needed someone to read it, so I felt the cycle was completed. I picked a classmate who encouraged my writing. She married an upperclassman who got a job with the William Morris Agency and my work vanished. I once traced her down to her roots on Long Island, but my creations had fallen to the wayside with no apologies.

After college, I continued writing and at one point had a wonderful routine. I journaled trips across the country and life moved on. I married and had a family, which seriously cramped my writing time. Still, it was all that was important in life and a wonderful trade off.

Now the kids are grown and I'm climbing life's ladder. I have the time and write often. I bring it to the Sterling House Writers' Group and before that the Milford Writers' Group. From these groups came encouragement, gentle criticism, and grammar aid flowed. Add to that the patience and kind words of a few friends and my cycle is again complete.

So thanks, in no particular order: Beth, Rich, Rosanne, Derek, Sandy, Pamela, Jack and many others.

Thanks also to Martha Reingold (Editing) and Joe Keeney (JK Indie Publishing) for helping to put it all together.

Stuff has come out of notebooks and journals where they have been sleeping for a few days, a few years, or more than that. Thank you for your time.
Dave Gregory

NATURE
Chapter 1

What would-be poet cannot tell tales of petunias; walks in the moonlight, and their wilderness?

Is Your Garden Well Tended?

Is your garden well tended?
Through the years has it been
Raked, weeded, tilled, and fertilized
Have you been satisfied at day's end?

The seeds that you've planted,
How well did they grow?
Have you reaped the enjoyment
And harvested the glow?

Do you allow visitors
Into your loving vines and blossoms,
Letting them enjoy nature's wonders,
Even seeing them out of control

Plunging deep in spring's frostless terrain
Withdrawing from summer's heat
Then digging down once more
Before the oncoming winter hardening

Sing to the colorful flowers
The bulb's emergence extraordinaire
The annual celebration of perennials
And the gentle smile on your face –

(6/29/09)

The Race

The race is on with crocus to daffodil,
Tulip to rose – we've rounded the
First turn – forsythia to azalea – here
Come the rhododendrons. Perennials now
→

Washed over by some annuals – vines
And weeds climb hand in hand.
Where, oh where has the magnolia gone?
Left in a heap on your front lawn.
Dandelion and buttercup – shooting stars,
Bethlehem stars, bleeding heart, blue bells and God.
Don't forget the herbs and vegetables
Bringing up the rear. Clusters and mounds –
Peat moss, fertilizer and mulches in great
Confusion. Each spirit lifted as we root
For our favorite – Grandma's geranium,
Hollyhocks, hydrangea, hyacinth and hibiscus.
Petunias, marigolds, salvia and ageratum
Start to fluff in the backstretch –
Racing for the light, soaking up the moisture.
Wild flowers, tamed and broken – regulars
Crossbred to become thoroughbreds –
Resisting all that God and man can throw
At them. Lilies, lily of the valley give
Way to day lilies – daisies rise up and
Pansies hold their own – the race continues
With color, with awe and excitement
With green thumbs and none 'til
Mums and such bring it to conclusion.

(6/4/05)

King

I'm king of the grass
You bet your ass.
My roots go deep
With a bright yellow smile
Still, I'm persona non grata

See the garden soldier
Hunting with trowel and sprayer.

But bad penny that I am,
I'll come back to visit

From your neighbor's land
Take my leaves for salad or for wine
That's OK I'll be fine

When my smile fades
Watch the little hand reach down
Break my stem and raise me to their lips

Child blows gently, watch me fly
Drifting on a breeze
Settling down in this yard
And of course on the next

I'm king of the grass
You bet your ass!

(5/3/10)

March Winter Day

Crumbling skies. God's dandruff
covers my world.
I am confined, stuck inside
the clock's pendulum insults me.
Outside, the window is frozen,
a pathetic imitation of Currier and Ives.
All that could be or was beautiful
seems tainted by shovel, plow and calendar date.
Instead of the promise of flowers,
muddied roadside creations reside.
The heat and the lights chug on from
morning to night. →

Wind carries on a monologue
as it rearranges the scene.
Some of the curtains move gently
from either the rising warmth
or the invading cold.
Without the child's anticipation
of no school and frozen construction,
there is little merit to this day.
It is full of "maybe I could have..."
"But in this weather, I certainly can't..."
Ambition seems to flag
as fast as the daylight disappears.
and now I must wait again
for the white to slide away
and, please God, the colors to begin.

(3/2/09)

The Little Garden

Slowly the sky slipped out of black.
The stars twinkled good-bye.
With great care,
The world arranged itself for a new day.
A fanfare of color introduced the sun
And carefully the sunrays spread,
Lifting heads out of pillows,
Sending things into motion,
Starting a new day of repetition or discovery.
In one hidden corner, just out of sight,
Hidden by fences and trees and time,
The Little Garden felt the first light.
The leaves shook off the dewdrops
And the residents yawned into smiles.
Flower blossoms stretched to the sky
Opened their petals to life all around.
Daffodils were trumpets, heralds if you will.
The wind, no just a breeze,

Stuff

Gently shook sleepyheads onto the ground.
Green grass soldiers stood tall, ready to march.
Bees hit the time clock
And butterflies fluttered in.
After the worms and the birds had played hide-n-seek,
When all the plants set to work
Stretching and growing and facing the sun
Out come the residents of the little garden:
Elves, gnomes, fairies and the like.
They are happy and laughing and all full of life.
For breakfast they suck on a honeysuckle blossom;
They drink a leftover raindrop
And hold buttercups under their chins.
Some grab their magic bags and head out to work.
Others talk to caterpillars and ladybugs.
The ones with authority talk to the weeds.
They explain that they must go
And send them around the corner to when
This world, kept so busy, has only one or two friends;
Dick and Jane, Jack and Jill, it's all the same
They bring water, day and evening and sprinkle it about.
These blossom buddies, for at least an hour,
Keep their secrets, especially this secret place.
Then off they skip to tea or dolls or trucks.
Back in the garden, orders are given.
Some were sent to pick roses.
They are arranged in a bunch
And handed from lover to love
Hearts beating quickly, life carries on.
Some daisies are gathered and brought to a door,
From there into water and set on a small table.
Then they face toward the bed.
The person full of aches and then pains,
Opens her eyes and behold… she feels better.
Finally, there is a big gathering of all the little flowers
Banding together and slipping into a white paper doily.
They're carried onto a sagging porch with a broken door,
Knocking softly, waiting for an elderly stranger to appear
Knocking louder, worried they didn't hear.
There is mumbling and fumbling. "Who is there?"
Finally, it opens a crack and a tired blue eye peeks through.
The nosegay is held stiff-armed out to the door.→

An eyebrow lifts and the door is opened wider.
Here is the mystery; there are no words to be said.
The shaky hand accepts the flowers with a shaky smile
And the donors don't run in fear;
They just feel warm inside from head to toe.
Back in the garden, the songs of nature continue.
The leaves in the trees clatter about.
Things sing and buzz and chirp all around.
Finally a cloud turns gray,
Or the sun starts to bow to the horizon.
Those that have left the garden return.
The growing is stopped; flowers close up shop.
To bed with elves, gnomes, fairies, and all the rest.
The night walks on to take control.
The moon rises and grows bright in all its phases.
Stars are arranged just so,
And all is quiet,
Ready for the next day
In the little garden.

(9/10/16)

The Last Bird's Song

The last bird's song
Comes with the sun gone,
But the sky is still light.
What declaration is made?
A scolding parent,
A braggart, a sage,
The tune of a full belly?
Is there a conversation?
A connecting communication
Or just some sort of noise?

(5/23/08)

Water to the Shore

Waves wash the shore
Move the sand in
Pull it back again
Hit the rocks once more
Patiently smooth them
Gently move up the beach.
Deposit your bounty
At the high tide line,
Give up your treasures
And then draw them back.
Tear mercilessly at walls,
Sand walled constructions.
Fill the castle moats
Then flood the castle
Then destroy the castle.
Swallow children's footsteps
And those of strolling lovers
Or determined and dedicated joggers.

Lift with the wind and tide.
Lay bare your foamy smile,
Rise higher and higher
As you move closer and closer
Then smash forward
Past your normal edge.
Collide with everything still,
Push at it, and then pull at it
Loosen it and destroy it
Vent your anger and show your rage,
Pound what's there.
Find the easiest passage
And dig in deeper.

Then, with the wind shift,
With your total exhaustion,
Run away to another shore.
Bring back your innocence,
Your gentle lapping, in and out, →

Reveal and cover once more.
Resume the restful monotony.
Steal a new shade from the sky.
Welcome once again the rivers,
Take in their contributions,
Protect your lodgers,
And tolerate those who would disturb you
With splash or hull.
Come back, go back...
Move in, move out...
Move in, move out.

(11/22/12)

Spring/Summer Day

Summer has come to play this late spring day.
Everywhere people are engaged.
A few lawns are being cut and watered.
Some weeds have met their doom,
But mostly people are soaking it all in
From umbrella covered chairs in the backyard,
To bodies giving the rays a destination on the beach.
Sailboats are running parallel to the shore.
Everything about the day is bright.
The new leaves do their best to shade,
Birds have their young ones in school
And time seems to have an aimless drift.
Summer rhythms and pretty soon the barbeques,
But there is no loud laughter by the pools.
The water is warming but still awakening
Yellow is moving west the clouds have the day off.
I'm hoping for a gentle night.

(5/30/15)

It Is Summertime

With windows open to catch faint breezes,
Complaints of heat, too little, too much,
Complaints of rain, too little, too much,
The sky a hazy blue or
Crowded with clouds bumping and crashing.
And the sounds; the sounds
Guided by a summer metronome of flip-flops.
From children's hysterical screaming
As they cannonball into the pool,
Or twist and turn into a pounding wave.
To the backyard, back fence conversations
Spreading news; some true, some gossip.
Ades and brews warm
As burgers and dogs cool.
Parties and picnics crammed
Into a few holiday weekends,
Vacations to where we've never been,
Or more likely where we've been before.
The trains are deeper in the night,
The planes louder by the shore.
Exciting spring colors have faded
To steady, less spectacular fare,
Fireworks and freedom celebrations.
It seems a frantic pace; uncertain.
Uncertain, that if we don't get our fill,
Maybe we never will.
Perhaps it's still a time for romance
Some to last 'til fall;
Some to last forever.
The ogling, check it out.
The late-night wrestling match
In the back of someone's parents' car.
Does that still go on?
A new love that can carry
A conversation through the night
On the porch or the deck
To watch the sun slip away.
Pull the weeds, cut the grass
Trim and prune and edge. →

Some watch from the window
To see the grass grow.
Is it high enough so I can cut it again?
The nights we sit quietly
And watch the birds settle in
Waiting, waiting as the sky darkens.
Our voices soften so as not to disturb
The twilight, the neighbors, the on coming darkness
To see the chase of the fire flies,
To swat the occasional bug;
Where you didn't spray.
There they are. One…make a wish…
Two, three, more, more, so many more.
And look over there. See it?
That lazy old moon peeking
Over the horizon, the neighbors roof?
Climbing sometimes orange to white
In all its phases reflecting on the water
Causing nighttime shadows and delight.
A voice from inside the neighbors' house;
 Maybe it's the television,
They've given up on the day.
Perhaps it's time to go inside
And leave the rest of it for the critters.
Good night.

(7/13/09)

A Day in the Clouds

There was a time when I was young
That I spent a day in the clouds,
Or at least it seemed that way,
It wasn't what I set out to do.

But it was summer; my chores were done
And nobody could come out and play.
It was a warm day full of noises.
I took the dog across the street
And into the wide open field there.

Stuff

Somehow I decided the dog should fetch.
With a little apple tree branch, lessons began.
The wonder dog learned in no time at all.
Over and over again the stick and the dog flew;
Flying through the air the wood went
And, with feet almost not touching the ground,
My mongrel followed and returned smiling.
This continued till my arm tired
And I sort of dropped to the ground,
Joined by a very happy, sloppy, kissing dog.

I rolled on my back to watch the clouded sky
Blue with puffs all across it.
Mother Nature must have taken one of my mom's *Kools*.
My still panting friend and I settled in.

Just at the edge of my hearing
I could make out the noise from the beach
Happy summer gibberish and boat motors.
In the other direction, a train passed through town,
But my eyes drifted upward to that crowded sky.

Somehow I felt the Earth spinning.
The clouds stretched in the sun
Moving on a blue tablecloth.
With a furry head on my stomach,
I spotted the camel and the elephant,
Easy finds no guess work involved.
Faces with eyes, elongated chins
Angry frowns would then wash away.
A caravan moving by… maybe a wagon train…
I saw the horse, and maybe that was an Indian,

But they were moving east not west.
Parade, carousel, dragons, monsters, time slipped past.
Time told in vague hours finally dawned;
It was time for man and beast to rise up.
A quick brush of whatever stuck
And a playful run back across the street
To the more civilized grasses of home.

(4/18/15)

In Praise of a Summer Day

Summer seems to have the advantage.
Winter has Christmas —
Autumn has turning leaves —
Spring the beginning of flowers.

But summer has so much more.
It is the time when school is out,
When many families plan their vacations,
And for all its energy, things seem to slow down.

Perhaps a stretch of too hot —
A night of thunder and lightning.
Beware the sunset mosquitoes
And traveling on a summer escape highway.

Walking a trail with good old dappled sunlight,
Floating in the water, complete independence…
The only decision to be made in a day…
Do you want your burger rare, medium or well done?

Picnics with or without cranky relatives,
Ice cream trucks, sailboats and summer camp…
The sun up late, beach days, the mountains,
"Happy Birthday America" celebrations.

Band concerts and streetlamp romances,
Neighborhoods alive and talking and laughing,
Trees in full leaf. And grandma's geraniums,
Lawn cutting, house painting, dandelion murders …

It is a world full of noise all around you
Or noises barely heard in the depth of darkness —
A child laughing on a swing, down a slide —
The admiration of what summer uncovers.

Nights full of moons and stars and blinking lights,
Where you can sit in your yard
Or on the beach, next to the campfire,
And enjoy your family, your life, and your love.
Finally, putting out the fire, turning the lights out,

Closing the door, leaving the dishes for morning,
Tucking little things in before you are all tuckered out...
Giving the night to lightning bugs and unblinking eyes.

(7/20/14)

Dandelion

Dandelionus Weedamoungus Misunderstoodinus.
Much maligned, my dandelion.
How many weeds turn to salads,
To wine, my fine young dandelion?
What harm, but to add color to the green —
Are we so hostile to a buttercup?
What makes green right and yellow,
Enough to drive my neighbor mad?
Could we have been brainwashed
By the likes of Scott and Ortho?
Come kill the little dandelion.
With spring, out come the spreaders —
Poison and pull at this plant.
Deep rooted we hack with trowel and hoe.
Or do we own a specialized tool,
A dandelion designate.
Whichever way we go, we've forgotten
The child... your child... you a while ago
Who pulls a past-bloomed stem
And blows the white fluffies to the wind.
Dandelion, "Tooth of the Lion,"
Your yard won't be free
If the wind is blowing right
And there's still a child in me.

(12/31/07)

*Previously published in "High Tide – 2008" Annual Poetry Publication

Rain Dancers

The rain dancers came.
A gusty wind brought them from the wings.
They performed upon the window —
Surging ingénues auditioning for the lead,
Pushing one another aside
"See me!" "No, see Me!"
Their music was their feet upon the glass
They moved across the pane
Pushing against the residue
And moving down in a quick step
Only to appear at the top once more…
Or maybe it was just more gypsies.
Finally, the choreographer changed the tempo.
Everything slowed and only the best called back.
Then the spotlight was turned on
To feature some fancy footwork
And then they all exited the stage
To thunderous applause.

(9/29/13)

Night of Whispers

Long after sunset, after twilight, I ventured out.
Carefully I stepped out on the deck and surveyed the night.
Grown restless of all I was doing and that had to be done,
I slipped into my chair with glass in hand.
My day's worries had been absorbed into ice
And mixed with surrounding liquids, thus becoming unimportant.

Settling in, I realized the quiet and calm —
No breeze, no zephyr pushed at the nearby chimes.
Neighbors had climbed back into their cubbies.
I could see a flicker of TV glare escaping the edges of shade-drawn windows

Stuff

And heat had also disappeared —
It had to be hiding with no wind to push it away. —
On the other side of the fence, — the next block.
Don't care, it's all gone and I'm not chasing it.

I maneuvered away from my neighbor's security light pollution
And focused low on my solar color changing lights.
Reds, greens, blues, even purples randomly rolled over.
That's when I heard the night's noise…
A thin chorus of crickets reached me through the darkness.
I raised my eyes toward the heavens, — how timeless —
No expert, — every constellation looks like some kind of dipper.
The problem was that the sky provided no lines to connect the stars.
There was nothing threatening about this night;
It was one that I felt could only hold whispers —
Two lovers, shoulder to shoulder, lazily pointing to this or that,
Turning and kissing, then returning to stare upwards.
A plane blinks across the sky, high enough to be silent,
Heading to vacationland or homeland.
Cool, late summer night, hinting of autumn
Whispers of the past, walks in long past neighborhoods,
Alone now with people ending their day.
A light goes out.

A noisy car rips the night in half;
It idles loudly until a stolen kiss is taken.
The car roars away and my neighbor's daughter enters her house —
A lingering pause — and the porch light goes out.
Another car's headlights brighten the street.
It floats into a nearby driveway and it's dark again.
The car door slams and then the house door.
Lights go on and off making their way to the second floor.

Now the night whispers that everyone is safe.
I look at my glass and everything inside is gone.
My back is tired, my head is empty, and one last look around
Then inside, and trail my lights to bed.

(9/18/15)

Mist and Rain

Mist and rain, mist and rain
Gray sky, the sun done
Wind coming down the street
Wind coming on to shore
Pushing closed the door
Warm weather is no more.
The cry of colors dying
Letting go and flying
All the beds and fields plowed under
Harvest done, all made secure
Doors and windows closed
Shut now for the longest time.
Frost on the gourd, sap headed down
Smiles to frowns, pretty much all around.
Worlds become smaller and quieter too.
No over the fence chitchat
Lawnmowers put away till spring
Shovels moved up into place.
Mist and rain, mist and rain —
Every year it's just about the same.

(10/3/15)

Tears From the Sky

A sadness of gray lets go
The tears from the sky
Falling in chaos upon us.
Bittersweet mourning
Draws the smells of the earth.

Hard driven anger,
Frustration smashing hard to the skin
Crowded with the noise of our silence,
Holding in all our despair
Echoing our tears —

Soaking our clothes
Pushed sideways with a wind.
Today has been lost
To the tears from the sky.
Fold in our shoulders —

Walk away from the mound.
It is only what's left —
That and the ricocheting sound.
Uncounted numbers gather below
Leaving lakes of reflection.

Still wait for your heart,
For the summer of your recovery,
When a leaf can catch a raindrop
Then unfold it on to your nose
And make you smile and love again.

(1/10/17)

Tonight

Tonight is warmer than tomorrow.
It is a still night, a windless night.
It is a quiet night — a black and white night
Full of an almost full moon's light.
On a night like this, the old man will be partially eclipsed.
I've looked at him, studied him, stared rudely.
His expression didn't change,
He gave me no clue.
I did ask questions, didn't I?
There were words wondering
Did I have to speak them aloud?
Or did these words ask for favors,
Was it a sort of prayer or bid for understanding?
The more I slip into it
It seems those were statements — declarations
Spread silently from my little porch
To the deep dark infinite starless sky. →

Then I paused and lowered my sight.
I retreated indoors and double locked the world outside.
I left the beauty outdoors
But double locked its memory
Deep in my heart.

(10/19/13)

Leaf on a Blossom

Leaf on a blossom, is autumn done?
Has the chill gone cold?
Are the frightening faces on Jack-o-lanterns sagging?
Colors have begun to drain.
The canvases are falling from the trees.
Hayrides and mazes have no more takers.
Soon candy-givers will be done,
Costumed candy-takers hobble home,
Tired, they sort their bounty —
A sugar high or two, and then
Getting ready for the transition.
Leaves raked, bundled, mulched or removed,
Yards are cleared and secured.
The last rose, a pretty pink,
Clashes with all the brown on the ground.
Cider and cinnamon donuts blend,
Cocoa becomes the warmer-upper.
Soups and layers with gloves and mittens
Complimented by sweaters and scarves.
Fireplace sitting replaces leaf-kicking walks.
Evergreens stand out, having come out of hiding.
Say good-bye to the neighbors as you climb inside.
Put up the storms and wash the shutters —
Almost time to sleep an hour later.
Transition quickly to Pilgrims and then Claus.
Put on that extra blanket —

Almost time to start the rush,
Thank the Indians once more.
Ham or turkey, what time, who goes where?
And what can I do to help?

(10/25/16)

Clinging

As I drove my everyday road,
I saw yellow leaves clinging,
Rookie skydivers afraid to yell "Geronimo."
I think of a boat upset,
Its untrained master clinging to the rail
While gray and wicked waters pull —
Acting as a primeval Siren's call.
There is the optimist clinging to hope,
The politicians and politicos to their beliefs,
The immigrant to his traditions,
The old man to his memories —
The Santa and Easter Bunny —
Clinging to the glass.
How about the dryer sheet
To the sleeve of a now clean sweater,
Or the hand of a three year old
To the edges of her mother's skirt,
Clinging to life till the leaf lets go?

(12/19/13)
* 2nd Place winner in 2014 CAPA (Connecticut Authors and Publishers Association) Writer's Contest.

A String of Woven Threads

A string of woven threads
Ties a wondering heart.
The sun smiles and lifts our beings.
Moonlight stark winter white
Or slumbering summer soft
Invites us to embrace.
We wander the shaded trail
Hand in hand with no destination –
Searching for a path in the snow
Staggering arm in arm for warmth.
A campfire or fireplace concoction
Has us together young and old
Telling stories to the flames
Releasing our pent up heat.
The satisfied smile of having each other
Worried glances to check if things are right.
Night coming to morning from either end
Life pushing and pulling smoothes the stones
By the seashore or in the mountains
And a child picks up the stone
And puts it in his pail.

(11/29/14)

Struggle

The grass has stopped growing
Most of the green has gone to brown
Leaves have changed from green to color
And they too cycle through to brown.
Temperatures flip-flop up and down
But each up is lower
And each down is lower.
The daylight is shorter.
People start looking toward the ground
But not at what's around.

Stuff

On a cloudy and rainy day
All we do is black – gray – black.
Shoulders bend and aches happen
Smiles become corrupted
Heavy hearts, blues, depression
Come down the street and turn the corner
They howl and fly from house to house
A Tarzan wind scraping all that's loose
Pushing it up into unnatural flight
Until the rain makes it too heavy to rise
Flopping for cover – caught by a bush
Or smashing into a curb or foundation.
The sun that never shone has set
And little peeks of light start to appear.
A perception of warmth has begun to take over.
Families gather, they talk, they argue, they laugh
Devices are turned on and things become – cozy
Fed, studied, entertained, disciplined, loved inside.
Outside the storm rips at siding and tears at shutters
Trying to pull shingles, a child's tantrum
Throwing garbage cans into the neighbor's yard
Pounding its tears against the windows
Finally too tired to fight anymore
It moves to a different neighborhood,
And the sky rips open showing its stars
Through drawn shades, the lights flicker out
Smiles return with bedtime stories
Tired and weary grown-ups pucker up
Then roll over all tuckered out.

(11/26/13)

Grumpy Day

Everything I saw outside was gray.
The sky was gray.
The water reflected that gray
With only smiling teeth of white,
Even the horizon was gray. →

And as I watched
A fog slithered in and pushed the gray closer.
It was a grumpy day,
A no-good-make people-frown day.
Birds were late at the feeder
Yet there were no cats or hawk in sight.
Maybe they overslept. Whatever.
There was no color among them
All browns and variations.
Color must have flown to another neighborhood.
It was a tightening day.
There was no spirit to be found
Go to work or run around
A bills-in-the-mailbox kind of day.
No miracles happened, no great breakthrough
The day was to be endured
Time was to dawdle along, drag its feet
Yank us early into night
Right there in the middle of the afternoon
Nothing to do but wait.
Great, wait for the gray to go to black.
Finally time to move upstairs
And search for the restful darkness.
It has been a grumpy day
And it has made me grumpy with it.

(11/15/14)

Jackets and Sweaters

This time of year
There is confusion and conclusion.
Summer colors clash with autumn.
The sun still warms us
But the nights forecast
Jackets and sweaters.

Impatiens still shine
Waiting for the frost

Stuff

Trees turn their somber rainbow
And mums cluster our doorways.
We venture out and turn back for
Jackets and sweaters.

Even the aggressive mowers
Must wait an extra day or two.
Soon they will become the mad rakers
Bagging and mulching their catch
Then standing guard in
Jackets and sweaters.

Our gardens are harvested.
All that remains is a tangle
Vines sinking to the ground
A few tomatoes green and cracking.
We plant our spring bulbs in
Jackets and sweaters.

The world turns orange and golden.
As we head towards white and gray
Nights lengthen as we secure our world
We cover and take apart the summer
And pull tight the collars of our
Jackets and sweaters.

(10/8/06)

Invasion

Into the wind they jumped.
As soon as their chutes opened
They were pushed off course.
The main invasion had begun
Crashing to the earth. somersaulting to a stop
Only to be pushed across the field
Before they could secure their equipment,
Uniforms of yellow, orange or crumpled brown.
Gamely they charged with no enemy in sight→

Diving for shelter, zigzagging always forward.
The first wave reached the closest enemy line
Some were pushed off and skimmed the edges
Others were captured by dying green troops
Veterans along the edges grabbing from their beds
Reaching for blankets and covers
Curling back to the earth as winter approached.
The heavier out of shape invaders still manage to hold on.
Others, faster, overrun the battle
And move on to the next expanse.
The sky is full as waves of reinforcements descend.
They too meet the same fate.
The place is littered, colored by their lives fading.
Eventually there will be a cease-fire.
Then the orderlies and custodians will take the field.
In years past the dead would be cremated
With their aroma giving meaning to the season.
Now they are gathered or blown into mounds
Then lifted on to crude stretchers or ambulances.
Most are carried away, their life history.
The war will drag on for weeks,
There will be no negotiations,
Eventually the fighting will end.
The homeland will claim an uncertain victory
Yet the enemy survives and watches
Watches from above, never letting go
Almost silent, they wait for new recruits.
Volunteers will arrive in the spring
And will spend the summer training
Growing strong, anxious to do battle
And so it will go on and on
History indeed repeats itself.

(10/12/13)

Falling

```
F    f    f           Snowflakes
  a    a    a            Bouncing on the wind
    l    l    l          A child's delight
    l    l    l
      i    i    i
        n    n    n
          g    g    g
```

```
Raindrops                    F    f    f
Sliding down a window pane     a    a    a
Staining a grown man's cheeks    l    l    l
                                 l    l    l
                                   i    i    i
                                     n    n    n
                                       g    g    g
```

```
F    f    f           Autumn leaves
  a    a    a            Natures colorful confetti
    l    l    l          Harvesting, concluding, preparing
    l    l    l
      i    i    i
        n    n    n
          g    g    g
```

```
In Love                       F    f    f
Giving, Celebrating, Discovery   a    a    a
Committing Ourselves               l    l    l
                                   l    l    l
Falling                              i    i    i
 Falling                               n    n    n
  Falling                                g    g    g
```

(3/1/09)

Snow: Morning Arrival

One morning it is there
A pristine sheet of beauty
Catching light from the sunrise
Causing joyous shouts from behind closed doors
Mixed with moans and groans.
Trees are one of the collectors
Fashioning themselves for festive praise
Or leafless branches a winter's declaration.
Even windowsills gather it in corners
To make looking out as beautiful
As we see them looking in.
Breakfast appetites are lost
Cabinets are turned upside down looking for cocoa
Little footprints appear following an army of "waddlers."
Great plans are made for forts and their destruction
Trails of green grass appear behind rolling balls
Soon to be standing tall in stacks of two or three
Complete with a fairly standard wardrobe —
That would be hats, scarves, pipes, carrot noses
And of course smiles and buttons from coal or stone.
The snowball factory is in full operation
While sleds and saucers are dusted off and waxed.
This to a background of scraping, shoveling and plowing
To uncover the family car and the road it drives on
And no one feels the cold, because their hearts are too warm.

(11/30/14)

Snow: Afternoon Arrival

Grumbling children went off to school
There was nothing but a weatherman's promise to keep them home.
The workers are working, head and bodies bent.
Everyone else is doing what they do, no reason not to.
Finally, sometime after noon it begins
Little teeny-weeny flakes, over-grown raindrops.

Suddenly big puffy cotton balls bounce from the sky.
Cars driving by first make that wet sound
Then it is muffled and we hear all the rattles.
But school will end and work will end
And all the villagers will arrive home.
Impatience reigns and wild promises are made
Books are thrown into rooms and mittens are found
Snow shovels exit through the garage door
And one or two super-dooper snow blowers appear.
Wild and aimless play begins through several generations
A race to the wilderness of darkness.
Snow angels big and small are created on a hillside
Only to be creased by downward moving objects
Sleds barrel by, a dad-cushion to a young one
Or masters of the art, hurtling with reckless abandon.
Saucers and toboggans smooth things down
As they too move top to bottom and pile up at the end.
Most of the spilled passengers are up and climbing topside
With their vehicles trailing behind them —
A few battle tears with bumps and bruises
But not wanting to be alone they climb less enthusiastically behind.

(11/30/14)

Snow: Evening Arrival

It has been predicted or sneaks in the back door
Dropping from a deep black sky, its clouds unseen
Falling fast, falling slow, pushed by the wind —
A dance, a confetti-strewn parade with no heroes,
Hitting the ground and sometimes scooped up again
The wind rearranging its winter collage,
Dusting all the objects below then building —
Building in drifts or just layers, flake upon flake
With the deepening night it also quiets the world.
Little snowflakes fall through the streetlight's beam.
The scene can be gentle or wild,
Anywhere from seasonal wonderment to winter disaster. →

The temperature slides in a deeper direction
And a sheen is set atop what's there.
Standing water pulls up its frozen covers.
What lights remain on, in all the houses
Seem duller, weaker and totally artificial.
A silly nightlight 'til first light appears.
Then the storm can stop and let the clouds pull away
Opening a curtain to reveal the winter sky,
A vast arrangement of twinkling lights
A holiday decoration available year round, on a clear night —
A night that could hold sleighs and singers
The beauty of the world and its residents
During this time of giving and caring and sharing God's gifts.

(11/30/14)

As the Snow Melts

As the snow melts,
The road is lined with frozen statuary,
Hardy survivors in changing shapes,
Slowly sinking into puddles,
Icebergs without an ocean.

As the snow melts,
It raises the curtain
On an interrupted spring.
The earliest flowers gather,
Each day their numbers increase,
While the ground softens to let them free.

As the snow melts,
Tentative neighbors emerge,
Chopping at a few remaining clusters
Or just lingering outside,
Relishing a new felt freedom
From winter's voluntary hibernation.

Stuff

As the snow melts,
Our plans for the yard and garden
Expand past any reasonable energy.
Everything is seen as lush green,
Or bearing a large harvest
Of fruit and color.

As the snow melts,
We see no crabgrass,
No dandelions or weeds,
No pests eat our crops,
No bugs or black and white friends
Drive us back inside.

As the snow melts,
We are full of life
And projects that can be modified,
With new and renewed dreams
Growing each day with
A budding, heart-felt optimism.

(3/24/07)

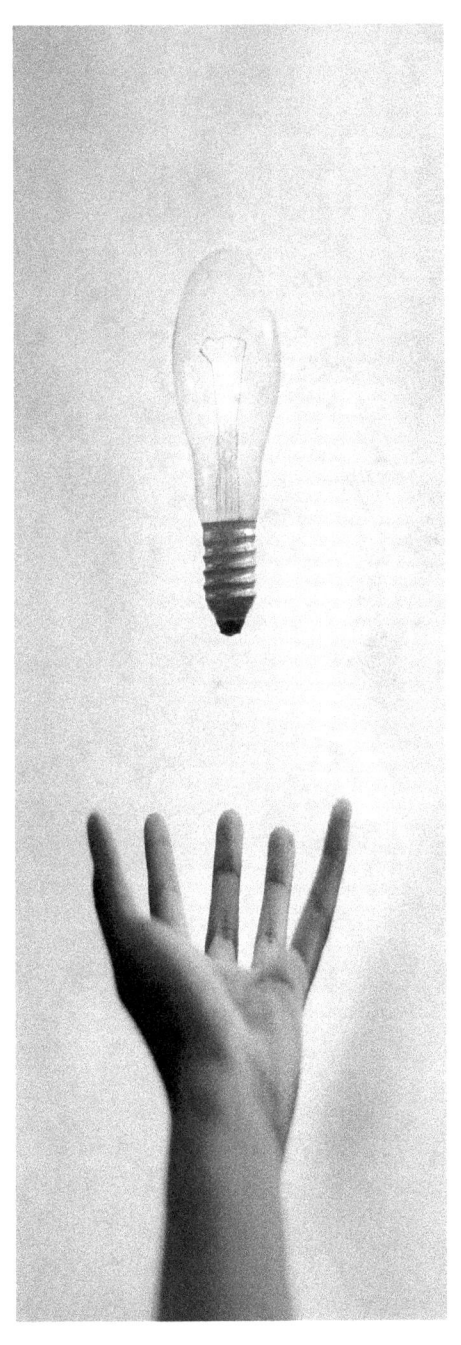

QUESTION AND OPINIONS

Chapter 2

This is a hodpodge chapter. Some of these works could go elsewhere but in the long run they seemed happy here.

Stuff

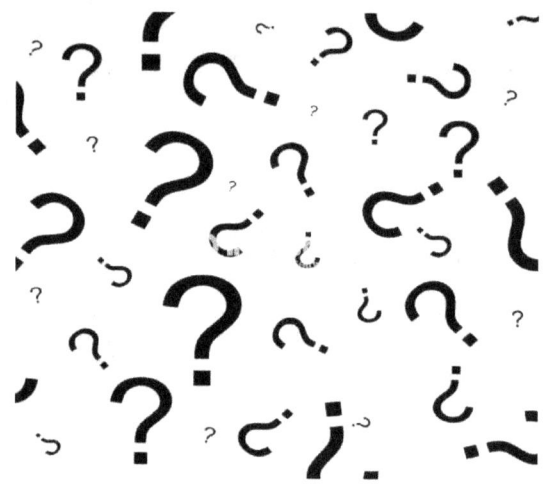

If I were

If I were a pineapple
Maybe I'd like this heat.
If I were a snowman
Maybe I'd like this cold.
If I were this and that
Maybe I'd like that and this.
If I were brown eyed
Maybe I'd like to be blue.
If I were purple
Maybe I'd like to be green.
If I were young
Maybe I'd like to be older.
If I were old
Maybe I'd like to be young – again.
If I were a soldier
Maybe I'd like peace.
If I were standing in the rain
Maybe I'd like an umbrella.
If I were in love
Maybe I'd like to be with you always.
If I were lost
Maybe I'd like to be found.
If I were looking
Maybe I'd like to find.
If I were alone
Maybe I'd like your company.
If I were in a crowd
Maybe I'd like to hold your hand.
If I were late
Maybe it hasn't started.
If I were dizzy
Maybe it's because I'm near you.
If I were right
Maybe you were too.

(7/8/11)

Age

Age has rounded my shoulders and thinned my hair
But I still appreciate the tension on a button.
Age has not taught me the difference between
An open door and a pile of straw.
Age laces the day with lists and memories.
Thrift and uncertainty have become my companions.
Perspective becomes a sloppy fit.
Moments seem to have more value.
Kindness is either greatly appreciated or expected.
Age slips into the mirror every single day
But it's still easier to smile than to cry.

(2/8/09)

Twenty Shadows

In a dozen years a prayer will be said.
The graduating class will be smaller,
Smaller than last year's
Smaller than next year's.
Some of those walking, diploma in hand.
Will have missed some nurturing
The smiling foundation to their education.
Out the door the graduates fly
Off to college, off to work
A firm grip on their future
Or a continued search to life's journey.
But those twenty shadows
Will hang back undiscovered.
They were to be our veterans
In wars still to be fought,
They were bankers, investors
The next generation of schoolteachers
Mechanics, housewives, shop keepers
Fathers and mothers who would be
Raising their children soon.

Stuff

They would have been firemen,
Garbage men, nurses, doctors,
Presidents of the United States,
Those jobs they wanted at their age.
They might not be sure what
Mommy and daddy did
But still they loved them.
And those parents are left alone
Finally left alone for years
For their lives, arms empty.
The siblings might not understand
And nothing they can do
Will fill the space.
Fill the space of those empty arms
And children who might come later
Maybe asterisks to their family's life –
Those twenty shadows, forever innocents.
Now the world's grief is fresh
And their final resting will be disturbed,
Disturbed by the sobs of family
By the tears of most beings.
The media will cover the funerals.
The first team reporters will move on
Replaced by the second string,
Who will continue to report.
And our TV screens will be full –
Full of Teddy Bears and candles
Of black and all that attends.
Next year there will be a follow up.
And every year some will remember
Perhaps a pink rose or a "Hot Wheels"
Perched on the cold December granite.
But for most, another tragedy,
Something as horrific,
Or, God help us, something worse
Will tear at our hearts
And pull tears down our cheeks
Leaving us hopeless once more
Searching the why.
Twenty shadows always smiling
Always laughing, suddenly alone.

(12/15/12)

It's What We've Become

No matter how much we try,
If we try,
No longer the athlete,
If we had it
Beauty fading
Despite repairs and creams,
At some point we're equals.

Perhaps the clothes still differ
Some with symbols and animals,
Names that aren't yours.
Others are just flannel or wool
Or perhaps even synthetic.

Our gate eventually slows
For some are even hobbled.
Backs tend to bend.
The heat has to go higher.
Some of the things we knew
We just can't seem to remember.
Things that are new
Become complications and puzzlements.

Sadly friends thin out,
Our knowledge is still harvested.
But now from experience
Rather than from books –
We see our youth disappear.
Then we see our young grow
And must tolerate their maturity.

If we look forward
It is to days or events.
But the frame is shorter
Gray hair, less hair, attached hair
Its what we've become.

(2/10/09)

The Time Will Come

The time will come
When my eyes won't see
When my ears won't hear
When my nose won't smell
When my mouth won't speak.
Will I be dead or just growing older?
But when I was younger
There were days I was too busy to
See the beauty before me.
I didn't always listen to life,
The birds singing, the wind.
I've lost the smell of the earth
Of burning leaves, my wife's perfume.
Words, words are easy.
They tumble from my mouth.
They spread across these pages.
But often they're clever and have no heart.
The time will come
When everyday will become important.
I will see sunrises, sunsets and quiet nights.
I will hear great truths and man's folly.
I will smell the salt air, the skunk.
My words will have meaning
To speak of loves lost and loves won.
The time will come
When I will see an end without glasses
When I will hear a cry without my "aids"
When the smell will be fresh and alive
When what is said is right
And what I touch is real and everlasting.

(5/22/08)

The Robber – The Thief

The flood of fear is held in check by such fragile gates.
A sudden pain – an unknown feeling –
Freezes the mind from reality.
A single thought – breaks down the walls –
And numbs the heart.

Where is the robber – the thief?
Is he back again?

An event, an occasion – something we've looked forward to –
Is reached with relief – there is no great joy.
It's over with little satisfaction.
Just the "we got through it" resignation –
Focus forward to the next.

This robber – this thief –
Hides behind our mind.

The milestones are reached – by day – by night
Each little step to try and recover –
A task – a source of independence –
All with the time – the tender time –
The unexpected time passing.

The robber – the thief –
Lurks ahead of the check-ups.

Fun and laughter – come from the unexpected –
From the out of the ordinary – the spontaneous moment –
The silly little thing – the "What did he say?" thing –
The head cocked to the side smile –
The nod of understanding.

But this robber – this thief –
Crumbles our daily bread.

As partner and witness – I watch mountains climbed.
Each day is not a success – some are gray –

But pointed toward cards tonight -
Or vacation in the fall - she fights daily -
She works for life's sunrise.

We wait each day for the capture -
And execution of this robber - this - this thief.

(2003)

To Watch A Child's Face

To watch a child's face
Awake or asleep –
It is free of subtlety.
You see the peace,
The calculation,
The reaction, free from deceit,
The happiness
The confusion
The concentration
The trust, the grasping
The new wisdom and understanding
The lies, the love
The whole thought process.
When do they pick up the mask?

(12/9/08)

Two Drink Courage

What does it bring?
That second round
With company
A careless wit
Some sort of relaxation
Letting down the guard.

Watch the slurring tongue
Perhaps too many truths
Walking on a tightrope
Watching from outside in
That sip close to the end –

Without company
A warm inside
A ticket to travel –
Not much about now
Keeping the future away –
But the black bright past
Comes clamoring back.

It's happy times
Captured in an embrace
Snippets of words
Flashes of faces
Times, good times back –

The price to pay
Seeing again, all
Pain and suffering
The could have been
Foolishness and sadness.

Oh, what a narrow road
A winding trail
Through ice cubes
And sloshes of this and that

(4/5/09)

Wren or a Sparrow

I figure I'm a wren or a sparrow
Certainly not a cardinal or junco.
I confess, like many, to a little peacock.
And I'm more dove than hawk.
But basically, I'm a wren or a sparrow.

Now I'm proud of my eagle
And like to think a mischievous
Jay or mockingbird is part of me.
Certainly not a dirty old pigeon.
No, just your basic wren or sparrow.

I smile at a strutting cockatoo
And question the wisdom of an owl.
I wonder at the grace
Of a gull on the wind
Or the anger of the swan and goose.

It's just me you see,
You're everyday wren or sparrow.
And if I have to choose,
I'll have to leave the wren behind
For God has his eye on the sparrow.

(9/29/08)

The Road Knows No Direction

The road knows no direction.
It tells you where you are.
It gives some orders and suggestions.
It is you who points and steers.

The roads lie – they say,
East, west, south and north
But their reality can be
All parts of the compass.

Some would say you couldn't be lost
If you have no destination.
Others would argue that
You are lost without a destination.

To that end, it is OK to wander
Yes, to stop and ask directions
Even to use a map
And a clearly marked line to follow.

Then too, you may stumble
Onto the right road
And join others on the highway
Or take a country road.

All the roads take you
From your beginnings
And bring you toward the end.
The scenery may vary.

The time it takes you
Is in your own heart
And it's up to you in the end
To reach, discover and be content.

(7/6/10)

Bruised Fruit

You come home from the store
And put away the groceries.
It is then that you may notice
The bruised fruit.

It's not always visible
No matter how close you look.
Perhaps it was harmed
By the environment it was raised in.

Then again as it matured
And was harvested
There's a chance
It was damaged then.

As it was packaged
And shipped to a different world.
It may have been bumped
Or mishandled more than once.

You might be able to return it
If you saved the receipt
And have the time.
But you may not be believed.

Maybe you ignored it
And left it on the counter too long.
In so many cases
There was no specific reason.

So what to do with bruised fruit?
Give up on it and throw it away,
Work at cutting out bad spots
And find varied uses.

Perhaps in an altered state
With love and understanding
It can be shaped and molded
Into a lovely centerpiece.

Something you're proud of
That others admire and praise.
It sometimes reflects upon you
That you are responsible for it.

And it turns out good.

(5/5/12)

How Do You Honor Them?

How do you honor them?
That old lady who gave you so much homework
So much that you remember today
What she taught you –
How to write, how to add, how to think?
How do you honor them?

They have you for a year
And then you move on,
That man who brought history alive
Or the woman who found fun in physics.
How do you honor them?

The one who got you through
The required stuff you might not use again
That extra push up, that short cut
That made some sense of it all.
How do you honor them?

Who look for ways to reach you
Who put up with all your excuses
And try to break through
That thick skull of yours?
How do you thank them?

Who take on a new batch each year
And try and find a way to teach you
To challenge and excite you
To make you stand higher than just getting by?
How do you honor them?

When they finally step aside.
A plaque, a dinner, maybe a scholarship?
And they step aside to their other life.
Oh yes, they have family and friends.
All these years they've balanced them
And perhaps short changed them a bit
So they could stay on top of things,
Look for a new way to help someone
Learn a new technique
Advance their education to then pass it on to others.
How do you honor them?

When you find they will take action
They will be the surrogate parent
And hide them and comfort them
And talk of Christmas and wishes
And lock doors and stand in front of them?
How do you honor them?

They have no uniforms, no badges,
When others come to grieve for them
There is no long blue line
There is no set formation
Taps is not played.

I have no answer, my schoolings done.
One of my children is one
I am a parent who is proud
Of her accomplishments
Of the fact that she struggles
Fights for a way to reach her students –
Not always the easiest way.
She challenges them and works with them
And is upset when the challenge is not accepted.
How do you honor them?
→

You work hard, as hard as you can for them
Because then you are working for yourself
And if you succeed,
You are their success.

(12/18/12)

If I Were a Wonder

If I were a wonder
I wonder what I would be?
Being something is to some
most important of all.
If I was something
how would it end?
Now, if being something
meant I was really someone,
would I tire of the acclaim?
So full of something
Busy letting others know
"I'm somebody, pooh, pooh."
You would all love me
because I am a Who's Who.
Still someone would see
I'm really full of *it*
and *it* is not the same.
It doesn't really matter,
What matters is me
Just being me.
I am what I am
I am what you see.

(9/18/12)

I've Been To

I've been to the Alamo, Bunker Hill and Gettysburg
But it was hundreds of years past doing any good.
I've been to Fort McHenry, Fort Sumter and Vicksburg
But only as an interested tourist.
I've put on a uniform and carried a flag
But I was a Boy Scout and a re-enactor.
I've read and heard words of freedom and independence
But I have seen hate, bigotry and segregation.
I've loved my country, my family and my fellow man
But I've seen death for all the wrong reasons.
I've prayed for love, peace and the souls of the departed
But I've seen people who see no future.
I've treasured my little life and its grand moments
But I've shed tears for loved ones taken.
I've watched the moon and nature all around me
But I've seen too many who do not care.
I've seen great men and women working for a better world
But often their voices are thin and lonely.
I've cheered for my teams and my children
But in daylight they don't always win.
I've climbed the many steps of life
But now I hold the railing and watch where I go.
I've had friends and family I'm proud of
But age pares down my address book.

I've lived in the present and looked to the future
But I wallow in my man-made wonderful past.
I've fears and reservations about what's to come
But let me nap awhile and smile in my dreams.

(11/16/16)

Infomercial 1

A restless night and already I've made
Thousands of dollars with tighter abs.
My rugs are clean, my make-up perfect
All sold to me by a blonde, a brunette
Dressed in clothes a half size too small.

Music from my past, kitchen gadgetry,
Who needs the FDA, just three clicks away
To health and wealth and greater potency
All sold to me by a blonde, a brunette
Dressed in clothes a half size too small.

It's all there waiting for me at 3AM.
Doctors and millionaires, they all swear
This is it; call in the next few minutes.
Will I talk to the blond, or the brunette
Dressed in clothes a half size too small.

No work, no strain, no interruption
Just send your money, grasp a straw.
Now they lean toward me, how sincere
This pair, this blond, this brunette
Dressed in clothes a half size too small.

(11/17/07)

Ice Cream

Some people say in this world
We get our just desserts.
In my world of desserts,
Ice cream is number one
Pie is pleasant once in awhile
And the earth should be covered with chocolate.
I grew up with a vintage 1936 refrigerator.
It had a miniature freezer above the top shelf.
Well that was fine, nobody ever heard of frozen food.
That freezer compartment would contain two things;
Ice cube trays and a pint of *Old Hundred* ice cream.
Still for some years, when I was a kid,
Those things would share space with aluminum Popsicle molds –
Mom would run a back door Popsicle business for the neighborhood kids.
Six cents with a penny back for the stick
Bought you treats made out of Royal Pudding or other sources.
I think the most popular was "orange ice," made from fresh oranges.
There was only one flavor a day and only so many a day.
She would raise money for her church pledge
And when that was reached she saved toward
Making enough money to take her boys to Savin Rock.
But I digress from my butterfat delights.
I know ice cream is not healthy for you
And the better the taste, well we won't go there.
We'll talk of a summer afternoon and a far off jingle
The Pavlov signal for every child in the neighborhood
To drop the bat, clear the bases and stop the mowing.
It was time to ask, plead, beg or throw a tantrum
For that money needed to stop the ice cream truck.
Would Mom say yes or would there be grumpiness all about?
Primarily we had a *Good Humor* man
Complete with white uniform and white truck.
That truck had those wonderful magical doors,
Each one storing our heart's desire behind it.
This man had the patience of Job
And a neat-o change dispenser on his belt
The envy of any dedicated newspaper boy. →

Studying the pictures, Toasted Almond
Regular Good Humor, maybe a cup or a Popsicle
Facing a gathering of sweaty, dust-covered faces
Ordering, changing their mind and grinning upon delivery.
But we grow and times change.
Howard Johnson's had their twenty-eight flavors.
Sometimes we have too many choices.
My go-to flavor is chocolate; wait, what's double chocolate?
I don't want brownie or cookie dough mixed in,
Maybe whipped cream and a cherry of course,
But only if it covers chocolate ice cream and hot fudge.
Banana splits or boats were always the most expensive item.
I don't or didn't need three scoops of anything.
But sometimes man must make sacrifices.
The basics: three scoops of ice cream
Sandwiched between two lengthwise slices of banana.
The three scoops were vanilla, chocolate & strawberry
Though various combinations of these three were permitted.
On top of the ice cream; chocolate sauce falling from on high
Sliced strawberries in their juices cascading downwards,
Then either pineapple or caramel (I can't remember which).
You could have a dip top cone, creating that wonderful crust
Top your cup or cone with chocolate shots.
In New England these are called *Jimmies,*
Or maybe you prefer multi-colored sprinkles.
I'm amazed at what some people have come up with for toppings
And being a purist (sort of) or stuck in my ways
I feel that old generation gap finding a new way to rear up.
Oh, and of course, if I go out to a fancy restaurant
 I've already put up with a waiter who is dressed better than me
A ten-inch plate with four inches of food on it.
And I'm paying big bucks for a little stack of mashed potatoes.
Peeking from that starch stack are six medallions of meat.
The meat has a name I've forgotten, but I guess I'm impressed
Over all of this is a tepee of three stalks of asparagus.
Obviously we have progressed in life from cook to chef.
I've gone through the wine ritual to my waiter's satisfaction.
Finally he asks, "Have we saved room for dessert?"
Hell, yes, and I may have to stop for a burger on the way home.
"We'll take a peek at the dessert menu."
I scan the list of delights with a sense of foreboding.
I've seen them all before and scan the details –
No cheesecake for me, no crème brulee

Stuff

Maybe an apple crisp if it comes a-la-mode.
I keep going through, no to red-velvet cake.
Most of these choices are too rich for me.
Wait, there it is way down on the bottom
In small letters and way overpriced
Plain old wonderful, comfort zone, little kid in me

ICE CREAM!

If you offer it with chocolate sauce please
Don't drizzle it, come on slop it on.
I'm not a drizzle guy, fine raspberry drizzle.
Didn't you people reach your drizzle quota yet?
You drizzled my dinner plate with some sauce.
Leave my ice cream naked or traditional.
Better yet, I'll pass on dessert
Sell off my kids to pay for the meal –
Get home, raid the fridge and kick back in the recliner
With a bowl of chocolate ice cream.

(8/27/16)

All Saints Day

There will come a first Sunday in November
When my name will be read and a bell will toll.
I will have been gone a week, a month, almost a year.
Some in the congregation will have known me
Family, friends, acquaintances, others not.
Yet, there will be a tear or two in life's recovery.
All share the solemnest of the moment
The name is called, but life is not alphabetical,
So there is a jolt as the face flashes in your mind.
I like it best when the bells build and spill out
A joy of celebration and remembrance for all.
I paint a picture of the congregation building
As the organ, triumphantly plays "For All the Saints"
And the voices climb louder with familiarity.
Just when our voices are silent again
As we file solemnly from the church
We are greeted by the day and more bells
Church bells, ringing, over and over again.
I see the most mischievous Sunday school child
Hanging onto the rope that rings the bell.
He fairly flies as he is lifted to his toes
And he laughs with all the life that is in him.
And the parishioners pause outside
As with each peal – spirits burst.
Butterflies, doves, bubbles climb above them.
Gradually we are lifted from hurt and anger
From frustration and loneliness.
We pass by the end and find the love
The warm memories and appreciation.
We find our strength in our beliefs
Our foundation, our God.
We discover how unimportant one person is
And how important life is.
What cracked off-key voice will fight,
Fight through tears with a smiling voice?
What flood of life will warm them in November?
Most of them will have done their best.
Those butterflies, those doves, those iridescent bubbles

Were the best parents they could be.
They were the best friends they could be.
They led life as best they knew how
And their spirits will climb to tomorrow.
Their faith, their love, their spunk
Will be at the core of their children
Their congregation, their friends
The stranger who felt their caring and smile.
And the bells will ring, the music soar
More and more and everyday.

(11/3/13)

Babble

I do believe there was a *Tower of Babble*
That might even be something Biblical.
There are many *babbling* brooks.
These are generally rambling and refreshing.
But just plain *babble* is what this is.
I've taken the word and I shall drivel on.
I'll babble about *babble* and never be done.
Usually you have a subject to *babble* on about,
A cute grandchild or one of your life's stories.
You carry on ad nauseam about someone or something,
Never mindful of your audience; you continue.
"I remember when…" is a launch pad
And questions are almost always rhetorical
Just to keep the flow going, the rhythm.
Because *babble* often requires a monotone
A flat expressionless disgorging of words.
You assume interest from another party
But only to get you going; once started
A true *Babbler* never looks back.
One favorite *babble* subject is one's health.
"How are you?" Can make a *babbler's* day
With an overview of general aches and pains
Segueing into more detailed information
Like recent doctors' visits and your take on that event.
Family health histories blended into your own,
How your ailment is more significant than others,
What and/or how many pills you take,
The various therapies and diets you are engaging in.
And the two most outstanding health *Babbler* lines:
"Let me show you my scar," coordinated with a visual,
Followed with "I happen to have my x-rays with me."
So it goes, from health you can move to
"When I was your age" or a simple "Did you know?"
One word of warning to *babble* encounters –
Never mix *babble* with *blithering*.
A babble may never end
But with *blithering*, you're an idiot.

(7/3/14)

How?

How far is the fair?
How long will it take?
How do you know that?
How fair is that?

                How many questions?
                How are you feeling?
            How did you get where you are today?
                How deep is the ocean?
                How high the moon?
                How come she got more?

                                  How ya doin' pal?
                                  How sweet it is –
                                  How did you win?
                                  How could you lose?
                                  How I pity you.

                How now brown cow?
            How many times have I told you that?
                How about another round?
            How do you get from point A to point B?
            How funny you should mention that.

How do you do that?
How long has it been?
How come you never asked?
How wonderful that you care.
How beautiful you look.
How about that?

                    How silly of me.
                    How does it feel?
                How did the world begin?
                How much are you paid?
                    How will it end?

    How come you don't ask who, what, where, why or when?

(9/29/14)

I Am Older Than the Super Bowl
(Things you might not know about me and probably don't care)

I am older than the Super Bowl
I am younger than Kellogg's Corn Flakes
I am older than only some dirt
I am younger than my parents
I am older than my children
I am younger to less people than I am older to
Because I am older, some think me wiser
I am no wiser than many
My memory can be longer and shorter simultaneously
I have opinions and make judgments
Some are right; others are wrong or uninformed
I'm probably a pessimist with optimistic streaks
I am older than the Nehru jacket
I am younger than plastic
I have been in love many times
I have been in love and loved three times
I do not adore babies, though mine were cute
I do not love infants and toddlers right away
I love watching three and four year olds learning
It is out in the open for everyone to see.
I like blue
I have no fashion sense
I do not like weather extremes
I dream of one to counteract the other
I am older than "Rock and Roll"
I am younger than "Swing"
I can't dance, but I can, when well oiled,
Move with a partner and forget to count.
I love to watch Nature; birds, water, skies
I am slow to wake, unless I have to get somewhere
I struggle with late night, unless with the right company
I am older than McDonald's
I am younger than Macy's
I like to shop for food and for others
I sometimes don't know when to stop...
Like a line or two ago.

(2/8/16)

My Son is the Sun...

My son is the sun, my daughter reigns.
I have a lady in the moon.
Words on the winds, smiles on the breeze
Memories in the tides
Pulling in the golden happy ones
Pushing out the clouds and heartache.
Scoop up some earth
Let it flow from your fingers
Sand to clay to rich nourishing dirt.
Wild tales waft to the heavens
And the simplest friend demands respect.
Some torrid heat intrigues our mind.
We are full of moments
Important moments that change our lives
And the sixty-second ones
That we live every day, one tick after another.
Gusts of faces glide down the street
Smiling, sneering, laughing and in tears.
Each one has a part of our lives
Actual or imagined, we see them our way.
There is no right or wrong way
They are ours, the same face two or three ways
As the years fall away
With full and wasted days
Always coming, always moving on.
There is the sun, and reigning princess
And there is my happy moon.

(4/9/16)

Why Do I Sit in the Balcony at Church?

Why do I sit in the balcony at church?
Do I think that it brings me closer to God?
Maybe it does, if I'm in third-grade Sunday school
When God had a very definite face
Flowing white hair and beard blowing in a gale
A combination of John Brown and Zeus
Slightly wild, to be feared, to be worshipped.
But I'm past the third grade and don't know when
I started climbing the stairs on the way to Heaven.
When I was young, in the 50s, and joined this Church
When not in the Plymouth Building, (Sunday School)
I sat downstairs and when my attention span departed
Well, there were the organ pipes to count and legs to swing.
I've been a member of the church fifty or sixty years.
I took two or three years off to be a Lutheran.
Anyway, it's nice up in the balcony
Because I'm shy and can't remember names.
I can wave to those I do know and shake hands with the few around me.
Being early lets me, I guess you'd call it meditate,
Stare through some wavy glass at some maple leaves
And pray, dream, sort things out, reflect,
Glance at the organ (now in the back),
Count how many choir members are singing,
Catch a bit of their warm-up and run through the program.
Some days, I go back in time, check out the plaques
See my mom sitting toward the back on the left-hand side
Wearing a hat and white gloves. Who's that little boy with her?
Oh, the Lyons a little farther forward, in the left center section
Earl and Betty sit with Betty's sister, Eunice Brewer,
Their daughter, for years now, part of the choir.
Who's preaching today? Pastor Adam, Ashley, Rev. Tudesco, Soper?
In this mood, probably Thursby, calm and measured.
He always looked the part, not a hair out of place.
And his son, typically always getting in trouble
Suddenly, amazingly our own *Amahl*, singing up front,
And... and the music, the organ, the choir, the bells, the soloists
The congregation singing with confidence, if they know the hymn

Phoning it in on the more obscure.
I can't sing well and will sometimes stop trying
And try instead to hear the words with the music.
So it goes when I'm there, but even when I'm not
I am there, looking down at the pulpit,
Listening to the stories and working on life
And being able to see when the sermon has reached its last page.

(5/2/16)

Little Girl Walk

Somewhere after toddler
A young girl finds freedom
Whether it is serious questioning
About ladybugs and ribbons
Or creating her own world
Jumping over different colored tiles
On the mall's food court floor
Still attached to her mother's arm.
It's the arms flying free
Wings swinging and dipping
As she moves across the grass
A serpentine dance of celebration.
There is no holiday – no destination
Except the event in her head.
Time will come soon enough
When arms will fall to her side
And she will walk rather than skip
Run rather than prance.
If only some of it remains
Hidden until she needs it,
She needs it to be in her core.

(9/24/10)

*Previously published in the 2011-2012 edition of "High Tide" by the Milford Fine Arts Writer's Group.

A Summer Dress

In an age of casual shorts and calculating jeans
There is still nothing more pleasant than a summer dress.
From a time before I glimmered
It was the style, the custom –
A little more fashionable than pedal pushers,
    clam diggers and calypso pants.
These dresses survive till at least a day ago.
Lesser quantities and not in every closet
Brightly colored or with broad prints or patterns.
It has skirt enough for a happy girl's swirl –
Plenty of arms, a scoop of a neck in back
A sort of a bold innocence flirting with the sun.
Not only does it catch the eye
But makes a little statement –
A tribute to the hot summer days
Ready for a cocktail on a veranda
Getting ready for a sunset.

(8/10/15)

Beauty

Beauty comes in a canyon carved by an angry river.
It comes at the shore as the tide pulls the earth away.
Beauty surrounds us with autumn leaves and winter's snow
Around the turn in the road or morning's sunrise.
Beauty is in the moonlight on the water and the night sky
In the flush of a good poker hand or life's little moments.
Beauty surrounds the heart and weakens the knees.
Sometimes it stands bold before us or gathers over time.
Beauty is obvious and subtle, a declaration or a smile.
It is maturity, emotion, appreciation and desire.
Beauty challenges the observer and his environment,
Take the surface and run or look much deeper.
Beauty can be special or the everyday.

The slightest morsel can be glorious to the hungry.
Beauty can be in the swagger or the sway.
It can be the touch and tracing of a lover.
Beauty can be in the comfort of one's embrace,
Or some great accomplishment finally attained.
Beauty is full of time and experience and love,
Being familiar or comfortable, but not taken for granted.
Beauty is a laugh, a smile and a knowing look.
It is the warmness and excitement of the heart
Beauty does not stand-alone, it is enhanced
By love, respect and understanding.

(11/13/13)

Old Dog

See the old dog sitting there, over by the wall
Looking left, looking right, forgetting to be lost.
Sixteen years I'm told, sixteen times seven
Older for sure, older than me.
Gone for good the running wild
Chasing stick and ball
Gone the fierce protector
Who was frightened by the Hoover.
Still a yowl and a whine
When the old stomach growls,
Doing his duty, appreciating a pet
But not knowing who it is from.
Not wanting to be alone
Still not fussy about the company
Cat or bird or little pup.
Sleep the hours, the days away.
Will that be me with add on years
Under the shady tree,
Looking left, looking right, forgetting to be lost,
Not understanding that I'm alone.

(2/27/16)

A Story for Henrietta

Henrietta is a cat. I told this story to her a few days ago, but I'm not sure she was listening. I thought I'd write it down so she could read it at her leisure.

When I talk to animals, it probably is the same way you do. We tend to talk to them as if they were babies or small children; we watch their heads for signs of recognition and understanding. For most, we look for the cocked head, the stare they give us, ears to perk, or maybe, with dogs, a tail to wag. What words do they know and are we really communicating with them?

With birds, we usually have a stunted vocabulary with only a few sentences, "Pretty bird," or the ever popular "Polly want a cracker," come instantly to mind. If the bird tilts his head and looks at us, have we had success? When the bird chirps, are we carried to heaven as "the Bird Whisperer" or is the bird merely saying; "feed me, give me water, change my paper (I've finished reading it), shut up and pull down the damn cover."

Dogs are man's best friends, right? There are so many breeds and mixes, all different colors, sizes and personalities; it is hard to isolate the reaction we search for –

I guess, different things for different people. Personally, I tend to roughhouse with a dog, once I know it. If it's small, I'll try to turn it over and tickle its belly. With bigger dogs I'll have tug-of-wars or play fetch (for a reasonable amount of time), as long as the dog is doing its fair share of the fetching. I'll accept big old sloppy kisses and see if it knows any other tricks. My dialogue goes something like; "Is you a good boy (girl)? Fetch, Sit, Want a treat (biscuit)? Do you have to go out?" and to give you a clue as to my political up bringing, "Dead dog or Democrat." Oh, and if it is not too early in the morning, I might ask the animal "Speak."

Cats seem to be a whole other ball game. They are independent; they socialize on their own terms and what is OK one minute may not be the next. Still, it is possible that some will give you unconditional love and still destroy the upholstery on your couch. I've had cats that wanted their three squares and clean litter; the hell with anything else. Others couldn't wait till I sat down, so they could jump up and settle in. Some you pet or chin-chuckle at your own risk, coming away with a contented purr or a bloody stub.

Henrietta is not my cat and, when I visit, she will give me some attention or settle close by. I was sitting at the dining room table and she climbed into the chair next to me and got comfortable. She was watching me, so I decided it would be rude not to say something to her and so I started the word game. Using her name, praising her and watching for a reaction. I went on to mouse and bird, she was still listening so I told her this story.

One spring day a family of mice gathered around a maypole. There were a lot of cute little *mices* dressed in their finest outfits. Father Mouse's name was Eisenhower; mother's name was Fiona and they raised a fine lot of kids, everyone happy and smiling in the springtime air. The day was full of freshness, pungent smells from flowers, trees, (bread baking and fresh cut grass.

Suddenly, out of the sun came thousands of birds, all kinds of birds, from colorful and exotic to plain brown and gray birds. Big and little, they dove in and about and, as if by magic, pulled yellow ribbons from the blooming daffodils and the sun's sparkling rays. Others took light blue ribbons from the light blue sky, while some grabbed pink ribbons from chubby-cheeked azaleas and the many fine blossoms of the magnolia trees that stood about. Finally, a flock of birds whisked light green ribbons from the fragile early leaves of the maple trees and with the rest of the birds tied one end of the ribbons atop the maypole while the other ends drifted arthward

When they came within reach, the Eisenhower children grabbed them and music erupted from the birds and all the other living creatures and the world was full of harmony and love. The mice began to dance, moving in opposite directions; some weaved in while mice going in the opposite direction weaved out. Slowly the pole began to be colorfully wrapped in pastel stripes that moved closer and closer to the earth. The music tempo increased as the laughing and singing mice moved faster and faster and the circle got tighter and tighter.

Finally, the pole was completely wrapped and some of the mice let go of their ribbons and fell to the ground at the foot of the pole, rolling on their backs, feet still pumping to the rhythm of the music punctuated by their laughing voices. But some other mice did not let go of their ribbons and the speed of these dancers launched them into the air in all directions. Odd numbers went north to south, even numbers went east and west, while still others circled or connected to one another making beltways and connectors.

And that is how we got ribbons of highways and Eisenhower became the Father of the Interstate Highway System.

Once I stopped talking, Henrietta slowly closed her eyes and turned her head into her body forming a little circle. I took this as high praise indeed.

(4/15/14)

POLITICS PATRIOTS PARADES

Chapter 3

Yes, I love my Country.

Yes, I love a parade.

Politics, not so much.

Lawn Signs

It's that time of year again.
Like mushrooms overnight
They appear to tell me who is who –
Red and white and blue
Surely a patriot true.
Green and white,
Ah, this one's for the environment –
Red and white.
Perhaps we have a communist?
No, one, two, three, four
Republican, Democrat, Independent
Some with no label
That might tell me more.
Oh, look there's another one!
Wait, no just an Open House.
Merrily I drive along
And see the candidate's names –
Over and over and over again.
Caldwell Banker is running I see.
Wonder what he stands for
Or any of them stand for.
These signs give me no clue.
Wait – maybe some of them
Are doing some remodeling.
Their signs are side by side.
Vote for me to be Mayor.
Tag sale Saturday and Sunday.
I'm running for "Planning and Zoning."
Take karate lessons, "House for Sale."
City Clerk, dental insurance
Challengers and electricians.
Know who's running for Alderman?
Yes, I do.

And I even know we're in Century 21.
Ah, this temporary urban blight.
It's a wonder you can see the grass.
Why plant any flowers
Paint them on a sign –
Then stick that in your lawn.
Why should politicians be the only ones?
Have some fun; write your name on one.
Perhaps you'll garner a write-in vote or two.
Where was I going?
I haven't got a clue.

(10/12/09)

"I Promise"

"I Promise if I'm elected…
I Promise on my wife and mother…
And my children pictured here."

"I Promise on my war…
I Promise to give you more…
Unless it's less you need."

"I Promise on this flag…
I Promise to lower taxes…
And smooth out all the roads."

"I Promise to kiss the children…
I Promise the old folks dignity…
And save the egret too."

"I Promise to bring in industry.
I Promise to save every tree.
All State and Federal Grants you'll see."

"I Promise good government.
I Promise this to get elected…
And my party promises too."

"I Promise if I'm re-elected,
To Promise this and more."

(11/1/10)

It's all red, white and blue

This time of year it's all red, white and blue.
They ask everyman what it means to you.
"Freedom" they cry, one after another,
"The right to speak my mind," from a malcontent.
It's marches, fireworks and military
Picnics, parades with chests puffed out –
Summer heat and everyone is proud
Hands over heart for flags and taps.
Prayers for those fighting, for those gone.
America is beautiful, is proud
Is not always right.
It's not one person or one person's view.
It's melting pots, discrimination and politicians.
It's personalities; it's trying to be better.
It's hardworking and scheming.
It's worshiping God, American Idol and the dollar.
America is natural beauty
Coupled with the attempt to destroy it.
It's being bigger and better than the next guy.
It's going farther than mom and pop
And they're proud; it's what they worked for.
It's loud and gentle, cruel and caring.
It's a hand to man: to push him down
Or help pull him up – It's hopeful and ignoring.
It's love for thy fellow man – unity.
It's love for thy fellow man, as long as he is…
Some appreciate it more than others.
Some are blind to all but their way.
It is good, it is bad, it hugs you
Or lets you wallow – it is all the
Opposites you can think of.→

For me it's some of these things
But most of all it's home.

(7/2/08)

"The Pledge"

The hand over the heart
The pledge so easy to start.
Why is it only small town,
A thing of the past?

When I was small
You stopped and stood
And the anthem played
All the way to the end.

"I pledge" I promise
Young men and women
Just starting out
Boy Scouts, Girl Scouts to Cadets.

"Allegiance", and loyalty
Crowds gathered on the green
Orations of red, white and blue
The words of Patriots and Politicians

"To the flag", the banner
The purity, the blood
Stars and Stripes
Fields by dawn's light

"Of the United States of America"
The growth from Revolution
Under pine trees and myths
Chilling songs and brotherhood.

"To the Republic", the Confederation
Imperfect and overpowering
Allowing its critics to be friends
And lovers to be neighbors.

"For which it stands"
Loyalty, Honor, Valor
Blood spilled to preserve
Legend taking on reality.

"One Nation under God"
All these beliefs,
Somehow, they bend and blend,
A single language in crisis

"Indivisible", to the point of war
States Rights – individual rights
All rights struggling
In this – their home.

"With Liberty", freedom
I am free – but a part.
I am a leg – an arm;
A head –and a heart

"And Justice for All"
Something we work for
Something we try for
Someday – Someday.

This flag-snapping day
Before the summers are gone
We need to listen
With our hand over our heart.

(7/2/08)

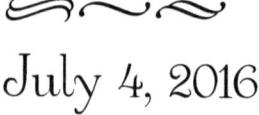

July 4, 2016

Firecrackers Under a Tin Can
"Bam"

Happy Birthday America
"Bam"

Picnics and Parades
"Bam"

Pools and Parties
"Bam"

Kids at the Beaches
"Bam, Bam"

A String of Chinese Firecrackers
"Bam, bam, bam, bam, bam, bam"

March Music and Military Movies
"Bam"

Summer at its Best
"Bam"
Apple Pie and Uncle Sam

"Bam"

Gathering by the Shore
"Bam"

Sitting in the Field
"Bam"

Sun Going Down
"Bam"
"Bam, Bam"

Blankets Spread
"Bam, Bam, Bam"

Baby hands to ears with the noise
"Bam, Bam, Bam, Bam"
"Bam, Bam"

Fountains in the Sky – "Bam"
Colored Clouds – "Bam"
"Bam, Bam"

Quick White Spray – Double Down Explosion
"Bam, Bam"

Ahs and Wows
"Bam, Bam"

Gold, Blue, Red, Green Inside out
"Bam"

Higher and Higher
"Bam, Bam-Bam"

Faster and Faster
"Bam, Bam-Bam Bam Bam **POW**!"
"**WOW**! Bam. Bam"

More and More
"Bam – Bam – Bam"

Finally the Finale
"Bam Bam Bam – Bam Bam B-B Bam Bam BAM bam"

Then No More
Fold Up the Blanket
And the Sleeping Child
""Bam"
From a Distant Shore

The Politician

When I was a child, we liked Ike.
I don't know why, he was a nice man.
The only thing I heard was
 Stevenson was too "brainy."
I didn't know what to make of that.
Then and now, but what was the thinking –
Rat-a-tat, tat here comes the parade –
Marching bands, scouts, veterans, floats
Come moving past me, clowns and politicians.
Queens and princesses wave to me
Elbow, elbow, wrist, wrist and pass by.
But my silver-haired politician
Wearing a fancy suit, everything in place,
My representative who has no clue
No clue how to live at my level –
He is not Jimmy Stewart.
And with rare exception, he is a party man –
Pachyderm or donkey. So many seem cookie cutters,
Flunky to their party and the backrooms
A platform that can be built
With no foundation, except to elect their people.
Why do I feel that most are corrupt or corrupted?
How sad, and yet I must vote,
And so must you.
But don't vote on labels.
Feel sad that millions of dollars
Filter into the economy, just to tout and condemn
Half-truths and lies cloaked in red, white and blue
Meant to turn your head and mine.
What a waste.
This is a presidential year
And so, the mud slinging increases.
As we move closer to November
Robo calls will start soon.
A voice that won't let you question
Flyers and letters draped in flags
And smiling families clutter the mailbox.
Ads on radio and TV

Appeals for more money to throw into the wind.
Local politicos will start knocking
But they want to deliver their message.
They're annoyed when you try to question and share –
This is meet and greet, "Hi, I'm so and so…
"I'm running for this and that,
I hope I can count on your vote, bye."
Well hell no, not till I know
And I hope you want to know.
On a local level, my vote counts.
Pick up my garbage, pave my road,
Plow the snow and don't tax me too much.
But, if you are running for dog catcher –
I don't care about your politics –
About how you feel about abortion,
The death penalty, the NRA, healthcare or the economy.
Can you catch dogs? What's your experience?
At the state level these questions,
These life changing and effecting things
Become topics of discussion.
And at the national level even more.
But I always feel that the higher the office
The less my vote really counts –
That whole Electoral College thing.
Still I want to vote for my choice.
Here's my suggestion, thanks for asking –
Watch the news on several channels.
Try to get a balance.
Never just vote the party lever.
Take the time to know who is who
And whom you think is best for the job.
Make sure you search yourself
To find what you really believe –
Then find the man or woman who represents that.
Don't get comfortable labeling yourself –
Don't lump yourself as one thing or another –
Take the time to tear apart the fabric
And find the quality of an idea.
Take apart a program or plan
And support what you think is good.
Fight to change what you think is wrong.
Send letters or e-mail to those people who wave.
They're supposed to represent you, →

Be a squeaky wheel, if only,
If only to say you tried.
When you pass the gauntlet of signs
As you enter the polling place
Have your mind made up.
Do your homework.
Yes vote, but vote intelligently
And win or lose, feel proud
That you voted for whom you thought best.
(9/8/12)

Am I Free?

Am I free? Am I free?
I've come to pray my way
Standing on this land.
Let us give thanks.
"God Save the King"
But give me liberty.
Don't tread on me.

Am I free? Am I free?
Principles and fears
Build that new nation,
Pray to Heaven.
God help us
Not again, not again.
Dawn's flags flying.

Am I free? Am I free?
Grow out – Grow up
Expand and be mighty
Build bigger – Harvest more.
He is a man.
Not a thing.
Give up the old.

Am I free? Am I free?
Let him go.
Free him now.
Listen to me brother.

So long sad man
End another war
Rebuild – Let me stand.

Am I free? Am I free?
Take me west
Trample the sage.
It's a new age
Gold and land
Farm and city.
Where are they all from?

Am I free? Am I free?
Charge up that hill.
We are a power.
We stand in isolation.
They won't leave us.
Stand behind them.
Tramp now over there.

Am I free? Am I free?
War to end wars
Ticker tape invincible
Peace forever – Never.
Roar and restitution
Flapper and bathtub gin
Buy an apple – Wait in line.

Am I free? Am I free?
Climb and build
With all those letters
Head rising up
Sunday morning bombing.
Come my brothers
Join in and join up.

Am I free? Am I free?
How many gone now?
Years and years of death
Sacrifices at home.
Another war – the second war
Is done – We won.
Is it finally done? →

Am I free? Am I free?
No, now we're the world's police
In snow, new ways
To kill and increase the pain.
We fight wars with no winners.
Years of dollars from our muzzles
Leave blood and tortured minds.

Am I free? Am I free?
With lives returning home
And others left to rot and ruin?
Sing songs of passion
Widow and wife
Gold star mother
Flat-footed brother.

Am I free? Am I free?
Not till all the bodies
Are buried beside the road
Or brought home to rest in peace
A field of crosses.
Who is the next evil?
Has he ever held a gun?

Am I free? Am I free?
Heart's lonely song.
I can't face another day.
Let me just rest and pray.
I fight in spite.
I fight for…
I want God on my side.

Am I free? Am I free?
My flag, my country
My brother, my son
My father, my mother
Walk with me.
Sing with me.
Think with me.

I am free. I am free!
(11/10/14)

Stripes and Stars and Bunting

Stripes and stars and bunting
Here they come 'round the corner
Behind the blinking police cars
Following the convertible politicians
And the hollow veterans of wars gone by.
It isn't peacetime; there is no more of that.
The little wars of hate, centuries old, continue –
A clown or two then an old, old fire truck.
Now I see them! Here they come!
A small, but bold service band leads the way.
Commands grow loud for such a little turn
A turn on to my main street and yours.
Spit and polish, row upon row they appear.
Where did they all come from?
Why are they all here?
Usually it's a little bunch, the reserve.
But not today, all the services stand tall.
Look at their faces, some so young
And others older, who've answered the call.
How strange these survivors
These men and women who have come home
Home to my hometown. Why, why do they come?
No smiles, eyes front, in step, marching
Reflections of all the years, sun shining
The color guard now passing, all salute
From VFW and American Legion doorways
Old bones on the side stand straight
To hands on hearts and children waving
With little flags they wave, they're just learning.
Mothers pass on the lesson of this special day,
No, not these ones you see right here.
Yes, we're proud of them and the others too.
But today is not for them; it is for their shadows
It is those colonial guys marching with the fife and drum
The bandaged soul in blue or gray,
The trench survivors from World War I,
My father, my grandfather, my friend next door,
The ones who rest on beaches and on the ocean floor, →

Those that never came home from World War II.
Here the steady drum, the beat, the heartbeat
The always winter Korea, the rainy, steamy Viet Nam.
Oh, thunder of the cannon, the yell of the attack
Echoes today on desert floors.
Why do they come, come to my hometown?
To honor all those shadows, who can march no more
And to lead the way for Cub Scouts and Brownies,
Boy Scouts, Girl Scouts, Karate schools and such,
Out of step and laughing, free to be out of step and laughing.
Join in at the end; come on, just down Main Street.
You're part of the reason, you are the reason
For stripes and stars and bunting.

(5/28/16)

When Johnny Came Home

"How long has it been?"

"Been awhile."

"What did you see?"

"More than I wanted. Don't wanna say."

"Come on, we've been through a lot right here at home."

"I know that. I appreciate that, still…"

"We was there when you marched out of town. All of you proud, marchin' with flag and drum. Dust rising with gun on shoulder, we cheered you all. Why I even sung."

"It was a fine send-off and our chests was burstin' right out of them new blue uniforms."

"Can't you just tell us a little of what went on? And where's all the rest?"

"I'm it. The only one left."

"No, that can't be, there must be more of you. Maybe just around the bend?"

"I wish it were so, but it's not to be. I see all their faces, every one of them. I see them that day we left here, twenty of us joining into the old 25th. We fell into the ranks and stayed in step; right happy we were to help old Uncle Abe."

"Yeah, I remember the sun shinin' off those bayonets and the officers on horseback, keepin' the line movin'."

"We left here in that big parade, figured we'd do a little trainin', be off to war and back again by the end of summer, Christmas at the latest."

"That's what they said when the word came down from the Capitol. 'Sign up for three, six or nine months,' that's what Senator Blackwell said."

"Yeah, that's what Blackwell said. They made him a Colonel with his beautiful black horse and special sword; he even had feathers in his hat." →

"Is he back at the Capitol?"

"No, he's lyin' under that big black horse on a hill in Pennsylvania. I saw him there, sword drawn, starin' at me from the ground. I seen his unblinkin' eyes starin' at me from
the ground."

"He's dead. Sorry to hear that. Please tell me about the others."

"I see them, I see them every night, each one of them. I see them happy and laughin' as we marched out of town. Pullin' tricks on one another at night, as we pitched our tents and ate by the fire. We marched a long time and them smiles slipped away. We asked where we was goin' to an officer. He said 'To war boys. Where do you think we were going?' We had one ugly old sergeant from Massachusetts who kept an eye on us. He told us what war would be like and how to take care of ourselves, our equipment and especially our feet. We practiced chargin' forward with fixed bayonets, yellin' and screamin' and stayin' in line. Most of us thought it were just a silly game. We marched day and night clear into Pennsylvania with nary a shot fired. We was given food by nice people along the way. They wished us well, but we couldn't stop. We kept marchin', mile after mile. The people would yell out names and where they was from, and tell us to tell these people they sends their love. We waved back, but we really couldn't make out all that they was sayin'."

"But you did fight, didn't you? I mean our boys didn't fall off the end of the world?"

"Oh yeah, we fought at a place called Gettysburg. Seems like we sort of bumped into Johnny Reb right there in the middle of nowhere. People was runnin' in one direction then another and we was right there. We marched into camp, were told to drop our stuff exceptin' for our rifles, powder and bullets and off we went."

"That fast?"

"That fast and we come out in the open in some sort of peach orchard. We lost three boys right there, before we had gone any good distance. We went back and forth 'til it finally got dark and we moved back to the campground. I don't think any of us slept a wink thinkin' about our friends lyin' out there with their faces in the ground. We were told that men from both sides were allowed out there to clear away the dead. Still there was no smiles, no jokin', each man was deep in thought and prayer. It was a long night and then two more days and nights of hell. The second night we was around our campfire eatin'. Ben Atwater got up and went to the fire; he was after some more beans. Well a shot rung out and Ben, he just crumpled to the ground. He had a hole in his head and some of his brains had spilled on his plate. A sniper had snuck up close and climbed a tree. We spotted him and shot him many times and then just left him dead in the tree."

"How could it happen? I thought we could beat them 'Rebs.'"

"I don't know. They fight hard and we fight hard. A dead soldier, whether he's dressed in blue or gray, is still dead. I'm not sure all of the officers on either side knows what they's doin', but most of them are right out there fightin' with their men and dyin' with them."

"How did that thin' end?"

"Well, old Robert E. Lee, he snuck out of there and took what was left of his army and headed south. We stayed there and reorganized and took care of the wounded, before headin' out. I found out I was alone. All the rest was gone."

"All the rest?"

"Yeah, and each day I was there I just prayed to make it till dark. But when it was dark, I saw all them faces dead or dyin'- In pain-with doctors operatin' in tents and orderlies pilin' arms and legs outside the tent to be buried later. I would wake with a start, feelin' a dead man's hand on my shoulder or hearin' the cries of the wounded as we crossed a battlefield. Finally they said I could go home and here I am. But somehow I have nineteen stories to tell and none are goin' to be happy endin's. And no mother, father, wife, no sister, brother or child will look at me with anythin' but contempt. Why I am standin' there and not their kin. Every day I walk through town, people will be starin' at me. I might as well be Jefferson Davis hisself. I don't like bein' the messenger of death. I mean, I may leave town and there will be no parade."

(8/26/16)

Politics

I am pretty much a
Conservative, Liberal, On the fence.
Republican, Democrat, Independent
Left, Right and ambidextrous
Person who hates politics.

Every year I start the study
Sifting through the issues
Listening and reading about
Candidates, incumbents
And those doing exploratory searches.

I'm not fond of politicians.
I guess I see them as
A necessary evil and
Only a few earn stickers and stars.
The rest I view with dismay.

Their vocabulary to me is foreign:
Earmarks, lobbyist, pork barrel
They have trouble with other words
Like ethics, transparency, honesty,
And in the end disappoint me.

Well if you want better, get involved.
I am involved; I'm an educated voter.
I'm not thick skinned enough
Or rich enough to be a candidate
And I'm not sure I could represent you.

I have trouble standing on platforms
Where there might be a loose plank or two
And I don't want someone telling me
How this or that should go
Because I don't have time to study it.

I pay my taxes, but don't always agree
About where it goes or how it is spent.
Pick up my garbage and pave my street.

Stuff

Let me have a sticker to park at the beach.
Don't tell me what you think I should think.

You see I'm pretty much a
Conservative, Liberal, On the fence
Republican, Democrat, Independent
Left, Right and ambidextrous
Person who hates politics.

(3/23/10)

Johnny, Billy & Muffy Too

As we rock from cradle to rocking chair
We follow trails our parents lay out for us
Or we take that famous different direction.
Often there is an unconscious competition
Undeclared and perhaps not mean spirited –
Time to jump in or walk away.

My Johnny is walking and talking and reciting the Gettysburg Address;
He's a perfect weight and height and has been accepted at Yale. Billy
has a great sense of humor and his hair won't stay combed.

Johnny wants to be a lawyer and then a senator;
If all goes well he'll be in the White House at forty.
Billy worked a year and took night courses.

Johnny is a "junior" or a "II" and joins his father's fraternity;
He is dating Muffy and they will marry and have two and a half kids.
Billy will graduate in the middle of the pack and travel a bit.

Johnny Jr. joins his father's law firm after graduation;
He becomes a junior partner after six months in the ranks.
Billy joins a fishing crew and later writes for a local newspaper.

Johnny is now a Senior Partner and a member of the Country Club.
Muffy has one child, hires a nanny and is totally bored.
Billy moves from writing obits to feature stories.

Johnny becomes Chairman of the Board and has a lover.
Muffy takes tennis lessons and a lover.
Billy joins a prestigious newspaper and becomes a foreign
correspondent.

The Republican Party endorses Johnny for the State Senate.
Muffy and her girlfriends go on vacation without their husbands.
Billy reports from hot spots all over the world.

Johnny is elected and leaves the law firm.
Muffy threatens divorce and now drives a new car and sports

diamonds.
Billy returns home, courts and marries a long time girl friend.
Johnny is being groomed and fast-tracked.
Muffy is drinking and is well supervised.
Billy is made the network's Chief Washington Correspondent.

Johnny is running for the United States Senate.
Muffy smiles and waves along the campaign trail.
Billy covers Johnny's senate campaign and becomes a dad.

Johnny wheels and deals and is a rising star;
Promises are made and money appears and disappears.
Billy turns down an offer to be Johnny's campaign manager.

Johnny and Muffy's daughter is in boarding school;
Johnny and Muffy smile and shake hands with anyone.
Billy starts to dig into Johnny's background.

Johnny makes policy statements and slings some mud.
Muffy is seldom seen after she spoke a few misguided words.
Billy and his family squeeze is some time for each other.

Johnny is leading in the polls and his war chest is full;
His power has grown and most consider him a shoo-in.
Billy talks to Muffy and her daughter.

Johnny is full of laughter, arms around blue collar,
Shaking hands in every state, sometimes three cities a day.
Billy publishes his articles and wins the Pulitzer Prize. →

Johnny is talking to the FBI, his hands in cuffs.
Muffy takes her daughter out of boarding school.
Billy and his family continue to have adventures together.

Johnny is in a minimum-security prison.
Muffy has divorced Johnny and lives in a small town with her daughter.
Billy anchors *The Evening News* and takes his son fishing.

(5/27&5/30/15)

Politics Jingle

Hi! How'd ya do? I'm for you.
See my wife, see my kids
I've fought in wars.
I'm red, white and blue.
Give to me; I'll do for you.
Hurry up it's the November after next
Never mind the text
It says I'm for you.
I'll give you that; I'll give you this
Here let me give that baby a kiss.
I'm against war; here's my purple heart.
But not that war.
We have to prove a point
Re-establish our power
Give'm this, give'm that
See my new gun; rat-a-tat-tat.
I hear you. I know your concerns.
Support me, work for me
Give me money to fight the evil.
One for you, two for me.
Fix my house, I'll fix – you know that.
My party's right, that's why you belong,
Don't let them scare you
You know they're wrong,
Red, white and blue – Lincoln too.
You hear my words.
Did I say that?
Let me clarify that.
I'll run on my record – what record?
I love America, don't you?
I know best, let me take care of the rest.
Give me your financial support
To stop them from ruining –
The government, the environment, the economy.
Let's jail them all – set them free
One for you, two for me.
Cut and drill, give to them
Don't take away from me.

Stuff

I didn't know, pay no attention to that.
I said this, I said that.
Here's some money – don't grow that.
What we're running low?
Print some more, don't let them in the door.
Can I take the floor? I love this country.
Where else can you say what you want?
Did you hear what he said?
When he was in high school, he wore red
And she burned this and that.
I'm not kidding, I'll have none of that.
I'll make you a judge, an ambassador,
Assistant to the assistant at a lot a year
But you stay home, just slip me some.
What sum? What are you talking about?
I have my rights; I'll straddle the fence.
I'm for you, vote for me.
Need a ride? I'll take you for one.
We need guns for everyone.
We'll teach you to shoot and when you're done,
We'll send you there; hell, there's a war to be won.
I'm sorry, a peace and then we'll have fun.
My wife can smile, she has a cause,
We're just not sure which one – because
The wind blows left – it blows right
And I'm ready for a fight.
I have the experience.
Give me two and I'll only tax you one.
I've done this – I've done that –
You didn't hear it from me, but he's a rat.
Hey good buddy, let me shake hands with you.
What are your concerns?
I'm listening to your every word.
How do you do? My hair is white and neat
I can roll up my sleeves
And wear your union jacket
Just let me step out of my limo.
Do you believe the price of gas?
It's his fault you know, what he did
What he left undone.
Here's one for you, I'll take two.
I love this country – every man,
Woman and child – green, purple or blue →

Have their rights and the futures' bright.
We'll have food, jobs, retirement,
The world's respect, flags flying,
Just for me – and you.
Sing the songs of freedom.
Pave the road to happiness.
Fill the potholes.
Fill my pockets.
It's great to be an American.
One for you, two for me.
The home of the brave, land of the free.

(3/26/09)

SILLY STUFF

Chapter 4

Sometimes I have a corny idea and there are times when there is no idea. So I'll start a silly rhyme or a miscellaneous word journey and it will take off. Some could be moved to "Politics" or other categories, but why not leave them here, after all they were lots of fun and deserve a place of their own.

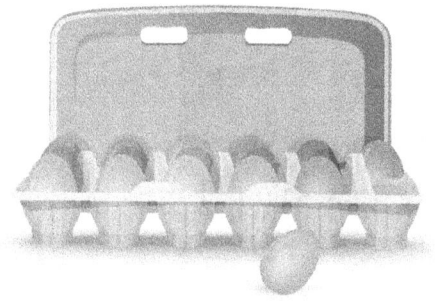

Eggs

They're mostly
sold by the dozen
I don't need a dozen
Too many are not good for you
I don't know how to cook 'em
I barely know how to crack 'em
I do know how to color them
Could never separate them
And always expected a baby chick to appear
They are lauded in literature
There's "Humpty Dumpty"
"The Egg and I" and don't forget
"Green Eggs and Ham" or
"The Agony and the Eggstasea"
People boil them hard and soft
They poach them, scramble them
Fry them sunny side up or over easy
Not to mention over hard and yolk broken
Kids throw them at Halloween
Grown-ups threw them at vaudevillians
Me, I'd rather have the chicken
On either side of the road
Deep fried, baked, rotissarized
Or plain old
Chicken salad
(6/20/09)

Doodle Dumb

Doodle Dumb, mean and evil scum
Never having been seen by some
Craggy face full of scars and jowls
Into the mountain winds he howls.

Most comfortable on a stormy night
Creating evil is his main delight.
Slugs crawl on his shirt and vest
Barnacles hang from all the rest.

Patches cover holes and eye
He gains pleasure when you cry.
Draining pus and drinking rust
Never can he be one to trust.

Slipping through the night of the quarter moon
He sings a carefully crafted tune,
Designed to tease and torment
The listener soon joins in the lament.

A chorus of shrill and unmerciful babble
There is no room for such ungainly rabble.
Twisting meanings and telling tales
Lying and cheating when all else fails

Blaming all that's wrong on the other
It's no fun having him for a brother.

(3/20/12)

I Should Be Eating Salad

I should be eating salad.
My figure to that attests,
Chilly iceberg or the stately romaine
Tossed with other tender greens.
Then the familiar additions

Shaved carrots, sliced cukes,
Chunks of any garden's tomato.
Perhaps a bit of mushroom,
A ring or two of Vidalia, a radish,
Raisins, nuts, assorted colored peppers.
Apple, chicken, shrimp, oh God sprouts. – Yuk!
And yes top it off with any vinaigrette.
Combine that with exercise.
Forget deserts and modify your snacks.
I could be that calorie counter.
Perhaps I should be that calorie counter.
But, Lord in Heaven,
There are so many
Meatloaf recipes to be tried.

(1/29/12)

RING

The bells call the faithful
They toll in sadness
And chime in joyous celebration.

Ring –

The fantastic digit decoration
Display of fortune and design
Symbol of love and commitment.

Ring –

Advertising's ultimate villain
Leaving its mark on collar and tub
Only to be spared by cleaning's heroes.

Ring –

The framework for man's competition
From Marciano to Ali →

To Gorgeous George and the WW something.

Ring –

The cross-sectioned count
That holds the age
Of your neighbor's sycamore.

Ring –

Spaced out circulation
Wrapped in cosmic mystery
Surrounding the Saturn planet.

Ring –

The big one has three
Enough to hold elephants,
Lions, acrobats and silly clowns.

Ring – around – circle – peal – and pickup before the fourth or "you have reached …".

(12/3/05)

Oh, Dear Mr. Gardener

"Oh, Dear Mr. Gardener
How do your ornamental grasses grow?"

"Why lass, how nice of you to ask.
They've grown as tall as your ass
And show all signs or growing past."

"Oh sir, your speech is quite crass!"

"Alas deary, I grow weary, old and clearly
Living in the past. Was a time I could
Speak my mind and people would hear

That I was sincere."

"Well those times are done,
So watch your tongue."

"Yes mum, oh dear you've stepped in the dung."

(8/8/11)

Padoodle

A long time ago, in the land of Padoodle,
Lived a prince with the personality of a noodle.
He owned a longhaired cocoa curly Lithuanian poodle
And both sat around eating nothing but strudel.

In Padoodle the sun would rise very fast.
But, alas in this community it didn't last.
It started right down and long shadows were cast
'Til long about quarter to three, the daylight was past.

People in Padoodle generally wore a frown.
They took little comfort that their comforters were down.
Rather they wanted poly something or foam to drown out the sound
Of all the night creatures that in their yards would abound.

There were weak-kneed willies and monks,
 Not to mention bitty bears and cross-eyed skunks.
Frosted flamingos that turned green, would eat flowers in chunks
And the moon was so bright, the children slept under their bunks.

The prince would walk his poodle at dawn
And this royal pet would puddle or dump on every front lawn.
The peasants would smile and generally fawn.
His nibs would just yawn and wait till "Poopsy" had gone.

Then one year in the part of a day
His royal ness saw a maid come his way→

He was immediately smitten and found words to say
"Would you like to walk with me by the bay?"

The lass cast her eyes to the ground
She nodded yes without making a sound.
They walked and his highness knew love he had found
And beauty and romance were all around

The courtship was rather simple and short.
The prince discovered she had but one wart.
And he asked her to marry with a sincere snort.
She paused but a moment before a positive retort.

The ceremony was held in the brief daylight.
People cheered as the now royal couple came into sight.
Things in Padoodle had never been so right
And the party lasted well into the night.

The prince, now happy with his new wife,
Started his new and full life.
Cutting the cake, he and his bride used an old hunting knife
Dancing and cavorting to the music of piccolo and fife.

The very next morning, the prince did declare
That sunshine would last longer and there would be a fair.
The peasants were wise and tried not to stare
It seems the royal beautician did poodle's and princess's hair.

Pooch and princess all full of curls
Now the object of imitation by a nation of girls
Round and round the earth still whirls
And the flag unfurls; oysters turned to pearls.

(7/18/11)

Wiggle Witch

Wiggle Witch waited for night
Resting, ready to take flight
Cats in order, all proper black
Cauldrons bubbling with potions
Most brimming with improper notions.

Bats hanging to rafters
Skeletons escaping the hereafters
Spider webs set, carefully woven.
Pirates with treasure sail by,
Headless horsemen outlined against the sky.

Wiggle Witch rocks and gives out a cackle
Thinking of tricks she will tackle
Gremlins and ghouls, gourds and pumpkins.
Full moon - hear how the wolf howls.
Wait what's that? Her face scowls.

Little children at the door knocking.
"What do you want? I'll put nothing in your stocking."
Timid and shaking, the little ones look up.
"Trick or Treat," comes a small voice from under a sheet,
"My mom's just down the street."

"BOO to you little kid."
And he ran behind the bushes and hid.
Haystacks, hay rides and mazes,
Summer colors rusting,
All the furniture needs dusting.

Wiggle Witch mounts her broom
Takes a few steps, then up, away, zoom.
She circles once around the house,
Lifts her head back, laughing with glee.
WHOOPS she didn't see the tree.

(10/5/06)

I'm Your Fish

No, I don't fetch
I don't attack balls of yarn
I just swim around and eat flakes

I don't want to go for a walk
I won't scratch the furniture
I'll just swim back and forth

OK change my filter and keep the water warm
But I don't make a lot of noise
Or go racing around bumping into things

I just swim forth and back
And give you fishy kisses
Nope, don't spin a wheel
Or hop around leaving colored eggs

I go up and down and round and round
The light goes on, the light goes off
Make sure the cover's on

Not gonna jump on your bed
Or your lap or beg for a snack
I'm quieter than a mouse

I'm not sure I care about you
But I'll race for them flakes
I don't spill my water

And you don't need a plastic bag
To scoop up my pooh-pooh
No litter to change. I won't try to get out

Gimme some grass or a castle
And I'll keep swimin', it's what I do
I'm your fish.

(9/23/11)

Rhyming Story - 1

Billy Crumb was a bum
Feared and hated by some
Never a full day's work done
And loved by no one.

He was born in Delaware
His parents just didn't care
The hugs and kisses were rare
For a young boy it wasn't fair.

Moved about for whatever reason
Rarely in one place for a season
Other kids never tired of teasing
Nothing he tried was pleasing.

Out of the house as soon as he could
Living a life that no one should
Scratching for love in a new neighborhood
Going bad, as his parents said he would.

Not expecting to get to a ripe old age
Never a job with a decent wage
Life was cruel at every stage
And with him only a constant rage.

His education was certainly slim
No teacher ever reached out to him
He roughed up people for a fin
Left cars resting on a rim.

One day he met a girl named Terry
Around women he was always wary
In a rare gesture, her bundles he offered to carry
The feelings inside him were scary. →

Stuff

She had sparkling eyes and a funny little smile
They stopped at her stoop and talked awhile
Terry wasn't afraid of him and had style
Billy's words stumbled and conversation was a trial.

But he mumbled on and she listened
God, how cute her eyes and her hair glistened
He touched her hand and there was no resistin'
It was quite clear this boy was smitten.

He asked to take her out next day
She knew his reputation and said, "No way"
Still they talked and talked
And found that they had walked and walked.

Terry asked some questions he had no answers for
Why he did what he did, why his behavior was poor
He was going to brush things off
But he couldn't, her skin so soft.

Layer after layer of hate peeled away
The paths he had taken, all the wrong way
And all the time she stared
The first person in his life that cared.

Time slid by in a flash
He offered an invitation, quite rash
She paused, looking deep inside him
Then flashed a smile as he turned grim.

Music poured into his ears
So close he came to tears
Play that tune once more
"Yes" was her answer, his feet left the floor.

They set the time and the place
And she hurried home at a rapid pace
He turned in circles, his mouth in a smile
Then he sat down and dreamt for awhile.

(6/23 – 9/15/15)

Composer

Twice upon a minute.
Betty Bennett sat at a spinet.
She plunked at the keys
'Til her hands fell to her knees.
As hard as she tried
No tune from her head could be pried.

In frustration she gave out with a <u>howl</u>
She had had it, all done, throw in the towel.
But wait, it was there, that <u>note</u>…
Quickly on paper she wrote
One right after another
It was here, oh, brother!

More than a catchy little tune
This would make publishers swoon.
Now from her heart she added the story
Down home and comfy she was in her glory.
A picture so real was painted
Anxiously the next verse awaited.

Two people falling in love
Being watched by an in-flight dove.
When the boy bent down toward the girl
The bird got excited and started to swirl.
The two lovers locked tight in a kiss,
Our feathered voyager did not miss.

Billy Joe and Sue Anne were a mess
Anger and disgust were expressed in excess.
Quickly the bird returned to its nest,
While amorous thoughts were put to rest.
Down the dirt road the pick-up truck raced
Sue and Billy looked up red-faced.

It was Sue's father, his dog Blue, riding shotgun,
Time was late afternoon, heading into the sun.
The truck hit the couple and then hit a tree.
The tune ended with Blue walking free.

(4/13/12)

"Drip, Drip"

"Drip, drip" the faucet calls through the night,
A steady pounding from spout to sink
"Drip, drip" the crashing pulls my attention
And tosses me side to side and pillow overhead.
"Drip, drip" the minutes stir my tired bones.
I don't want to rise – I have an early day.
"Drip, drip" my head tries to tune it out
My eyes squeeze tighter as if to shut my ears.
"Drip, drip" can it really add to the water bill?
It will help keep the pipes from freezing.
"Drip, drip" no I'm not sneezing
And I'm so comfortable – so warm.
"Drip, drip" I hear you calling.
All right I'll stop stalling.
"Drip, drip" wait – hold on – I'm coming.
The floor is cold. Where are my slippers?
"Drip, drip" I'm on my way – half awake
Hitting every piece of furniture along the way.
"Drip, drip" light on – crack a look
Yes I see it – turn the handle tight.
"Drip, drip" wait now I thought it was done
Maybe not so tight – loosen just slightly.
"Drip" Oh that's it – almost there.
One more minor change then – silence
Light off – stumble – fumble – OW!
Oh God – now I'm awake – no relax.
Sandman and nymph carry me through.

I can still get a good night's sleep…
Ah – yawn – no light through the windows…
(Pause)
"Drip, drip, drip."

(3/13/12)

A (Abner) Meets B (Bob)

Scene: *Late afternoon on a dirt road passing along a fenced in field. Abner is on the far side of the fence resting against it and is dressed in typical farm clothes. Bob, in well-worn traveling clothes enters stage left heading towards stage right.*

A-	Hey there!
B-	'Lo
A-	Where you headin'?
B-	Down the road.
A-	Yeah?
B-	Yup.
A-	Down the road?
B-	Yeah.
A-	How far?
B-	Some.
A-	Where you from?
B-	*(Pauses and moves towards fence)* Back there.
A-	Yeah?
B-	Yeah.
A-	Goin' down the road?
B-	Yeah.
A-	Been here before?
B-	Yup.
A-	Really. When?
B-	Some time ago.
A-	Know anybody in town?
B-	What ya got planted?
A-	Hmm, oh, potatoes.
B-	Good crop?
A-	Fair. →

B- Well got to get goin'.
A- Been travelin' long?
B- Some.
A- Got far to go?
B- Some.
A- You know which way to go at the fork down the road?
B- Yeah.
A- Be careful, we've had quite a bit of rain.
B- Yup.
A- Need a place to stay tonight?
B- Nope.
A- Already got one?
B- Maybe.
A- If you go right at the fork, Clara Hobbs rents rooms in town.
B- That so?
A- Yeah.
B- Hmm.
A- I could give her a call; let her know your comin'.
B- No thanks.
A- So you goin' left at the fork then?
B- Have any problems with potato bugs?
A- What?
B- Potato bugs? Problems?
A- Oh, no.
B- See ya around.
A- They say it might turn cold tonight.
B- That so?
A- Yeah, that's what they say.
B- Hmm.
A- Might want to go right at the fork anyways and get a nice hot meal at *Millie's Place*.
B- Hmm.
A- Sarah makes a mighty fine meatloaf.
B- Sarah?
A- Yeah, Sarah, she runs the place.
B- Millie's?
A- Yeah, Sarah owns it, does the cookin', serves ya and takes your money.
B- And Millie?
A- Oh, left town with Sarah's husband years ago, talk of the town back then.
B- Hmm.
A- So you're headed west?

B- Would appear so.
A- Comin' from the east?
B- Hmm.
A- I'm not tryin' to be nosey; we just don't see many strangers. My name's Abner Nelson.
B- Hi.
A- Um, What's yours?
B- Bob.
A- Well, Hi Bob. Glad to meet you. Um, don't want you to get lost or nothin.'"
B- No.
A- I mean the roads get a little tricky around here and there ain't many signs tellin' ya which way to go.
B- Hmm.
A- Yeah and it gets dark quick, once the sun hits them mountains, turns real cold too.
B- Hmm.
A- Listen, I'm just about done for the day. Why don't I head down the road with ya for a little while; my place is just down the road on the right.
B- Suit yourself.
A- *(Moves up stage to gather tools)* Yeah, I can show ya the fork from there, Midville to the right and Flatt's Landing to the left.
B- Hmm.
A- You headed for Flatt's Landing? I got a cousin down there, Bill Turner, know Him?
B- Nope.
A- You are heading for Flatt's Landing?
B- What kind of potatoes you grow?
A- *Red Bliss* mostly, good market nowadays.
B- Hmm.
A- Let me get my stuff over there and we can head out.
B- See ya. *(Continues toward stage right exit)*
A- Hey wait, only take a minute!
B- Got to get goin'.
A- Long way to go?
B- Long enough.
A- Well OK, we'll see ya and don't forget about *Millie's* if you get hungry.
B- Right.
A- So long Bob, nice talkin' to ya.
B- Hmm.
 (6/1/14)

Mesquite, Mosquito

Mesquite Mosquito was danger on wings.
He was born in a birdbath
A forgotten birdbath that the owner never filled.
It would collect a little rainwater
But the shade prevented full evaporation
And a green mold would be born.
Not long after that, Mesquite Mosquito was born.
This aviary tub was located in the western part of the yard.
Mesquite was not an only child.
In fact, Mesquite had a huge family
And sharing was not his, or his siblings' strong point.
Mom and dad were not providers.
This flurry of bugs was left to their own devices.
No regurgitated snack, no wiggly main course…
They were all out for blood.
Now, it's not like they could travel a long way;
A trip to the center of town was beyond their range.
Even if they found the Red Cross building or the hospital
These winged nasties probably couldn't tap in.
They needed local dining opportunities
And the man in the hammock, the lad in the sandbox
Was the type of menu items that suited them fine.
  Mesquite was quick and constantly alert.
He made great landings, vertical or horizontal,
Picking a place not easily reached by the victim…
No lingering; in, bite, suck, out and away.
Watching for the slap or the spray
Ignoring the garden bug light
The fly swatter was a joke that was for flies.
He would take solo flight or lead a whole flock
Brothers, sisters, cousins, uncles, aunts would cloud up
And ride the wind looking for an unsuspecting food supply.
Then it was "dive, dive, dive" and dinner was served.
Mesquite got his name because he lived next to the grill.
It was there that the mesquite chips were stored
And Mesquite just blended in.
It wasn't an easy life but he was a hardened veteran.

Too often he had seen relatives slapped and smeared
Leaving just a little itch on the killer.
Now, the only thing the mosquitoes would do,
After successfully loading up with assorted blood types,
Would be to stagger up to the nearest tree branch.
There they would plop down in a long line.
A moment of silence for those lost in the day's battle,
Then a deep voice would begin to sing, almost a chant.
Gradually others would join in with their tiny voices.
Perhaps you thought it was the rustle of leaves
Or two branches scraping together,
But listen harder; you can almost hear the words
"A, B, AB, O – A, B, AB, O – All the positives, don't forget the negatives
We suck it up all day, hey, hey, what do you say?"
And so it goes day after day until the frost.
Some say, that mosquitoes die off then.
They don't have the range to fly south.
Inside a house they become vulnerable.
Still after a hard frost, I find no huge pile of dead mosquitoes.
Do you cover your grill in winter?
Bring the gas tank in or leave it empty?
My thought is that one dangerous villain
One named Mesquite Mosquito lives on,
Under the grill cover, in a pile of leftover mesquite chips
A stubborn hoarder works through his supply
Softly singing,
"A, B, AB, O – A, B, AB, O – All the positives, don't forget the negatives
We suck it up all day, hey, hey, what do you say?"

(5/16/15)

Would You Help?

- What if Jiminy Cricket gave a little whistle, because he was in trouble - would you help?
- What if the third pig's house was poorly constructed and it too came tumbling down - would you help?→

- What if the villain has tied the heroine to the railroad tracks and is happily twirling his mustache, the train is coming and "our hero" is busy kissing his horse - would you help?
- What if the Three Bears have caught Goldilocks and turned her over to the police on charges of breaking and entering, damage to personal property, theft of food goods, and wrinkling the sheets - would you help?
- What if the mustached twirling villain from above has the mortgage on your grandma's house and is threatening to foreclose and throw her on the street - would you help?
- What if Cinderella is busy scrubbing floors upstairs and doesn't hear the guy with the glass slipper arrive and Lucifer has cornered Gus-Gus and Jacques and is preparing lunch - would you help?
- What if Brigadoon never comes back, Johnny sings more than one note, Red Riding Hood isn't little anymore - would you help?

Of course you would!
My Hero (Sigh).

(11/29/14)

Choices

Coke or Pepsi
Left or Right
Up or Down
Soup or Salad
Friend or Foe
Paper or Plastic
Believe or Not
Truth or Consequences
Coffee or Tea
Right or Wrong

(4/30/08)

You Are My Creation 1

You are my creation

You are outside my door
You are inside my heart

You have three toes
And they grow out of your nose

Your hair is a lovely lavender
Your eye a ravishing red

Your feet a clown's desire

When you smile
The sun must hide

When you speak
The beagle howls

Bugs crawl from your lips
And from your skin

Only a *chia* pet competes

You are my creation
Now go back inside

(8/26/06)

You Are My Creation 2

You are my creation
You are outside my door
You are inside my heart

We are younger
We are together
We are alone →

Stuff

Your hair is long or not
Your eyes are deep
Your smile a little uncertain

We talk and chatter
At first the words tumble
Sharing, confiding, asking

Then laughing, then crying
Hands held tight
We ride and walk

And we are together

We are in all seasons
We are at the water's edge
We are on a path

The rain is soft
The breeze is steady
The sun, the shade
The moon, the stars

We grow tired
We rest – your head nestled
We are both safe

Sunrises, sunsets
We grow older
But we are the same

You are my creation
See you tomorrow

(8/26/06)

A Day of Celebration

People awoke to a cloudy day
But that would not deter their spirits
A day of celebration had begun.
By noon the sun had found us.
Gradually from dawn, until deep into the night
Things were sorted and bagged
And all joined in rolling, carrying or dragging
Their collection to curb's edge.
Greetings and gossip were exchanged.
Joggers, walkers and animal care givers
Were included in the building excitement.
People costumed in assorted outfits
From hastily covered sleeping garments
To the neat and coiffed workers
As they headed out for daily grinds took part.
The ancients usually were first
They were up early with nothing better
It was on the top of their lists anyway.
Here then the discussions range
From weather to some event in World War II
That neither was old enough to remember
Perhaps some incomplete facts
Proffered as a God given truth.
It didn't matter - they became distracted
A car traveling too fast down the street
Gave them cause to raise their voices
In an instant duet of "Slow Down!"
Then they would wander back into their yards
To putter and mumble and get the job done.
Still others were uncertain, is it true?
Are you sure this is the celebration day?
Finally convinced, they joined the parade.
It was indeed Garbage Eve
And a recyclable week as well!

(6/25/14)

Jack

"Half a pound of tupenny rice"

Alone in the dark
Unable to move
Noises outside
My bones caved in

"Half a pound of treacle"

No time for friendships
Pushed down into blackness
Behind the door
Lifeless with no sound

"That's the way the money goes"

Those times of freedom
That first Christmas morning
Turn the handle
Here I am!

"Pop! Goes the weasel"

At first it was up and down
All day, up and down
Quick peeks at what's around
Colors and faces and then.

"Every night when I get home"

Another journey into midnight
Once or twice up for air
Then the big deep void
And longer times waiting.

"The monkey's on the table"

One time I was out
And they left me there

What a wonderful time
Slightly bowed, I saw all

"Take a stick and knock it off"

The ins and outs
Of their daily life
Busy, too busy to see me
Nights full of quieter sounds

(softly) **"Pop! Goes the weasel"**

Then one day, I was dusted off
Closed back in
And moved once more
It stayed so lonely.

"Up and down the city road"

Tilted upside down
Then falling on my side
I heard panic around me
Little sad voices and crying

"In and out of the Eagle"

Time was lost for everyone
Dolls and soldiers whispered
They shared their past
And imagined no future.

"That's the way the money goes"

Suddenly I heard my song
I sorted myself out, ready
Sprang to a face, a new face
A giggling, joyous face!

"Pop! Goes the weasel"

"All around the mulberry bush
The monkey chased the weasel→

The monkey stopped to pull up his sock
Pop! Goes the weasel."

(11/30, 12/15 & 12/21/14)

Sillies

W E L L, Tilly Wong Wong
Sitting, singing a song song
Spitin' at flies
Meddlin' in lives.
What do you think is next?
Could it be Wonder Dog Rex?
Fighting for justice and right
Sad his collar's too tight.
Swell the music, loud and clear
Come take a walk with me my dear
Shall we travel to the sun?
Step by step, skip and run
Hand in hand across the land
Tripping on tulips and turnips in the sand
Working our way up the valley
Stop by the Palmettos – let us dally
Green and rich, damp with morning mist
Sample the fruit – if you insist.
Now the sky opens wide
And our feet can play with the tide.
What's this – no lake goes in and out
Up and down perhaps and turn about
Float the fisherman and all his tales
Minnows and trout all covered with scales
Pockets of vacationing swimmers and waders
Splishing and splashing, these summer invaders
Talking in tones and vowels and gibberish too
They start a sentence and never get through –
Up to their cabins, with clothes on the line
No TV or Internet – give me the Checkers; they're mine.
Stuck in the woods with no reception
Oh, those evil adults, what a cruel deception.
This was supposed to be different and fun

Stuff

Getting us off the couch and into the sun.
Now I have dawn, bugs and the day's catch dinner
It's lucky that the kayak race had me the winner.
Yeah, all the scenery is pretty, pretty boring
And my big brother, father and mother are snoring
So I'm hangin' by the backyard swing
And suddenly there is something I find interesting.
She's about four foot nine, lives next door
Dressed for summer, I can't ignore.
We take a casual walk toward each other
Turns out she has a horrible little brother.
Her name's Barbie, don't laugh my name's Ken
We talked and talked about this and then
Then we walked and walked on woodland path
She told a joke and it made me laugh.
Then the time passed and we were lost
We wondered if we'd be home by frost
Which way to go, neither of us was sure
Oh, the wilderness, dense and thick to endure
Quiet now and maybe some lips were trembling
It's only been an hour, but the world is ending.
Then we both heard it, a babbling brook
Together, wordless we turn to look
Our savior, a swift little stream
Racing downhill out of a dream.
We stumbled and tumbled to the end
It spilled into our lake, this watery friend.
I guess we had come quite a distance
A suggestion for home met no resistance
We happily bounced along the shore
And were home again with time to ignore.
Adventures in the next days ensued
My summer was saved, my spirit renewed
Talk upon talk and a few hidden smooches
We walked younger children and their family's pooches,
Till our time came, too quickly, to an end
Still I had the e-mail address of my newfound friend.
We packed all our stuff and said good-bye to the lake
Leaving happy memories drifting in our wake.

(12/17/14)

What's in That Drawer

What's in that drawer, you know the one?
The one where you stuff the take-out menus
And the coupons you might use from the mail.

Elastic bands gone stiff and useless.
A tack to stick your finger with
Never found when you needed it.

Birthday candles from the ages, some burnt, some new…
That little piece of string, to tie up a roast
To tie a package or fasten a pull chain or shade pull.

Plastic ware bundled with napkins or loose.
Oh, what's this, a cherry pitter, red plastic?
A prize from Avon days or a catalogue free gift,
Never has it seen the inside of a cherry.

A miniature screwdriver, key tags and markers,
A pen or two and a AA battery, not corroded –
Assorted picture hanging devices, with a wee bit of wire.

Look, instructions to run that gizmo.
Do we still have that gizmo?
Then there's this thing that came off of something
I was going to glue it on, maybe tomorrow.

Now, I came in here for something;
Don't remember what.
In the meantime, why don't we order Chinese?
Here's the take-out menu.
Just let me close the drawer.

(3/26/16)

Birdfeeder

I put out suet and seed
Expecting a yellow-bellied monk
Bluebird starling wren cormorant
And then a red-winged grackle
Goldfinch sparrow finch
Or perhaps a grosbeak eagle,
Tern cardinal gull or plastic flamingo.
I add extra sunflower seeds
Hoping to attract a blackbird
Hawk owl woodpecker towhee.
With a flicker of hope that maybe
I'll see a blue jay chickadee
Maybe a junco wood hatch
Or, be still my heart, a titmouse.
A mourning dove after ten.
Forget egret sandpiper or goose
Not much waddle room for a duck
But maybe a nuthatch oriole waxwing
Mocking bunting catbird swallow
No not even a nesting plover.
Day after day I look out the window
And plopped in the middle of the seed
With its' orange eye staring at me
Is a damned pigeon.

(8/16/08)

* Previously published in "High Tide – 2009" – a publication of the former Writer's Group of the Milford Fine Arts Council -

Dust

Tonight, I'm thinking of what's on my list for things I want to get done tomorrow. Near the top of the list is *dust*. That would be the act of dusting the *dust* off the furniture mostly.

Dust is that stuff that steals into your house and plops down wherever it wants. It gives a gray covering over furniture, small appliances and generally anything that doesn't move a lot. I have found dust on my person when I have awakened from an unexpected nap in my recliner.

This coating does not make a good pet despite how much you might like the designation, "dust bunnies." Besides it doesn't hop or bring you Easter eggs.

Drill sergeants and mothers-in-laws carry white gloves to prove what a slovenly person you are and every company in the world has a solution. From *Endust* to a magic micro-fiber cloth, the solution is only a few dollars away.

I give you fair warning, this is not true. Whether you dust yourself, or have a trusted housekeeper, one that has been retained by your family for generations, that dust will be back.

Way back, when I had chores instead of lists of things I wanted to get done, dusting was usually mine. Growing up, the dust cloth was a square of light black material about the size of a handkerchief with a thin line of red stitching around the edges, to keep it from unraveling. I would rub it across the tabletop, shelf and visiting Aunt Clara. Then race to the closest door to the outside world, stick my cloth holding hand out the door and shake vigorously.

Wood was waxed and polished, countertops were scrubbed to their original color and Aunt Clara was bathed and groomed. Still, in a week, everything was covered again.

Dust enters through the pores of the house; it follows children who forgot to close the door and hides in corners and closets and behind curtains 'til the minute before someone checks on how well you've done your chores. It sneaks into places in an instant and makes the designated duster a shrugger of responsibility, a person who will never make something of himself, a failure in life.

It is a rare few who see any benefits to dust. Yet, I consider myself one of those few. If there is a math problem to be solved, I mean in the heat of an argument when a point must be made, you have an instant blackboard.
When there are no misted windows nearby, how can you draw a heart with an arrow through it to express your love for someone? Maybe that someone is even the inspector!

(9/6/15)

Who invented

There are days when I get a number of things done
There are days when I find excuses.
Somewhere in-between those days
There are days I have deep thoughts.
I question the reasons for things.
I wonder about the origins of things.
Today I sat at the table paralyzed in thought.
It wasn't even morning... barely afternoon
When I came up with one of life's eternal questions.
      WHO INVENTED TOAST?
Bread has been around forever – right?
Leavened – unleavened – wheat, rye and pumpernickel.
Some combine multi grains, like some sort of a bean salad
And, as you might expect, my favorite is white.
We know bread goes back thousands of years,
Just look at those references in the Bible.
So just who invented toast?
I was thinking, the Earl of Sandwich
Accidentally knocked two slices of bread into the fire,
He reached to grab the bread back
But it was hot and he almost burned his fingers.
Frustrated, he had only managed to flip the bread.
In the meantime, his tuna salad was getting warm.
Finally, he grabbed once more and pulled them free.
Using the ancient five-second rule, he picked them up,
Examined them as if biting into a gold nugget.
Pleased, he built his sandwich and had lunch.
No, huh?
Then perhaps a caveman made the discovery,
Right after he had bonked his woman on the head.
She had left the dinosaur out all night
And the big something, a saurus, was getting a cold.
He opened his loaf of Wonder Bread.
Taking two slices, he held them toward the heavens.
You can guess the rest – lightning struck...
The bread was toast, but then, so was the caveman.
Knights of the Round Table may have played a part.→

Now these guys were pretty good fighters.
Yes, they were grumpy, but so would you be
If you walked around all day in a metal suit.
So if they weren't sitting around the table
Or trying to get scarves from ladies,
They needed to find some sort of fashion statement.
Well maybe they could go for a ride in the country
After a few hours they might be getting hungry
So off the horse and rustle up some lunch
They're eating with their fingers, stuff they brought along
Spread out on a "blankie," a mini feast.
Wouldn't you know that a dragon shows up?
Yup, a fire breathing dragon to boot.
He does his fee-fie-foe-fum-rum-a-dum-dum bit
And spits a few flames the knight's way
It bounces off the metal outfit and voila',
The bread on the blanket is toasted.
No? Well I just don't know then.
We have hold bread over an open fire things –
Side opening, pop-up two, four or more machines.
We can have it light or dark or in-between.
But, toast – When? Who? Why?
A chef or cook disguising stale bread?
Something to crunch and annoy your mother-in-law
Who just moved into the spare bedroom?
You don't hear much about peanut butter and jelly
Being put on toast, but you do hear
About jelly, preserves and marmalades being served
On a single slice of nicely toasted bread.
Maybe it was named after someone famous?
Then I wonder who was the first "Toastmaster?"

(Unknown Date)

My Sister

My sister got caught in a twister
Where she received not one, but two blisters
Not much on looks, the army guy said "Hey, Mister"
And tried very hard to enlist her.

To this she took great offense
Jumped right over the fence
The soldier man had no defense
And was pummeled into obsolescence.

Well she was arrested and taken to trial
Had to sit in a room covered in green tile
While the judge studied her file for awhile
Finally taken down a hallway almost a quarter of a mile.

She stood before his honor, head bowed
The judge sought justice he vowed
He ruled the military man had been rude and loud
And threw open the doors of freedom, whose threshold my sister was allowed.

My sister left court in the rain
She thought of traveling to Spain
But that idea went down the drain
As she waited, she hoped, not in vain.

Soon the judge came out the back door
With a grin you couldn't ignore
He gave her a kiss that said more
They were married in the chapel next door.

(10/23/13)

I Tasted Yogurt and I Didn't Die

I tasted yogurt and I didn't die.
I took steps and didn't fall.
I rode my bike and didn't fall.
I understood what you said.
I tasted green stuff – it wasn't good…
And the fine line between mold and penicillin.
I tasted tofu and it had no taste.

I knew a woman who served tofu to her husband.
They divorced but maybe it wasn't the tofu.

I kissed a girl and she kissed back,
I stood in the rain and got wet.
I stood in the rain with a girl and got wet.
I kissed her and she kissed back and wet didn't matter.
I weed in my garden and it doesn't seem to matter.

Night almost always follows day
Unless day decides to follow night
And that depends on when you wake up
Unless you hit the snooze button
But I don't think God honors a snooze button.

I generally make a list of things to do.
Some days I do all that is on the list.
I have learned over the years to curb my frustration
And make short and easy lists.

I never have to go to school again, never...
But I love to learn about stuff I love
And if you love, you never learn enough
About the people you really, really love.

(8//18/14)

A Gerbuttal Fish

Found in the depths of the North Atlantic
Deep down at the ocean's bottom
That place where light has never been
Resides the prehistoric Gerbuttal Fish.

The Gerbuttal Fish has eyes wide open
But because of the darkness sees nothing
He is not blind, just unseeing
And what he doesn't see, he doesn't believe.

This unbelieving fish comes in a variety of lengths
And is usually, but not exclusively, white
One might describe him as an old fossil fish
He just doesn't know he should be dead.

He feeds on rumor and innuendo
Thriving on distrust and half-truths
Quick to bite on any weak or different species
Happy to hoard his abundant pantry.

To help build that food locker
He will take many shapes
Posing and posturing, preening and promising
Painting Holocaust pictures of every man's dream.

The Gerbuttal can bury his head in the sand
And suck the nutrients from the ocean's floor
Always looking to the right
While stealing from the left.

His horny skin repels rebuffs
And he spins on a wheel
Denying what others see
Finally sticking his own butt in his mouth.

He points his fins in the air
And wags danger everywhere.
Moving farther away from the middle,
The Gerbuttal Fish continues to spout his drivel.

(4/4/14)

Flipity, Flopity, Gizmo Delight

Flipity, Flopity, Gizmo Delight
You wind it up and it goes out of sight.
It's red and blue and yellow and white
When it gets close to a table it takes a bite
Flipity, Flopity, Gizmo Delight. →

The man at the mall made it go fast
He swore on his bonnet it would last.
We got it home and the guarantee was past
The gap in performance was vast.
But the man in the mall made it go fast.

It was a "I gotta' have it" buy.
But soon into the toy chest with a sigh,
With other fantastic bargains it will lie.
No matter how hard I try
I couldn't get it to sit, spin or fly.

So, I'm sorry I asked you to buy it.
I'm sorry too; I threw a God awful fit.
You were right to make me go to the corner and sit.
I promise next spring I'll only ask for a mitt.
Don't you admire my candor, frankness and wit?

(10/9/10)

Whatever Comes Out

Jibberish, Jibberish
Monday Night
Mumbo, Jumbo
Succotash
Silly Lilly
Hello Billy
Getting scared
Here comes Willy
Hash to Trash
I once rode in a Nash
Dinty Moore
It's on the floor
My teams playing
What's the score?
Kitty scratchin' at the door

Stuff

Well Mr. Dillon, want some more?
Chester wears a Sou'wester
Raining buckets over board
Sailor's knots tar and feather
Who's got the scarlet letter?
Quarter moon left some change
Went 'round the clouds
Just hanging out
Taking the night off
Sitting on his butt
BUT rumination – great elation!
Flags a flyin' - no ones dyin'
Catch some fish for fryin'
Rubber boots, tall ones – waders
Casting flies, swatting flies
Let's go camping just for fun
That ain't Smoky, run, run, run
Mountains and forests
Trees and grass
Laugh, laugh, laugh
Edit, edit, edit
Sittin' on my ass
Things to do one two three
Open the door – who's to see
Secrets hiding? Surprise!
No way today
Say what you want to say
Say what? Putt, putt, putt
Skateboard, surfboard
Kids standing around bored
Back to moonlight and gardens
Lovely lady, handsome man
Nineteenth century, she has a fan
Arm and arm away from the light
He touches – his hat
And says good night
Willow walls and climbing wisteria
She's lost and rushing to hysteria
How could he? – How dare he?
Leave her standing on the garden path
Perfume rising – energizing
Why, here comes the gardener
Full of weeds and wit →

He's tired and dirty
She moves over, kind of flirty
He sits on a statue's apron
She spins a tarantella
And sits next to this fella
He looks over and shows his – ivories
She flirts and fusses
His fingers walk across the marble
She reaches over and touches the granite
Oh My God!
It's Jeannette MacDonald and Nelson Eddy
They burst into song
And old Jeff Davis on his horse
Smiles and says, "The South will rise again!"
His horse climbs off the base
And joins in the race
"Old Dan Patch" and "Call Me Madam"
Ain't seen this since Eve and Adam
Getting late – all's slowing down
Why look at that, it's almost eleven
Roll a seven – all good children go to heaven.

(6/12/12)

Protractor?

There is no more fun in September
Than getting some new school supplies...
A pencil box, a foot long ruler, pens, and pencils,
And a protractor.

The gloom of a new school year
Hangs depressingly overhead.
Mom and dad seem happier every day.
I guess I need a protractor.

Dragged to the store for clothes
No more vacation trips
Less time at the beach...
I think the teacher requires a protractor.

Questions are asked about reading lists.
Then there is this week's sweetheart.
The girl who lives around the corner…
Can I at least get a colored protractor?

The days are getting shorter
And one is blazing hot.
The next is a little chilly.
The protractor doesn't fit in my pencil box.

So now the grind begins,
Up before dawn to slog to school…
Home with homework and little time to play.
I don't ever remember using a protractor.

(8/15/14)

P E O P L E   **S T O R I E S**   **T H I N G S**

Chapter 5

This is a loose grouping of stories and poems, some based on a snatch of an image as I wandered by or sometimes as I just sat and watched. Also some are total fiction.

My World

They say I should get up,
That there is no reason for my not getting up.
"There is nothing physically wrong with you."
But I can't get up.
I can't move from this bed.
My world is four feet wide and six feet long;
My world is my caregivers.
I can move about and relocate my body,
But the effort is exhausting.
I can't talk, but I can point.
I play a daily game of charades
And that gets me food and a bedpan.
I'm able to turn the pages of a book
But my mind will only focus for a few minutes.
The room is always the same…
Three walls with little or no change.
The fourth wall, is the window, it is everything.
It looks out on to bricks and other windows.
A few large branches of two holly trees
Are the green leaves of things.
They flap stiffly in the wind,
Reaching from behind a six foot wall…
But they have red berries.
Pigeons come every day and "coo" loudly.
Someone must feed them regularly.
They drop through my view from top right corner
To left lower corner and linger for a while over their meal.
 Their dinner conversations are soft repetitions of that "coo" word.
Then they flutter up loudly and disappear,
Headed for their next adventure.
Last night the snow was falling,
Softly, gently and steadily past the upper left window.
It fell through a shaft of light.
Still I couldn't see the cloud it fell from
Or where it finally landed.
The room is hot, but one window is opened at the top.
Through it some fresh air gains entrance,
But not a steady breeze, →

Just an unpredictable gasp of coolness and relief.
My world of wall and windows across the way
Never changes much.
Days are bright with a few shadows
Or days are gray and faded and not far from darkness.
Night is pitch and long
With only window lights across the way
Going on and off.
There are no people to be seen,
The angle is too steep and I wouldn't want to pry.
I saw a head once - a young woman's head
Hair brown, shoulder length
It peeked out high above me
To check the weather above or the source of noise below,
But it was gone very quickly, never to appear again.

I am not in a bedroom; I am part of a living room.
The bed is in one corner with a TV opposite.
There is a couch and chair facing us,
Us being the TV and me.
Beyond that is a work area and a double door –
That leads to the dining room, kitchen, bedroom,
Bathroom and the world.
People come and go in small numbers –
Caregivers in their regular shifts – puttering,
Watching TV, or moving into the other room
To talk on their cell phones, help me, bring me food.
I also get a small cluster of friends and family
To sit opposite me and chatter
Sharing events of the day, telling a joke
With the punch line bringing a polite smile.
It's hard to miss the slight glance at the wristwatch
Almost from the minute they sit down.
What is the accepted visiting time? I wonder.
I confess that I don't help the situation.
The family, I have alienated long ago,
Mostly from lack of attention or caring
Which is graciously returned in like form.
Friends on the other hand, a few of them,
Come into my world with no obligation.
They come because – they come.

There is no agenda. They just want to visit,
To make sure I'm OK, tend to my needs…
Sometimes I try to interact, but communication is hard.

My world is best when I find a comfortable position
And I am left with a lifetime of thought.
I try not to think of the future.
If forced to, I would not be very positive.
I don't foresee getting well because I'm told nothing is wrong.
The present is eating, going to the bathroom,
Staying awake long enough to be tired.
I have a clock, but it does not tell my time.
The TV goes round and round but rarely stops
It's on for others entertainment, just noise.
No, my best times are when left alone to dream,
To remember or to create something I can make real
Sliding into comfortable memories, closing my eyes
To see children, buddies, happy times
Bringing in unknown faces to join the crowd.
Early happy days all cleaned up
Threats and hurts removed, sanitized for viewing.
I don't want to talk about how I got here.
What's the point? Besides I can't talk.
I have my space. I can move my hands. I can see.
Not everything was taken away.

I am routed out once in awhile, put in a chair
And wheeled into brief world encounters.
These are called doctor's visits.
I am poked, prodded and tested.
"There is nothing wrong. You can walk"
And the psychiatrist waits for me to write answers.
His probing questions don't help a bit
And I think he is as happy to get rid of me
As I am to get rid of him.
Not much pleases me – self-pity I suppose.
It's not that I'm home from the war,
Giving my mobility and voice for a just cause.
I am walking down the street, on the crowded sidewalk.
The day is cold and my head is bowed to the wind.
At the corner I glance at the crosswalk sign. →

The little white man in the sign is walking, so then am I.
How did the car get there so fast?
Why was the car there at all?
And I was in the air, my body detached,
An old-fashion rag doll of skin and bones –

No feeling – just surprise.
And the landing is a crack into blackness.
Voices are far away and all around me
And time again is forever.
And then the light goes on a few floors up –
The building straight across, behind the wall,
Behind the holly branches…
Wait, the shade is rising…

That Deep Night

Deep into the night a fluttering fell from the trees, bouncing shadows in the bright night light of the hunter's moon. The blackbird, already nesting for the night, was startled as two young people passed under his branch. He gave forth with an angry shout, but it was lost in the vast darkness of the woods.

That almost full moon seemed perfectly aligned with the path the two youngsters traveled on. One wonders if, without it, you could even find your way to it much less travel upon it.

The moonbeams extended down the path and across the still lake before climbing back to their source. Those "fluttering shadows" were actually an assortment of falling leaves bleached by the bright evening light.

The man and woman held hands as they moved toward the water's edge. They had been hand in hand almost from the time it was allowed, risking teasing from friends and some raised eyebrows from the older folk.

They were next-door neighbors and played together, fought, laughed and grew close as season passed to season. Sitting on a porch on a summer night, talking for hours on the phone while they stared at each other from their bedroom windows.

Growing and learning, sharing and maturing they both made assumptions. And those around them, friends and families, made the same assumptions about the couple. Plans for the future took a natural turn as they grew older and yours and mine became ours.

Now, finished with High School and having spent yet another summer together, when time never seemed to be a problem, it was always at their feet and it was passed without any stress and they were comfortable even in their silences.

Tonight, like no other night, screamed with quiet. Hands held together with a surprising tension, they moved toward the lake, pushing aside a few low hanging branches. They were headed for "their" spot, their refuge away from everything and everybody.

They came here often, as a place of adventure, a place of sampling, a place that was truly theirs.

Their plans had been disturbed and they strangely could not find a resolution. Both had planned to attend college, State College. Both had been accepted and it was here that they would continue their preparations for a life together, even planning their course loads to compliment the direction they were headed.

But that all came screeching to a halt a couple of weeks ago. She was still scheduled to start college, but he had a different destination. He had been drafted and was to report to boot camp in three days. He and his parents had argued with the local draft board, but to no avail. Yes, he was a student, but because of some loophole or messed up bureaucratic paperwork, he had not actually started college, so he was vulnerable. No amount of showing an acceptance letter or pleading for common sense would move the board and they blocked any appeals. Everybody continued to try for a better solution, but none had been won and time was almost up. All promised to continue the fight, but it was agreed he had to go unless something miraculous happened.

Finally they reached the edge of the lake and moved right along the shoreline. A handful of steps and they turned into the tall branches and high grass that bordered the lake. They disappeared from sight, but were on an almost invisible trail that led up land parallel to the water's edge. The beach area of the lake in this spot ended abruptly, leading to a rocky cliff that was able to support a gentle little forest before meandering down to shore level again as it curved toward the northern portion of the lake.

Suddenly the couple appeared on a rock outcropping completely hidden on three sides by pine, cedar and beech trees. Only from on the lake could this spot be seen. They sat in each other's arms and stared out at their secret world. They did not speak for a while. Looking out across the moonshine and all the mysteries contained in the night, they harmlessly touched each other within their embrace, as if to reassure each other that this time was real.

"Peter, I don't want you to go. I don't want you to leave. It's not fair."

"I know it's not fair, but there's nothing that can be done."

"Sure there is. We can get married; we can elope to where nobody can find us!"

"Amy, Amy our plans we can't run away. We have no money and our parents wouldn't understand."

"We can go to Canada, I don't want you going to Viet Nam, and I don't want you to leave me, to die."

"No Amy, our dads wouldn't understand, they're both vets and as much as they love us and want to help us, they won't tolerate us running away."

"But why? Our plans... all this time... we've waited and now it's almost our time and it's been taken away."

"It just sets things back a little. When I get out I'll go to school, the Army will help pay and then we'll be together again and for always."

"No, it won't happen. You'll go away and you won't come back and I'll be alone - alone forever."

"I will come back and then we can marry and start a family."

"No," she sobbed, "You won't come back. You'll be dead or changed and you won't want me. I don't want to lose you. You're the only man I've ever loved. Don't go. Please Peter, please."

"Amy. Look across the lake. See that trail? That path of light that comes from the moon? I'll walk that path right back into your arms and everything will be right again."

"Damn you Peter and your stupid poetry. I ache for you. I need you. I want your love. I want to have your children. Don't you understand, can't you understand?"

"I understand and it will all happen, just like we planned, just a little later than we expected."

Amy was silent, quiet as the tears that flowed down her cheeks. These were not gentle tears, no way, they were sloppy tears from her eyes, from her nose, from her heart and they could not be stopped.

Peter held her close, trying to stem the tide of tears, trying to stop the quivering of her body, but nothing worked. He cooed into her hair, shushing her sounds and tried to calm her. Finally she stopped, and Peter thought he had finally got her settled. She wiped her eyes and nose with the sleeve of her shirt like some ten-year-old tomboy. Amy took some deep breaths and gave a weak smile up to Peter's shadowed face.

They sat for a minute and then rose. No issues had been settled, no compromises, no communication and this - after all those years. They moved down their trail and climbed out of their hiding place away from all that was said and unsaid and headed home. Very little small talk carried them away from the lake and Peter kissed Amy goodnight on her porch and walked across the lawn to his house. Amy waited on the porch and watched as Peter went to his room and turned off his lights for the night.

Amy looked aimlessly around her porch and at the door that lead into her house and Peter's darkened window and at the deep, deep night. She moved off the porch and walked. Walked through the darkness and felt her footsteps and needed no light - her way was lit from within.

Soon she was on her way down to the lake and the air was not cold. She felt no breeze - perhaps a little tired making this trip again. To the shore, to their spot and now the moon was almost gone. The trail of light was narrow and dim, as she stood unseeing into the now early morning hours. And she saw only one path to take, one course of action. She knew she was right, she would have her happiness if only in her heart, in this night. Amy moved forward along the trail he said would bring him home again and when he came back, then they would truly be together. →

(8/11/11 –Prompt #2)
(11/18/13 – Balance of story)

*"Silvery flakes drifted down, glittering in the bright light of the harvest moon. The blackbird..." Re-titled and slightly altered for a contest. (Didn't win).

Oliver

Oliver was gentle.
Oliver was kind.
He would save your place in line.
Raised to be a gentleman
Holds the door open
With just a hint of a bow.

Oliver would smile.
Oliver didn't laugh.
No, it was more like a titter.
Dressed up so neat and clean
Buttons buttoned and ties knotted
Not one hair was out of place.

Oliver had eyes of blue.
Oliver had a nose turned up too,
Ears a little big and dimpled chin.
I'm not sure you'd call him handsome.
Certainly he was good looking
But, I don't think he believed it.

Oliver was a loner.
Oliver hadn't many friends.
He kept all his feelings in check.
It was hard to tell if he was smart
Studying hard, but testing average
Always quiet, no idle conversation.

Oliver rose the same time every day.
Oliver stuck to his routine,

Ready for the world on his time.
Seasons passed to years
Clock hands spun
The world pushed its sun.

Oliver picked the day.
Oliver had waited long,
Breakfast done and out the door,
Down the street
Around the corner
To the store.

Oliver looked over the counter.
Oliver nodded to salesgirl Betsy
And lo and behold he smiled brightly.
Betsy knew him for many years.
In-between times her life went up and down
But it all circled back to the neighborhood.

Oliver's smile had grown to a grin.
Oliver's heart was beating a bit irregularly.
Still, after a pause, he was able to speak.
There wasn't a word of small talk from his mouth.
He made a simple declaration
And followed that with a request.

Oliver now had to wait for the response.
Oliver thought all time had stopped.
The air was crowded with his dreams and wishes.
Betsy, for some reason, was not surprised.
Perhaps she thought of this some time ago
Now she weighed and reasoned.

Oliver some time later wore a tux.
Oliver had a flower in his lapel,
And a nervous smile waited at the end of the aisle.

(7/14/15)

Morning

Dawn came running through the night.
It tripped on the edge of the world
And spilled orange paint on the morning.

As early birds searched their quarry
Old "Sol" woke and washed things yellow.
The world was now awake. Amen.

Those who needed to get somewhere started.
"Rise and Shine" happy or grumbling,
Coffee beans gave up their flavors
To raise lids to the new day.

Young children hit the ground running.
Older children and the "stay outers"
Tried as best they could to roll over.

But it wasn't to be. The alarm had sounded.
There was work – there was school
There were adventures – there was laundry.

Flags to raise – flowers to water in summer
Birds to sing – animals to be fed
Newspapers to be read – the world to catch up on.

Smiling and waving or bitching and moaning
The day people left for work.
Up the street they drove and turned the corner.

Round the corner and down the street
Came the fixers, the builders and the lawn cutters,
As the population in the houses decreased

So the trimmers and hammer swingers increased.
Some of these daytime visitors went inside.
The sinks stopped dripping and the walls became pretty.
Dogs got walked and healthy people got healthier
Jogging and running and talking and biking.

The cats got on the windowsills to watch.

And so it went as the clock kept climbing
The flowers bloomed the whole day.

(8/28/15)

Mrs. Madison was too busy to die

Mrs. Madison was too busy to die.
The invitations still had to go out.
She and Muffy had seating plans to set
Alterations to the ancient wedding dress
Menus and venues and the church of course.
They hoped that the Reverend Cleveland would preside.
His parents were not fully committed.
It wasn't known if they knew the protocol.
The rehearsal dinner was supposed to be theirs to pay,
No word yet if they would or not.
That reservation had to be made and discussed.
If nothing were heard soon it too would be on Ralph's shoulders.
Poor Ralph Madison seemed in a perpetual daze.
His only daughter, Muffy, was getting married.
Ralph called Muffy, Patricia, her given name.
He was not proud of his daughter or his wife
But he loved his daughter and his wife.
Quietly he watched them strive to be...
To be something they weren't... high society.
Buffy (Patricia) and Mrs. Madison (Ethel)
Had no final plan in this race
But ran the race nevertheless.
Ralph was a blue shirt not a tuxedo.
With regards to his family's current controversy
He walked away from the intense discussions
Of a crisis involving silverware patterns and napkin color.
Ralph didn't care about outdoing the last wedding,
The one where he sat politely nodding.
He danced with Ethel once and Patricia was occupied.
Patricia had a new circle of friends to hang out with.
Ralph was surprised and disappointed when he was told she would marry.
He even had a hard time remembering the guy's name →

It was Lester something the II or III.
Ralph thought that anyone with a II after their name
Had only been spared the ignominy of being called "Junior."
Ralph had met Ethel in high school and was instantly in love.
Ethel liked Ralph well enough when others weren't around.
Back in those courting days they would embrace
But Ethel's eyes searched over Ralph's shoulder.
By senior year, it was settled, they would marry.
It was settled because, not without trying, Ethel had no other takers
Ethel's family had left responsibility behind years ago.
They had provided her a roof, but had other interests.
Ralph's Dad had left life while Ralph was young
Too young for Ralph to know what was missing.
Ralph's Mom did the best she could, working hard,
But she had an empty heart to drag around.
She was proud of her Ralph, but it was hard for her,
Missing her husband every moment of her life,
A lot of affection and warmth was buried with those bones.
Ralph always worked, helped bring money home –
Paper route, delivery boy, jobs part time, full in summer,
Thus the wedding, right after graduation, was simple.
Small, simple and not really to Ethel's liking.
Her dress was off-the-rack and practical,
He had to buy a suit and the tie was always too tight,
It was what Ralph could afford in time and dollars.
Ethel, from day one, dispensed her love as a reward
A treat for her pet when things pleased her.
Ralph savored these moments and knew no more.
Over the years some ladies would more than smile
But Ralph never picked up on their clues.
It was decided that Ralph wouldn't go to college –
A few courses at the Community College
To strengthen his business skills.
Ethel would stay home and mind the house.
Ralph had been working for a large firm
This while a senior in High School.
The company liked Ralph and took him on full time.
Ethel had friends over for coffee and didn't like to cook.
Eventually she announced her pregnancy.
A surprised and joyous Ralph looked around
And no one except himself cried hurray.
Her parents made almost no comment.
His mother wondered how they could afford it.

Stuff

Ethel took this time of growing discomfort
To wonder if this had been her best plan.
Still, other classmates in town were popping babies.
She was not pampered to her liking.
And poor Ralph would again pay the price.
"The house is too small and we need a nursery."
And so the time passed without a smile.
Delivery was normal, nothing special,
But to Ethel this was quite enough
And took steps with the Doctor
To make sure this baby was an only child.
It was a girl, small comfort to Ethel.
Ralph was overjoyed; wife and child were well.
So time would pass; a day, a year.
Patricia grew into childhood under Ethel's guidance,
"American Girl" dolls more than "Barbie,"
Birthday celebrations to top others.
And even with Ralph's undying love
Buffy may never have been "Daddy's little girl."
There were dance recitals and school plays.
These proud family moments brought cheer to Ralph,
But Ethel generally found fault and harsh criticism. –
Not for Buffy, but the teacher, the director, the other kids.
She did this loudly and in front of her child and others.
As the calendar clicked down to that special day,
Lester's family had come through to pay for the rehearsal dinner.
It was not at the fashionable restaurant Ethel had suggested
But more of a family place specializing in "their" kind of food.
Ethel let it go; there were more important problems.
The RSVPs for the four hundred plus invitations they had mailed
Were coming back slowly with regrets leading the way.
Lester's list of invites was small and most were coming.
Ralph's list was made up with some of the people he worked with.
They had replied with great joy and generosity.
Buffy and Ethel's list was quite another story.
There seemed to be a wide divide.
The society they aspired to gave token responses.
There seemed to be a huge exodus that particular Saturday –
Vacations, family visits and the all-encompassing previous commitments –
 But some were coming, because they were obligated.
Finally, they reached the desired number
With a few High School alumni planning to attend. →

And then the day and the chaos began early.
Once it was up and running it never stopped.
At the church there was a flower mix-up to correct
Ralph stood in the Narthex nodding to friends and strangers alike.
Finally the audience was seated and the principals assembled.
Lester and his college fraternity brothers went out and around
To enter from one side and Reverend Cleveland was robed and ready.
What was left were the maids of honor and an angry bride
Ethel and Lester's parents had already been ushered to their seats.
Buffy's problem, whatever it was, had been resolved.
The music began, two little flower girls struck out.
They spread gobs of rose petals clumped here and there down the aisle.
The ring bearer, who wanted to be anywhere else,
Was threatened, pleaded with and finally bribed to follow.
Next the maids of honor spaced themselves evenly
And stutter stepped to the front of the church.
Buffy gave Ralph a sharp "Dad" that brought him from his reverie.
He positioned himself next to his only child.
She gave him a once over and sort of shrugged.
There was nothing she could do about this moment.
As soon as they entered, Buffy's smile was applied.
Ralph observed and tried not to react.
Down the aisle they proceeded, Buffy nodding
And it seemed almost blessing the who's of who,
Ralph's eyes carried on conversations with the few he knew.
At the end of the aisle he gave Buffy away –
Sadly he had given Patricia away years before.
His part done, Ralph sat next to Ethel.
There seemed to be a wall between them
The rest of the day was much the same.
He did get to dance with Buffy.
The music was some slow tune Ralph didn't recognize.
He talked to some well-wishers and friends from work
But mostly he was quiet and embarrassed.
He looked at Ethel flirting and dancing with several men.
The food was there and he ate it, he had paid for it after all.
Still, it tasted like any other big event food.
Day went to evening, with dancing and drinking.
The Bride and Groom finally left for their honeymoon.
Some guests were leaving and he bid them farewell.
Ethel wasn't in the room and Ralph wondered where she was.
He found her after he had used the upstairs bathroom.

She was in their bedroom, on her back
Her skirt was up and her panties down and chest fully exposed.
Two of her dancers attended her, taking full advantage of her wares.
Ethel saw Ralph in the middle of a grunt and a smile
The smile grew bigger as she continued this new dance.
Ralph was frozen; one of the dancers saw Ralph.
Ethel's face moved on to hate, as she pumped harder.
Without words, he could see in that distorted, vicious face
What his future would be and it would be his fault –
He would never be able to do things right.
His mind filled with images of the years to come
And on and on it ballooned in his head.
The second dancer had felt Ralph's presence rather than seeing him.
He withdrew from Ethel and faced Ralph with no embarrassment.
Ralph nodded once, more to himself than the assembled company,
Then he turned silently, walked down the stairs
Through the party remnants, with a still, blank face.
He got in his car and maneuvered across the front lawn to reach the street.
Ralph drove 'til Monday and then made a few phone calls.

From a prompt. (2015?)

Time with Ann and Al Malt (z)

I had never met Ann and Al and they weren't there,
We had a lovely time together nevertheless.
We spent our afternoon along the 59th Street
Entrance to New York City's Central Park.
The tall tree in front of us had seen so much.
It had grown tall and full of shade sharing
The young top leaves acted wildly, jitterbugging in the wind.
How like the youth of any age, dancing up a storm
Moving so fast and ignoring the wisdom below.
Those older and darker leaves could only suggest
And of course the top leaves only wanted to climb to the sun.
One of the branches had decided to grow sideways.
A perfectly healthy branch parallel to the horizon,
There it stood twelve feet off the ground→

I 95 in the squirrel's roadmap to life.
Suddenly there was a commotion a few feet away.
There was one - no two, three, four sparrows and a bagel.
They pecked at this straight piece of bagel causing it to roll.
Circling and chasing it, they had just about hollowed it out
When all their fun ended under the foot of a hungry pigeon.
Settling in near me, on my left, was the Chicago baby.
A young dad with his charge in a stroller
I confess to sneaking peeks because the cherub's eyes were piercing.
This child was in a sponge stage of life, taking everything in.
He couldn't talk yet, but was filling his head with stuff,
Stuff that interested him, which at the moment was his toe
Or perhaps all of them on both feet.
He managed, with the skill of a future gymnast,
To stick both feet in the air, in a Churchill "V" for victory way,
And grab on with both hands and at one point insert toe into mouth.
Dad's phone rang and there was a short conversation.
Then Dad turned the phone so the youngster could see.
That next moment made my heart sing and laugh and be happy.
I guess it was a "Skype" phone and the baby saw his Mom.
Right there in Central Park, there was a smile,
A smile as wide as any ocean, an ocean with waves of love.
The age this child was at wasn't a shy time.
What he felt he shared and you knew it.
After Mom went away he was hungry
And Dad couldn't move fast enough.
Once Junior spotted his yellow spoon, forget it.
It was a one-track mind that led to the stomach
I had seen Dad's Chicago Cubs baseball cap
And I knew the "Cubbies" were in town to play the Mets.
I ventured the obvious. Yes he was from Chicago.
The Cubs has lost the night before.
And yes, Dad said, his son knows his Mom.
Eventually they moved on, but that face will stay with me.
There is an ebb and flow to people walking by
Or perhaps it is my imagination.
It seemed that a parade was moving by
First going in one direction
And then a group comes from the other.
There doesn't seem to be much of a mix
Almost like movie extras strolling by
Quickly changing costumes before heading back.
Now there is a soundtrack for this afternoon

Stuff

Two musicians, guitar and keyboard
Sitting directly across the path from me.
To my way of thinking, they were not that entertaining,
More annoying than good and not drawing a crowd.
The guitar case was open on the ground
And a shekel or two were dropped.
I was hoping it was payoff for them to move on
But they stayed and stayed and stayed.
The bearded guitar player did most of the vocals.
I would call them the "Monotones"
Or sometimes the "Louder Monotones."
They were not showmen and did not interact well with any passersby,
Rather they seemed to be annoyed with the interruption.
The can't-quite-grow-a-beard keyboard artist
Would sometimes put down his instrument
And then venture to the middle of the walkway and listen.
Then he would go back, sit down and make adjustments.
Fortunately none of those adjustments made
Them loud enough for me to hear them well.
Mr. Guitar seemed to be able to play all right.
Mr. Keyboard was a rank amateur pretending.
This particular stretch of walk was an entrance to the park
So people would often pause for a moment
To get their families ready for the zoo and the park
Or to organize them to once more enter the real world.
Such a family took up noisy residence
They were on my side about twenty feet away
But it felt like I was in the middle of it all.
They had stacked coolers, knapsacks, and tote bags.
Anything and everything was being rearranged.
Two brothers squabbled, being ignored by their parents.
This was so the parents could squabble with each other.
From this chaos emerged a girl of seven or eight,
I'm not great at guessing ages, but I think I got this one right.
She moved about halfway between her family and me.
The young lady was not interested in me,
She had already tuned out her family.
No, her quiet expressionless face had eyes for Mr. Guitar.
Two things gave it away - the unblinking stare
And the very slight finger-tapping to the music,
Not obvious, but in time as it tapped the beat on the bench.
If I'm not mistaken, I believe I witnessed a girl's first crush
But the loud family was finally organized →

A quick call and off she went, perhaps wiser.
For awhile I became fascinated with wheels.
In the distance I could see the spinning wheels of the horse carriages,
Gaily decorated wheels trying to recall or maintain the flower of ages past.
Side by side with the carriages were the peddlers.
I forgot their real name, but one man peddles while two passengers sit.
This always reminds me of a rickshaw and Pearl Buck's "The Good Earth,"
Closer to me there were stroller wheels of all shape and sizes.
Inside those strollers were passengers of all shapes and sizes –
Babies who in past ages would be in a full-size baby carriage –
But maybe those are a thing of the past, only found in Grandmother's attic.
There were some who were too big for the stroller
But perhaps too small to make the journey on their own two feet.
Mostly these kids seemed bored and embarrassed.
This leaves those who fit in just right –
A wide variety, many who are way overdressed
These to be shown like a prize poodle with a blue ribbon,
Others quite content to see the sights
While banging something in one hand
And holding a pacifier or other object in their mouth with the other.
More than a few were tipped sideways,
Eyes closed, having given up the fight to the rhythm of the wheels.
Some in every category had to share space.
A few had a serious problem
It would seem Mom and Dad had made purchases
And once they filled pockets and pouches and balanced things on top
They seemed to have closed their eyes
And stuffed things in with little Johnny or Sue.
Maybe, if the child didn't scream or the package fall,
Well they have to get the stuff home somehow.
I saw two selfie-sticks in use,
Both were attached to people of Asian features.
One stylish young woman was on the clock.
Quickly she moved through the area snapping away.
It was she in front of this and everything –
And fifteen minutes later she walked rapidly the other way.
No more picture taking, it was all done and she was out of there.
A middle-age woman held the other selfie-stick.
She and her husband stopped across the way.
She was angling to get yet another picture of her love –

And then the two of them together.
He had an amused expression on his face,
Way past saying "cheese," he had been here before
Well, not here, but a hundred different places.
Long ago he had given up protesting
And now he settled for his wife being happy.
I say beware neighbors and friends of that next dinner invitation.
The last camera incident belonged to a thirty-something power couple.
No selfie-stick involved, merely an over dressed self-absorbed pair.
Out for a stroll I guess, but she had a purpose
She found her "mark" and stopped,
Handed her friend the camera and struck a pose.
It took him a moment to recover from his sudden duties
And he was having trouble working the thing.
Still, with that winning smile, she grabbed the camera back.
Once again, she pointed and directed, as if to a two-year-old,
Maybe mumbling a few unkind words through the smile.
Without losing his pasted on smile he took the camera back.
Finally the picture was taken and she led the way up the path,
All the while searching for her next perfect background.
Now all over the park there are varied artists
Plying their trade, demonstrating their talents for your loose change.
One of the most popular artists available was the portrait artist.
For ten dollars you could get a charcoal drawing of your child –
Maybe it was twenty for a couple.
I watched one of these artists work under the shade of four blue umbrellas.
From my distance, he was doing a creditable job.
He wasn't rushing and seemed quite secure with his talent –
These were portraits, not caricatures.
A mother and son were his current subjects,
The son first, who was patient as his age allowed.
Once done with him it was mother's turn to sit.
He worked quietly and quickly recreating her face.
The boy was on the left-hand part of the paper
And he fit the mother into the right side very nicely.
There was a moment or two of conversation after –
No smiles here, I think the cardboard frame was extra.
While waiting for another customer the young man practiced.
I submit that the young man was Chinese
As he copied a postcard with the likeness of Chairman Mao.
For years I never felt comfortable in New York City.
I still move my wallet into my front pocket. →

But in the last few years I have seen more of its good side.
Its diversity is incredible, a worldwide range that is hard to match.
Languages from everywhere live here or visit here
Today tourists and locals share the same park
Enjoying the sun and a holiday weekend.
Carnival or merry-go-round, what's just over the hill?
Pond or lake or softball field, what's just over the hill?
Shade or sun, wilderness, rock climbing, just over the hill
Dedicated runners and bikers, horse carriages over the hill
The universality available on this Saturday afternoon.
How nice to share it with Ann and Al
And how nice of their family and friends
To dedicate this bench I sit on to their memory.

(7/2/16)

Just Before Bed

The little girl sat on her bed
Covers were pulled up and over her head
Only her face could be seen.
Her chin rested on the back of dolly's head.
The little lady with hair overflowing
Whispered secrets to her best friend
Eyes focused somewhere on this day
With not all the understanding of yesterday
Spoke her own gibberish with words thrown in.
The conversation was all about everything.
Events of "High Tea" were recounted
About who behaved and who was naughty,
What had happened in Nursery School.
Relating all that her girlfriends had shared
And how dumb most of the boys were.
She talked about Mommy and Daddy
And about Grandma who was real old.
Her friend sat wide-eyed, unblinking
This confessor understood how important to listen.
The jumble of words went on and on
Details punctuated by bits of songs
Things she was learning

Stuff that was silly and made her laugh.
Even trying to understand things
Why the teacher had scolded her
How sometimes people didn't listen.
Her eyes began to blink
And she rocked to her side.
Dolly did the same.
Almost instantly, one pair of blue eyes closed
And in just a minute more, the other pair followed
A quick flutter open, then closed tight
Closed tight till morning.

(12/25/14)

Picasso Lady

Picasso Lady with a "Madeline" hat
Her back straight as she moves
Holding her plant at arms length,
It's stem a reflection of her spine
The buds or blossoms crowded to ends
So it's silly sticks in the midst
Of traffic, raindrops and population.
How fast she's gone
Disappeared among the circling tourists,
The ambling natives from elsewhere,
The man carrying conversations to the wind
And getting angry at its answers.
The handed offers to deep discounts
On the upper floors.
Taking it home or to the office,
A rescue or a reason,
Exotic or sickly,
Up three flights or twenty-fifth floor please.

(1/17/2009)
*Previously published in "High Tide – 2009" – Annual publication of the Milford Writer's Group, Milford Fine Arts Council.

Raindrop – 2

Raindrop on your nose
Flowers between your toes
A field of color
Where nobody goes.

Run for the nearest shelter
Stand in the doorway
Of that deserted barn
Rain heavy and dancing now.

Two people move in a little deeper
Thoroughly soaked, hugging to stay warm
Smell the chilled life
Gone from this place sometime ago.

Dirt, dust and straw
A shutter slams, the lovers jump
They share a nervous laugh.
Shouldn't they be headed home?

But the sky falls in a torrent
Let's wait a little while.
Climb the ladder carefully,
Up into the cozy loft.

The rain continues almost unnoticed.
Somewhere in the pile of hay
Love has grown and blurred
Buttons and zippers all undone.

Time will pass and the sun comes back
Just in time to settle down
And throw some color
Across the sky and resting lovers.

They wish the time would stop
Never do they want to move
Nor reality to cross their path
One more kiss, never done.
In time for crickets and fireflies

They climb on down
Rearrange the still damp coverings
And remove the clinging evidence.

Into the early evening
Heading back to where they're from
Either to make excuses
Or announce a love unbounded.

(11/28/15)

The Face

The face appeared first in a dream
A time moving in or out of consciousness.
It stared from behind a windowpane.
Then it was in the water's reflection…
The other side of a mirror on the wall.
You could call it a blank stare
Perhaps a vacant stare
But you would be wrong
Not even a hard stare.
The face was set, mouth drawn even –
A girl, age twelve, maybe fourteen,
Not beautiful, but fascinating features.
The body not to be seen
Just the head with a rural do
Black and white captured.
The face is unmoving
Still, not to be ignored
Eyes boring out into the world
Nose a little pug.
She will always look young.
I tried to walk away
It came back - not judging
No, I think it is hiding something,
A secret, promised not to tell.
Something she saw has frozen her. →

The face is now in my head.
I haven't seen it for days
Yet now it is haunting me,
A *Grapes of Wrath* vision long overdue
Bubbles to the surface.
In memory now, there is emptiness.
Nothing recently done gives me a clue.
There is no sound, no crying, and no laughter.
Is it a Tuesday several years ago?
Then suddenly it is back
The mouth, the eyes, just the same –
But the face is dirty
Cheeks smudged, hair in disarray.
Something has happened in that world
And she is not allowed to share.

(11/28/15)

The Point

He stood at his second floor bedroom window and stared out into the morning. It was winter, it was early and it took a moment or two for him to focus in on the day.

The street was dry, good thing, the house across the street sat empty and alone. It would see no life till late spring at best, like most of the houses on "The Point" it was empty from early fall until the sun found its warmth.

Beyond the house was supposed to be water; if he opened his window to the cold, he could probably hear it, but all he saw was gray. Layers of gray that shredded open to find a thicker gray with mist and fog covering everything starting at the shore's edge, - when suddenly a gull knifed through and dove for breakfast. Lenny was startled into the present. Yes, Good morning world. He was up, he was awake and he was ready for COFFEE!

Still he lingered a moment or two more at the window. Today was Saturday so he didn't have to go to work, but even then, for nine months a year it was an easy commute. While growing up, he had spent time, with his parents, on The Point. They sometimes rented a house for a month or more and he and his mom became full time residents and his dad joined them on weekends and for the last two weeks full time. Lenny had come here often enough over the years so he had some locals as friends as well as other returning transient vacationers that shared more than memories with him.

As the years had gone by and mom and dad had gone, he found himself coming back for a few days, maybe a week, almost every year. Finally, when he had his job of dreams in the city, he found he was just a short distance on the highway and a few twists and turns 'til he would be coming through the gnarled and stunted pines and cedars to the place he was most happy and content.

Lenny took a few years to make the decision, looking at all the pros and cons. Could he find a house that suited his needs at a reasonable price, factoring in the commute against being crushed into the city and feeling imprisoned by everything around him? Living in the city was expensive and after weighing everything, his sanity won out.

He had found a year-round house across the street from the water and took up residence. A nice little house, nothing special, with a view of the water sitting on a small, low-maintenance lot.

This time of year, The Point was down to the regulars and that suited Lenny just fine. He had a choice of two restaurants and two bars and one little grocery store. There was a small emergency clinic and a few retail shops that stayed open year-round. →

When Lenny left work, he really left work behind. Still, he did bring it home with him electronically, and on bad winter days he was able to do his job from home and feel no guilt if the roads hadn't been plowed yet.

Lenny knew how to cook; in fact he was a pretty good cook. Still he often went out to dinner as much for the company as the food.

Sometimes, on a rare occasion, he would eat in the city, perhaps with someone from work, but more than likely he would eat on The Point. He would come home, dump his stuff and head for one of the local eateries. Other times he would stop at a bar have a

drink and then come home and fix something. Either way he had a comfortable life.

There were three other types of people who lived on The Point out of season: the native, the local and the transplant.

The native was born and raised here. Only a few lived in the town. Most retained land and properties that served as mini-farms, or had rickety docks from which the fishermen set sail. They stayed pretty much to themselves, only interacting with the rest of the population as necessary. Their kids went to the local school. They sold their fish to the market and restaurants, as did the farmers with their crops.

The locals and transplants were separated by a fine line, one to service the needs of all and the other who mostly marketed to the summer tourist trade. Lenny was almost in a class by himself; he was, perhaps, the only commuter.

Local artists and artisans would spend much of their time painting or building to replenish their stock for the tourist season, or were well enough known to carry on business off-season and off The Point.

At the same time, the bars, stores and restaurants were run by the other transplanted locals and carried on with life in anticipation of the invasion.

In early spring there was a local guessing game. Which seasonal proprietor would return, who would be new owner and which places would be left empty. Talk in the bars or in the aisles of the grocery store would often focus on the up coming season, long range guesses about the weather, before moving on to sports, idle gossip or a recent scandal.

Lenny loved to listen to all this and would even join in on a conversation once in awhile. After all he had been on The Point over the years long enough to have a sound and respected opinion, especially after a couple of beers.

As to Lenny's social life, it wasn't very big. Once in awhile he dated someone from work, but the relationships didn't last long and he almost never brought them to The Point. Usually he would end the process with some feeble excuse of incompatibility, but the truth was that he would get bored. The sex, when it happened, would be fine, but it seemed that almost all the women only wanted to talk about work and careers, his or theirs. He couldn't care less about the subject.

On The Point he was more careful. After all he lived with these folks and had to deal with them on a day-to-day basis. He didn't want to estrange anyone, nor become a subject of the town's gossip. Several women had flirted with him and he had returned the favor. He was even the recipient of some casual sex from a woman who tended bar at one of the "drinkeries." They always got along well and knew how the relationship was and were both happy with it.

Finally Lenny got himself in gear and was about to head downstairs. One final look out the window and he froze. In front of that gray background and along the high tide line a solitary figure walked. He must have not been focused on the outside for a few minutes, but there she was almost opposite his house. It was a woman that could easily be determined by long hair being tossed in the breeze. Tight jeans were also a not-too-subtle clue and she had a bulky big-necked sweater that she hugged in a feeble attempt to combat the cold.

She continued on along the beach and Lenny headed for the first floor and that coffee to be made. Still he wondered about this mysterious figure. In season it would be no big deal with young couples with arms around each other as they walked and tried to
escape civilization, or an older couple, hand in hand remembering what it was like to be a young couple.

Once he got the coffee going, he stepped out of the kitchen on to the little deck that ran along the side of the house. He loved these moments of soaking up The Point. In one form or another he had been doing it for years, absorbing the smells, the noise, the quiet, the tranquility he felt here.

Before he moved back inside, he saw the woman on the street now heading in the opposite direction. Now he had almost no front yard, so he was not far back from the road and as he did often with joggers and dog walkers, mostly in season, he called a cheery "Good Morning!"

The lady stopped almost mid-stride and then it seemed she had a small debate before turning toward him. Even then there were several beats before she echoed; "Good Morning." There was no smile on a rather lovely face, but instead he felt there was an inspection in progress.

Now, more than a little curious, Lenny decided to continue the dialogue.

"Weather's a bit strange this morning with the gray sky, fog and mist."

"I suppose," was the non-committal answer, but she did take a step closer to the curb.

"Everything O.K.?" was his next step and he knew it might end the conversation.

Again the pause, but no nasty retort. What finally came was a totally insincere, "Sure."

Now what? Where to go from here? →

"I'm just making coffee. Want a cup? Ah, I guess I could find a paper cup. It's a little cold for the deck. You're welcome to come in, but I don't want you to be uncomfortable."

Finally she smiled as he fumbled along trying to find the proper invitation. She stepped up on the grass and said.

"It's OK. I'll come in for a minute and don't be afraid. I won't bite and I won't take advantage of you."

Lenny laughed and ushered her up onto the deck and into the kitchen. He motioned her to one of the two chairs at a small table by a window overlooking the deck.

"I'm going to make toast, want some?"

"Fine" she smiled. Framed in that long mane of chestnut hair was a not-perfect face. It was just off enough to be beautiful, with a more rounded shape than oval, sculptured cheeks that still held some of the cold from outside as rouge. Her nose was narrow but not hawkish, her lips were full, and her eyes – God - big deep and smiling.

Lenny managed to cover his staring by grabbing two plates and two cups from the

cupboard. In the refrigerator he found the bread, butter and some marmalade. He popped the bread into the toaster and took silverware from the drawer. He approached the table with the coffee, poured two cups and set the pot on a trivet already in the middle of the table. Before he sat opposite her he went back to the fridge and grabbed the milk and placed it near the coffee pot.

Those gorgeous eyes were looking out at a mourning dove that was returning her stare.

"He's waiting for breakfast," Lenny said.

"Well go to it man, I can't eat with those accusing eyes watching me."

Lenny sprang to the job, scooped some seed from a small barrel by the door and started out the door. The dove moved about six feet to the neighbor's fence and waited patiently for Lenny to finish the job. There were a few sparrows on the hydrangea bush, all brown sticks waiting to produce spring leaves. The sparrows sat confidently, sure that they blended in and were tying napkins under their beaks.

When he came in, the toast was divided on the plates and she was busy covering her toast with the marmalade. He sat opposite her again and wondered, what next?

"Well," she said, "Shall we talk more about the weather, politics, the state of the world economy? My name is Megan."

"I'm sorry, I'm Lenny and I play the part of nosey neighbor in the forthcoming MGM release."

A very slight pause. "Hi Lenny, thanks for breakfast. You want to know what a girl like me is doing in this place, your place, a place like this?"

"Well, it would help me get in character for my forthcoming role, but it's up to you."

"All right Lenny, for the sake of the arts then." Her eyes left the kitchen and moved back to the feeder, but he felt sure she was not watching the birds chow down. "I have a rented car down the street at the head of the beach. I've run away from home and this is the only place I felt safe escaping to. I had a boyfriend who I thought was my perfect mate. I've had other boyfriends over the years, but finally, Ben seemed just right for me and frankly I was ready to say 'yes' if he ever got around to ask me to marry him. Then awhile back as Ben got comfortable in the relationship, I found Ben loved Ben more than me. Fine. An ego. Nothing wrong with that until that ego seemed to resent me. A few nasty comments, a few fights that never resolved themselves before we went to bed and lately some serious anger and some serious blows, but never to my face, always where they could be covered by clothes."

Lenny started to say something, but she raised her hand off the table in a quick "stop" gesture. She was telling her story, maybe for the first time, and she needed to keep going.

"The last time I saw an awful smile on Ben's face when he hit me. He made up a situation and became the administer of his justice. Each time was worse, my ribs must be bruised, and I had to get out. It was time to stop looking for fault in me because
he said there was fault. I grabbed what I could and called a cab while Ben was at work, and then I rented a car and took off for The Point. A few hundred miles of driving and I am back where I came years ago almost every summer. My parents rented a place down on..."

"The raft!" Lenny interrupted "The raft, you used to swim out to the raft and lie on it forever."

"How...?"

"I remember you. Quiet. Always by yourself and not quite as pretty as you are now, but still quite a looker."

She stared at him in silence for a moment or two. Tension drained from her face. Megan reached across the table and gave him a little push.
"You pushed me into the water, you rat."
He giggled, back in a distant summer.
"Yeah, well it was easier to do that than try to talk to a girl."
"Well I'll be! I used to be jealous of you because you got to spend more time on The Point and everybody was your friend."
"Yeah. Well I've always come back and now I live here and don't really want to go away."
Megan glanced down at the table, took a bite of toast and sipped some coffee. Lenny drifted back to the present and addressed what he saw as the immediate needs of the situation. →

"There's a little clinic that is open on Saturday, maybe they could help you out."

"No thanks, I think I'm going to be alright."

"OK. How about sticking around for lunch or dinner?"

Megan stared at her hands around the coffee cup, then looked up at Lenny.

"I'd like to do that."

(Jan. 2015)

Lonely Road

I walk a lonely road.

Carrying a lifetime on my own,
See this young man all alone
A stranger in his home.
Angry looks and no good words
To help me win a day –
Something a little different
That no one understands.

I guess it's time to hit that lonely road.

Wandering along those dusty times
Looking for what I never had –
Friends and a place to love.
Growing up willing to work
Taking jobs that go nowhere
No roots take hold
And clouds close in.

On to that lonely road once again.

There came a time those years ago
When I joined my only uncle.
Sam taught me order and responsibility,
Love of country and duty to be done.
Still confusing with no victory
And home again with no honor,
No parades or celebrations.

Hit that long and lonely road.

Somewhere in the middle of life
I walked into a little town
Eyes cast down as I walked through a door.
I wasn't looking for a welcome there
Just some coffee and some eggs.
I got those and so much more
There were smiles going all around. →

Maybe I'll wait a day to hit the lonely road.

With just a little talk and few questions,
There was honest work to be had,
A place to stay and friendly greetings.
One day slipped to one week and more.
I wasn't making for the door
With the eggs and oatmeal
Came a handsome woman's care.

I lost sight of the lonely road.

Worlds united in conversations
Casual touches blossomed into handholding
Telling secrets, peeled away the years of hurting
Smiles and laughter and trust
Built friendship into love
And two people took a step.

It is away from the lonely road.

Now years have passed
And life has comfort and adventure
Arguments and laughter, loving and sharing –
Pass the days into year after year.
Gray has become the order of the day.
Aches and pains greet each sunrise
But one cares for the other.

What's this about a lonely road?

(11/22/15)

Sit Down

"Sit down. Stand up. Watch out I'm coming through."
The old man shuffles by, his cane almost tapping.
He's headed from here to there and there's no stopping.

Stuff

You know where he's heading, there can be no doubt —
The food is on the table or the bathroom is not far.
His trails are narrow, his days so long.

He still remembers life's siren song
So tempting, yet so far out of his reach.
Before it was a cane, it was a walking stick.

His world was full. See him. Yes that's him —
A happy little tap dance, a swirl around the floor,
Love of life and the love of his life in tow.

Waltzing through the years of happiness and tears
His wife, his children and his mom and dad
On the dance floor, on the carousel of life,

Round and round, reaching for the golden ring.
But he already had it all, including the golden ring,
The one he wore and the one he gave that day.

Good and bad at raising kids —
Sometimes not enough time with her and them —
Still plenty of good times, big adventures, little things.

Slowly the carousel emptied of love and life.
Fallen off riders by death and miles
Left alone and not telling stories.

"Sit down. Stand up. Watch out I'm coming through."

(2/27/16)

Ms. Diana Savannah at the Planter's Tavern

(On a night we walked in)

Down the stairs to the basement of "The Olde Pink House" we came.
As we entered, noise from the long bar on the right.
From the left came the firm notes
Of the black piano in the corner
And the voice of Ms. Diana.
If smoking were allowed, it would have been smoke-filled.
The music would cut through that smoke
And reveal a summer, southern, go-to meeting hat,
A bright pink hat covered with flowers.
Peeking out from under the hat came two eyes
And very red lips crying the notes of a song.
The piano never stops as it passes between the numbers.
Perhaps the player no longer needs applause
Or fears that there will be none.
Some songs climb back in time, deep in a heart;
Others seek a Carole King medley then vamping.
Over the music, Ms. Diana introduces friends
And carries on a monologue about things,
Strange and not so wonderful things happening to her
Stitches of memories wrapping around a few bars of music,
Trying to learn an "Adele" song on the run,
Enlisting the aid of a young woman nearby.
Hinting of her life before, seemingly in her world
But sharp and watchful around her, reinventing herself.
And, at a break, accosting a waitress,
Joking with her and leaving her space behind the piano empty.
Her friends and acquaintances, as well as her audience
Is an interesting blend, with each aware of the others' history.
Here comes a song we can all sort of sing.
The strong voiced woman, in a black dress, with a fan
Works singing "Happy Birthday" upstairs, downstairs is another thing.
She joins Diana with bits of a few songs
Now she must return upstairs to play that crowd.
Diana's friend, the lady with the big red hat
And the red dress, works a dialogue with Diana

The other lady who came in, also in red
Reminds me of Lee Remick, joins us for small talk.
You know it's a good night because you're on another drink
And the crowd has increased, pulling from the bar,

Moving closer in and around the piano,
A body of listeners, singers, observers, all in a moment.
Sometime the moment will end, and we will, because
We have to, move on tomorrow and find other things.
In the meantime, the voice, the hat, the night is always ours.

(4/22/16)

Disconnected

It drops from roof to nowhere,
A leafless piece of mechanical ivy
Anchored securely to the brick.

Sometime ago it was severed,
This wire from the heavens,
Disconnected, but not removed.

The cable guy from the old company
Or the installer of the new
Cutting it far enough away to make it useless.

Maybe it's not a cable.
It's hard to tell from a distance —
Perhaps a wire, electric or antenna.

What it has become
Is an eyesore, a blemish,
A tail that goes nowhere.

The party in 4B has moved out.
There is an empty space
Until the next story begins. →

How old is the building?
How long was a family there?
How has their life here ended?

Was it back in the early 50's?
A young couple is moving in —
Freshly married and deeply in love.

Times are good, we all like Ike.
It is safe to start a family
And the black and white television is attached to the antenna.

It is a time of confidence and these people are typical.
He works, she cleans and prepares dinner —
A pause perhaps to watch *Queen for a Day*.

The family arrives, he works harder and longer.
She cleans, shops, tends Junior and gets dinner ready.
Finally, Junior sleeps and this family loves Lucy.

Dad has two jobs, but still has quality time with the family.
Mom gets Junior off to school.
As she does the ironing, she watches *The Edge of Night*.

Junior comes running in and announces his arrival.
Mom has a snack for him.
After a brief interrogation, the TV asks, "Hey kids, what time is it?" –

Dad has climbed the work ladder step by step.
Mom does charity work and gets together with the girls.
Junior gets home from High School in time to watch *American Bandstand*.

The television is color, the screen bigger, and the sound better
Junior has introduced his parents to a new game
Better than *Scrabble* or *Monopoly*, it is called *Pong*.

It isn't long before *Pong* is left behind.
Junior is shooting alien invaders or
A little yellow circle chomps everything in sight.

Mom and dad are soon left behind.
Off to college goes Junior, with his new computer
And cable television has arrived.

Junior has graduated, sown oats and married.
Dad has beaten the computer to the finish line and retired.
Mom still volunteers, but she tires easily.

Junior is embraced by the world of electronics
And he flourishes amidst new software and technology.
Dad has some health issues and life slows.

Junior and his family come to visit.
The grandkids spend the whole time on their tablets,
While Mr. and Mrs. Junior are concerned about mom and dad.

One morning, 4B becomes a huge canyon
And the Mrs. is left wondering.
Junior offers housing and hospitality.
(Continued)

The Mrs. politely declines for now.
She has her friends, though shrinking in number,
And enjoys watching her programs.

Time passes slowly or quickly, depending on point of view.
Mrs. catches a lucky break, no nursing home.
She sits in her chair, a cup of tea on the old TV tray.

She has found that Johnny Carson has come alive.
Reruns make her smile and nod off.
Finally, Mr. wakes her and they walk down the hall.

(2/13/16)

When I See

When I see a family getting ready for a week in the country
It's time to just sit back and enjoy the scene.
There is the preparation for this pending safari —
Rented or purchased camping equipment,
Cute gadgets that collapse or fold flat.
Every possibility is covered as the family wanders the aisles.
A full turkey dinner in a can could be fun.
Canteens, knapsacks, fishing gear, hunting gear, gear gear...
Back home, the purchases are added to the pile already gathered —
Clothes for everyone, for every weather possibility,
Food and snacks for any and every appetite,
A first aid kit large enough to stock a small emergency room,
Toys and toys and more toys,
Books, cards, flashlights and lanterns.
The packing begins and mumbling starts softly.
Cubbyholes are filled, and then the rest is filled —
Pause — half is removed and the children nested.
Then priorities rule and something is left behind.
Whatever it is, it is crucial to someone's very existence.
So, a quick run to the sporting goods store and back again.
The new luggage rack is mounted to the roof and quickly filled.
Bikes are strapped to the car, front and back.
Finally, all is loaded, the driver checks that he can see
Front, and if he maneuvers a bit, most of the back.
Shotgun is mounted with maps and car entertainment games
Driver starts the engine and they start down the driveway.
"Wait, I got to go!" comes the voice below the inner tube.
The journey is paused, relief to everyone.
Everything in the house is again secured and alarmed.
Soon the end of the driveway is reached.
There is discussion in the front seat, "Turn left. No right,"
While in back, war has broken out.
Shouts of "It's mine. Leave me alone. That's not fair."
Echo loudly, as that early start has matured to mid-morning.
After hours of bickering, rest stops and a fast food lunch,
After every boat has rowed gently down the stream,
And every bottle of beer on the wall has been accounted for,
And license plates from thirteen states have been discovered,
The campground and the campsite has been found.
The children disappear with vague promises of staying close.

What is needed first is buried deep, so the car is unloaded,
Everything is laid around in a circle and the tent is found.
There are no directions. Still, how hard can it be?
The muttering of the morning has grown to yelling and cursing
Blame is spread from salesman, to the one who's supposed to know how,
To the one who came up with the whole idea,
And eventually to questioning marriage vows and the lineage of everyone.
Finally, the center pole is found and put together,
The tent has the right side up and is draped over the pole.
One person holds the pole and their breath
While the second untangles and fastens the guidelines.
Tent pegs are driven into the ground and the lines pulled tight.
One by one the lines are pulled and tightened.
Slowly, the tent rises from the earth.
The tent is up, the pole holder released, except
The tent is only about eighteen inches tall.
One by one the tent pegs are pulled from the ground.
The pole holder now pulls each line harder.
The other takes the end to make it taut
Then re-drives the peg into the ground and slips the rope over it.
A truce is declared, as the couple stands back to admire their work.
At that moment, a gentle breeze finds its way into the area
And the tent in very slow motion collapses.
The third time's a charm and the circle of goods is loaded in.
Next, everything is loaded out; some is loaded back into the car,
Some left outdoors and the necessities brought inside again.
The fireplace is reconstructed from some ancient ruins,
Wood is gathered and stacked and a fire is lit.
Gradually the troops return with tales of adventure
As well as tales of tattle and tales untold.
Gifts from the offspring are presented.
A bough of leaves gathered by one —
Quite pretty with its three shiny-leaf pattern —
Eventually established as poison ivy. Let the scratching begin.
The first frog of summer, which earns a resounding
"Ech, get that away from me."
The captor has brought knee-deep mud as well as the frog.
The final gift is also living and breathing,
A bored kid from two campsites down
Who lives two streets over at home and has been here a week.
He shares tales of all the disasters that have befallen his family. →

And asks if he can have something to eat.
He is sent packing with a "Twinkie" and the family gathers.
An organizational meeting is held 'round the fire,
Sleeping arrangements are outlined.
No one is happy.
Chores are assigned.
Cries of "we're on vacation" ring out through the air.
The nearest outhouse location is revealed.
The general sentiment can be summed up in one word, "Yuck."
There is discussion, even compromise,
Realization that some co-operation is needed for survival.
As tensions lessen, a family-friendly existence appears.
So likewise does the first raindrop or twenty.
Chaos again breaks out, as everything is grabbed
And moved from car to tent, trying to keep it all dry.
The fire starts to sizzle, as the ground softens.
The frog is now at home and croaks loudly
As the damp and musty people try to find places to sit.
Someone hears the first drip, drop from the tent roof —
A leak, one place, no two, drip, drip – drop, drip.
Drop, a third has appeared directly above someone.
Buckets and containers are found and aligned.
The rain gathers strength and starts to really come down.
The wind, 'til now relatively idle, joins in.
Flaps are tied, stuff moved from the edges,
Light is established within and crackers, already soggy are served.
The rest of the food, all dry and safe from bears, resides in the car.
The vacationers turn in at seven, hungry and mumbling again.
On the morning of the third day, as the rain continues,
There arose from the tent a chorus of cheers.
Quickly the food is removed from the car,
The children move off to distribute it to the hardier folk
While those who remain collapse and gather all that is left.
On top, behind, in front and within, gear and clothes
And all there is gets bent and shoved into place.
The children are added in crannies and crevasses.
The shotgun guider points in any direction.
The driver does a muddy wheelie toward home.-
The frog watches for a moment
Then turns and starts hopping for home too.

(12/29/15)

Whistlin' Willie

Whistlin' Willie was the most feared man in the territory. He was ornery and mean and ornery again. Willie had more notches on his gun than stars in the sky. That's on a clear night too. It was said, all you had to do was breathe on a deck of cards the wrong way and Willie would introduce you to the six-gun two step.

Now, he was called Whistlin' Willie because he always whistled. His words were few but his tunes were a-plenty. You couldn't always recognize the tune, but you didn't want to interrupt. What a silly tenderfoot you might be, to ask Willie what tune that was he was whistlin'. The least you would get was a cold hard stare and from there it was only a bad batch of whiskey or his eggs cooked wrong that would turn that foolish youngster into one miserable human bein'.

There wasn't much law where Willie lived. Grimy Gulch had a sheriff, a good man and a family man who enforced what laws there were, for those who lived by them. That was most of the town and actually the town looked better than its name. It was set in a little valley with a good number of trees risin' up the sides of the hills that surrounded it on three sides. Grimy Gulch had a general store, a church, a schoolhouse, a small hotel and a big saloon.

You sort of had to look for the town; there was just one small passage that led you in and out from the plains and desert that surrounded it. It was sort of an oasis on your trip north or south or east or west. There were a few farmers, but most of the town made its money from the travelers movin' by. Cowboys drivin' their herds of cattle north to the railheads in Kansas City and Dodge or returning home, as well as adventurous families movin' west in wagon trains would hold up on either side of the Muddy River that ran from the hills and along the southern edge of town.

If you were comin' into town from a wagon train, it was generally daylight and you would be lookin' to get some necessities at the store or if it was Sunday, to join the townsfolk at church. The cowboys headin' north with their herd, didn't have much money, but they too might need some equipment or need to get a bath and generally get cleaned up before movin' their steers farther north. The cowpoke headin' back south had been paid for his work and he wasn't savin' for no special occasion. He had a mind to have some fun and have it wherever and whenever he could. Yes sir, he needed a drink or more to wash away the dust from his throat. He needed someone to tell how pretty she looked and he needed to play games and have fun.

This was where Whistlin' Willie lived, his hometown, and he really never traveled far from it. The sheriff took care of most of the town, but the Empire Saloon and a few buildings on either side were their own settlement. Each pretty much left the other alone and rarely did one cross the line to the other.

Willie had a room two doors down from the Empire and pretty much ruled the roost. He gambled for a livin' and he managed to do quite well.

Now, there had come one Saturday night at the Empire that had lasted clear into Sunday mornin'. The music had finally stopped, the ladies who worked there had finally been able to get some rest, and the last of the cowpokes were packin up and gettin' ready to head home a little lighter in their pockets.

Well, Whistlin' Willie had done all right and had celebrated long after the last game had ended. Now with the sun grinnin' through the Empire's front windows, he decided it was time to get home. The only thin' he had to figure out was how.

Willie could hold his drink. He could hold it till it toppled him over, and then time would begin again a day or two later. Anyway, this particular Sunday mornin', Willie was weavin' without a loom as he fought his way through the Empire's swingin' doors. They even helped him on his way as he dallied too long in the doorway.

Willie took offense and almost drew on the hinged villains, but then laughed as he swung his body back around. Well, this move was entirely too fast for his well-lubricated parts to handle and he ended up staggerin' off the wooden sidewalk and into the Gulch's only road. Finally, reinin' himself in, he paused tryin' to figure out how he got where he was and where that was and how to continue the rest of his journey.

Sunday mornin', except around the Empire, meant church and most of the good folks of Grimy Gulch were headed there. Decked out in their Sunday best, they marched righteously toward the church buildin' on the far edge of town. From the farms outside of town, a collection of buckboards, buggies and wagons came from all directions with the same destination.

Willie stood frozen in the center of the road as a team of two horses pulled a wagon right at him. At the last second, he dodged the fast approachin' vehicle with an awkward and ugly dance, stumblin' away from danger and the saloon. His feet had
forgotten their dance steps and spilled Willie to the sidewalk opposite the Empire and into Polly Prue and Mamie Jefferson.

Whistlin' Willie lay on top of Polly in a mess of intermingled boots, buckles, skirts and a parasol. Mamie was totterin' into the wooden Indian in front of the General Store and then fell to the ground or rather into the Polly-Willie pile and the heavy and weathered cedar savage rocked forward as if to crush some scalps below.

Willie was once more confused and furious. He rose to his knees, drew both pistols and fired at the Indian who he blamed for everythin'. The insulted and wounded fella sat back solidly onto his base, having had enough exercise for the day.

The gunman, now more alert, perhaps because of all the noise, finished the trip to his feet. With his dawnin', he became aware of his presence amongst the toppled ladies mumbled an apology and offered assistance. First he reached out to Mamie who shrunk back and went to use her former enemy, the still silent and stoic native to help her to her feet.

Turnin' to Polly, he again offered a hand, which she accepted and was helped to her feet. It was Willie who was nervous and again apologized as Polly straightened her yellow-striped dress and petticoats.

"Oh, don't worry about it. Are you all right?"

"I'm fine," mumbled Willie.

Mamie, now up and wantin' to get back on the path to church, asked Polly "Are you ready?"

'You go ahead. I'll catch up."

Clearly this was not the answer Mamie expected and with a not-subtle look of distain toward Willie, moved on.

Polly smiled and extended her hand once more.

"I'm Polly Prue."

"I'm Willie. Willie Davenport."

That last name came out kinda dusty, he was not used to usin' it and he was not used to making chitchat with anyone, most of all a pretty young woman. "I was worried when I saw you stumble as you crossed the road and that wagon was going much too fast. I'm glad you're all right," Polly said.

Now what, mister mean and vicious fella? He knew it was his turn to speak and normally there would be some conversation endin' insult or worse, just so he wouldn't have to continue to be social. But instead he gave a quick, maybe you call it a smile and said, "No, I'm fine, just lost my balance, that's all."

"Nice day isn't it?"

"I guess."

This was painful, almost worse than a hangover, but she was such a fine lookin' woman. Polly's face was alive, with a huge smile, as she adjusted her Sunday bonnet. Willie just stared, hands at his side again, nervously twitchin'.

Polly's warmth just climbed into Willie's darkest corners and shed light all over them. The fact was obvious that Willie was shy around women. His ma had died when he was quite young and the only women in his life, while growin' up, had been a gruff and grumpy old maid aunt who helped raise him, but had no love for him and an even older teacher who Willie never got along with.

Willie stopped goin' to school early and nobody seemed to care.

"Will you walk with me awhile?" Polly asked.

Willie almost looked around to see whom she was talkin' to and finally said "Sure."

And they moved awkwardly in the same direction that Mamie had taken.

After walking together for a while, they began to fall in step and they went through a weather dialogue and then Polly sort of kept things goin', gearin' the conversation so Willie could get away with one, two or three word answers.

Willie was a bit surprised when Polly drew him onto a path not headin' to the church, but toward a wooded trail that lead to the Muddy River.

She was the schoolteacher in town, Willie learned. She had come from the east and when her wagon train had stopped here, well she felt like this was where she should be, this was home.

Polly had easily gotten the job as a teacher. The town desperately needed one.

The schoolhouse was empty the last teacher had married and moved farther west. And "No," she said, though Willie never asked the question, she was not anxious to get married. Polly had started west to get away from the boy everyone assumed she would marry. But she didn't love him and she was not very important in his life, but he was willin' to believe what everyone was sayin'.

As they walked farther down the trail and deeper into the trees, Willie began to relax and started to whistle, can't be sure he even knew he was doin' it. Polly snuck a
look at him and puckered up and joined in. Willie hesitated a second, but Polly gave him a nod, urgin' him to continue.
So the pretty young thing and this rather awkward cowboy continued on. What a picture.

Polly found out secrets that Willie never let on with anyone else. He couldn't read; most of his schoolin' was hard knocks learnin'. He knew cards and other ways of gamblin' and those he had shot had always been the first to draw.

He was gruff, because then he didn't have to deal with people who thought they were better than him or who would make him feel dumb. Willie wasn't sure he was happy, he wasn't sure he knew what happiness was or what to do when he felt that way, except to have a drink.

On and on they talked as they reached the river and sat by its edge. The water rushed by, as did their conversation and the time.

Polly finally said she should be getting' back. It wasn't goin' to be easy to explain to Mamie and anyone else who deserved an answer to what just happened.

Willie rose and helped her up once more, but their hands held together for a moment or two and they both sort of stared at them and wondered, now how did this happen? As they walked back to town, the talkin' was sparse and hands or shoulders bumped on uneven parts of the trail.

Polly carefully offered to help him read and after a long pause, Willie said;"Aw, you don't wanna do that."
"Sure, I've had a lovely time and it would please me if I could help. You wouldn't have to come to the schoolhouse, we could meet somewhere and nobody would have to know."

And so the odd relationship began and grew. The schoolteacher and the gambler became friends and, yes, eventually more than friends. It wasn't a secret, but they would go to different places to study and talk. The whistlin' became brighter and the two of them would often take a break and give voice to the wind with their music.

Willie still gambled and won, but he didn't have to threaten the other players. Polly got some strange looks from Mamie and some others, but eventually they saw the attraction and left the couple alone.

And indeed, a couple they became and started to talk about some kind of future together. Polly suggested that maybe he might become a farmer, but Willie would have none of that.

Well time wandered on and Willie even showed up in church one time or another. He bought the Empire Saloon and gussied it up some, tastefully of course. He turned the girls into waitresses and redid the rooms upstairs to become guest rooms. The Empire Tavern was born and had no problem sharing the customer business with the other hotel and restaurants in town.

After a time, Polly and Willie made a trip to the church on a Saturday and got themselves hitched.

She moved over to the Empire and Willie moved the gamblin' out. He was makin' a good profit with the restaurant and the rooms upstairs and couldn't have been happier, his mood brighter and six-guns out of sight.

The new Empire Inn gained a fine reputation over the years and flourished for its owners. Willie and Polly would cordially greet their guests and there was no more division among the townsfolk, - no good side or bad side of the street and the sheriff watched over the entire town of Grimy Gulch.

As the years passed, you might take a stroll on a summer evening. As you passed the Empire Inn, with its big front porch, you might hear the steady noise of a glider goin' back and forth and servin' as a background for a gentle tune bein' whistled into the nighttime sky, carryin' the wind's voice.

(11/17&18/14)

The Man and His Land

I saw him standing in his yard, a few steps from what he calls home. It never was much and now looks less. Just a couple of rooms thrown together under a sagging roof. Dressed in blue jeans, blue shirt, work boots, his face looking away from me, but this is a man who has worked hard all his life. He is older and by stature, looks even older, wife gone, children, if any, moved away and everything about him is tired.

The wooden steps leading down from the front door are more than weathered. My guess is that he built those steps in a youthful time, when life had not sat so hard on his existence. Though he has worked hard all his life, it is 11:00 AM on a Monday and he is home. Maybe he has a night job, but I'm thinking he could have no job.

He is surveying his land, measured in feet not acres, outlined by a toppling series of posts with a few rusted strands of wire connecting them. In the far corner is his fancy car, the one besides the ancient pickup on the side of the house. This fancy car is slowly melting into the ground, a souvenir from a rare time of money. It too is not working and probably last touched the road as Eisenhower became "Father of the Interstate."

The man has one of two lots carved out of a fallow field. The neighboring shack is empty; the field closes him in on two sides and the road I am traveling on completes his borders. I wonder if the field was originally his, or his father's or his father's father, and that circumstance have left the family in everlasting bad times.

What grass there is mixes with weeds and grows unattended. Other spots are down to earth and packed by years of neglect. Other remembrances of life past dot the yard, a mixture of discards. And I wonder if he is not the latest one.

(8/11/11)

The Couple at the DQ

It is near noon and my head says, "hungry or not, it's time for lunch." So I pulled off Route 102, in New Brunswick, Canada, as soon as I see a food sign. I am after a turn or two at a DQ – Grill & Chill in the town of Memrancook. I have never eaten at one of these places, so it takes me a minute or two to order what I hoped would be the least harmless food option.

I am given a little stand-up number thing (#42) and told my food would be brought to me. The emptiness inside of the restaurant belies the busy drive through; still, I pick a table with two seats, leaving larger tables for others who must be entering soon.

I face a view so as to be distracted while I chomp down my chicken something or other. "You're from Connecticut?" a neatly dressed elderly woman asks as she sits at the four-seater right next to me. Surprised, not by the question, I assumed she saw my license plate as she passed in behind me, but that she was speaking to a perfect stranger and initiating the conversation.

"We always sit at this table, this is our table," she volunteered to answer why out of the whole empty place she sat right next to me. I asked if she meant where I was sitting and she said no. "Are you sure, I'd be happy to move," and again she said no, where she was sitting was theirs and if someone was sitting in their place they would move to the next four-seater, in the opposite direction.

It wasn't long before I learned she had been working in her yard yesterday and cleaning the inside of her house today. The house was being shown today and they were moving to an apartment. Two bedrooms, two bathrooms, no shoveling, no yard work - it sounded like a brochure and there was no life in her voice. I asked, "No yard?" She answered sadly, "No yard. But my husband has been asking for two years, I had to say yes."

"How long in the house?"

"Twenty-six years."

At this point, hubby arrives with their drinks and their order number card. He is in the middle of a conversation with himself or one he's having with his wife and oblivious to the fact that it is an ongoing monologue, I'm guessing about his son-in-law.

"He's no good. He's from Ontario and he swears too much around the kids. I never swore like that when I was young; it's not right."

She could be coming or going to church, he was in, what shall we call it, his Farmers best. All browns, but otherwise a mismatch of plaids and stripes that blended with his sun-darkened skin. There was one opinion on a subject and it was his. →

Since "Hellos" didn't seem to run in this family, I joined right in with the conversation. It was beyond the point that I could pretend not to be listening or get up and move, besides it was so bizarre, it was fun.

I took a slightly different tack on swearing, saying I had tried to control mine around the kids, so that when I did lose it, they would know it was pretty serious.

He said all he did was - and he sat straight in his chair and pointed - and I flinched a little. He was a tall, strong, big man, and should have been flabbier or feebler at his age; he did move stiffly, but with darting, deliberate steps.

Their food arrived, brought by the store manager, who began explaining that their chicken, different from mine, had a new batter that just came in yesterday and she thought lighter and better tasting.

I was done and said good-bye while the manager continued to ramble on and repeat herself to her regulars.

I felt sorry for the lady who, though she may have had the opportunity to speak, was not often heard. And how her life would become trapped in an apartment with new walls and strange neighbors. I wondered how far away from their present home the apartment building was and how many friends she had. I think if he had friends, he met them away from the house and did not share them.

I thought maybe she belongs to a church group.

Memrancook, New Brunswick, Canada (9/4/13)

Wrinkles

It was there on a misty morning
His escape from a life he hated.
At fifteen he was a tool in the shed,
Up at dawn, working into night
In a loveless home. Now the escape.
Upon that field just out of town
The circus had come to play for two days.
It didn't come every year,
But when it did most of the plows were put down.
Rising into the sky, the mysterious
Tent poles put on end,
Canvas raised up and stretched,
A vagabond village rose with the sun.
 It was summer but the heat had not risen.
Watching this all was a small group of children,
Free from school and evading their chores.
They marveled in silence as color entered their life.
Cautiously they moved closer, our hero among them.
Some lucky ones were given duties.
Carrying a bucket of water to a mysterious tent
Was more exciting than carrying a bucket of water into a tired old barn.
This was better than any show, to be in the midst of
Men and women who would, later in the day,
Be transformed from work clothes to glitter
Bright and shining costumes, dazzling.
They would become acrobats, trapeze artists,
Animal trainers and loud-mouthed barkers —
"Try a game of chance and try another world."
And our friend did on the circus's last day in town.
After the last show, everything was packed up
Truck and trailer ready to move to the next field.
In the gentle folds of some canvas, in the back of a truck
Two wide eyes watched familiar change to strange.
The miles ticked off and now pushed away the past.
When he was discovered, he wasn't the first.
There were questions asked, but not many.
An age ago, the inquisitor had done the same thing.
He was bunked with some other single guys
And given all the worst jobs there were to offer. →

But they were done with unflagging enthusiasm.
Traveling from town to town, state to state,
Traveling through the night, through the year,
Following the sun from north in the summer
To the south in winter, highway to dirt road,
Nursing trucks and rides, keeping them running.
Once in awhile, an act would get a call
Up to the *Big Time*, good money, rest and fame.
Perhaps it isn't the same nowadays
The *Big Time* played in arenas - no more tents.
Other acts would break up and leave.
Affordable replacements would be found
From Europe or the Far East, somewhere.
This was the proving ground or the way down
When the spring was going from their step.
Our hero has no name; let's call him Ben
That's not his real name, but who he has become.
He flourishes and others accept him,
Tease him, teach him and befriend him.
Ben is young and strong and handsome.
He sees that some of the glitter is faded
But he's there to help make it shine again.
More than one woman has matured him;
Still he is not cocky, he remains caring.
Once in awhile he is given a part.
Someone gets sick and he learns the part.
He is always watching the acts during the show
So when someone is too ill or too happy,
Ben can slip into a hastily put - together costume.
And he knows how high to hold the hoop —
Tah-dah! The dog has jumped through.
He holds the net tight and steadies the descending trapeze artist.
Helping the acrobats move their equipment in and out of place,
Taking care of the animals, packing and unpacking,
Always there for his job and ready to help with others.
Around the food table or a rare relaxing evening,
When they play two or three days in one town,
Ben hears the stories of past glory, of dreams.
He hears his story time and time again.
Eventually he shares his story and absorbs the others.
There is a tight-knit group of three
Three men who are slow to warm to him —
To anyone. They keep to themselves

Stuff

In one corner, in their own trailer.
They are not young, rather ageless —
And these are the ones Ben is inexplicably drawn to.
The clowns, those who engage the public the most
Are withdrawn, sullen, it would appear unhappy.
Two were veterans who had once worked for *Ringling Brothers*.
The other one never quite reached that high on the ladder.
Ben watched them do their make-up,
White-faced with exaggerated features,
Carefully different, unique and always applied the same way.
It was as if it were a ritual and each element held meaning —
Meaning to their lives and what they had experienced.
Sweeping and returning confetti after a show,
Helping to refill seltzer and reset tricks,
Refolding an unfolded bouquet, keeping things ready,
Keeping things running and watching, always watching,
Pulling a punch, a little sleight of hand,
And most of all how to work the crowd,
To keep the people laughing year after year.
One corny trick after another and yet
The older audience has a double delight,
Willingly forgetting what is about to happen
And watching the newer generation fall for the same trick.
Quietly, on his own time, Ben practiced and practiced.
He learned the old tricks and developed some new ones.
Slowly the established trio warmed to Ben.
Any jealously quickly vanished in light of the adoration they were shown.
Eventually they shared their lives with him,
How their dues were paid, how they learned,
One of the *Ringling* pair was old enough
To have known and worked with Emmet Kelly.
Road to highway and back again,
One's life in the circus is narrow.
The world you are in is the only world.
You don't earn much money, but that's all right,
You have no place, really, to spend it.
Life and death are as common to this world
As it is to those sitting they're watching them.
So one day a clown crumpled in the ring
A heart that had given laughter stopped beating.
It is doubtful anyone sitting in the bleachers knew,
A quick cover-up and even a funny final exit. →

He was buried that night in this town.
He had no other family but his circus family.
They remembered him that night and then carried on.
His spirit however, would move on to the next town;
He was and would remain in their stories forever.
The owner of the circus called Ben to his trailer
Beside him were the other two clowns.
"Can you do his job? Do you want his job?"
Wrinkles was born.
The act was running smoothly within two performances,
And the circus moved on to the next town.
It was all the same, but different —
Arriving in town after driving all night,
Moving through a town full of circus posters.
The advance man had gone store to store
He had fastened them on fences and poles.
Now the trucks and trailers found their spot
And circled their gaily painted vehicles
Like a gaudy wagon train moving west.
There was little need for giving orders
Everyone knew their job and wanted it done.
Putting up the big top with bleachers inside,
Then the midway and ticket booths are assembled,
They construct their magic world on a muddy field.
One truck is then opened and the prizes are distributed,
Rides are assembled and plugged into life.
They are tested and tested yet again.
A quick meal for everyone and a short nap for most.
Next the local inspectors come; maybe there is a donation.
Finally the lights come on, the music plays,
A small parade of dungarees with suspenders,
Year-round flannel shirts and summer dresses.
Stagger in awe or suspicion through the main gate.
This is the repetition and this is the life.
Wrinkles grows stronger and more confident.
With the others permission, he slowly breathes new life into the act.
They start to interact with the other performers.
We see them now as a thread throughout the show.
The other acts work well with their friend, Wrinkles.
There is more life, more excitement, something new.
And miles and days and years wander through.
Wrinkles has become the oldest in the act
Replacements are either jobbed in or developed from within.

He is their leader, their teacher and their friend.
His relationships can last for years —
But they don't survive.
Some want to leave the circus and find a life,
A stability that doesn't exist on the road.
Others leave with their act to different adventures.
But Wrinkles is home and wants only to do well.
He has received offers to move on and up,
To marry and have children.
Still, in the end, he is where he wants to be.
Early on in his *Wrinkles* career they had played his hometown.
He made his entrance and had soon gathered laughter.
At one point he had switched a water bucket with a confetti bucket;
Dancing about in big floppy shoes he had teased —
First one part of the audience and then the other.
People would laugh and put arms overhead to protect themselves.
Finally, he headed for his target, a stone-faced couple in the second row.
With a great flourish he poured the confetti on top of the couple —
It wasn't water after all and everyone laughed
Except for the sullen couple; they found no humor here.
Wrinkles walked away with an exaggerated shrug
Good-bye mom and dad, I'm sure you think your money was poorly spent.
There was always excitement for Wrinkles.
He would get to know towns where they stayed for a few days
Little adventures or sightseeing thrilled him.
On and on it went until Wrinkles grew into his name.
The circus owner and he were longtime friends now
And he had earned a share of the business.
He was good at making suggestions,
Watching the show day after day.
Wrinkles could politely tell someone how to improve things.
He was able to twist it around so that it would appear to be the artist's idea
And that was fine; he didn't want credit, just a good show.
Duties changed for people as they aged or when others moved on.
Wrinkles, most people had forgotten any other name long ago,
Would supervise the goings on, help where he could,
Make sure all was going smoothly toward the next opening.
One day all was ready and the show began.
Everything was "perking" and the clowns had become the featured act.
Wrinkles was working hard, helping the newest clown break in, →

A young runaway, a mirror of his youth
And the young man was thirsty to learn it all.
With the show done, the entertainers retired.
This was the first of three days and the midway was alive.
Wrinkles paused near the tent exit and played with the exiting audience.
When all were gone he sat on the edge of the first row of bleachers.
Slowly he took in all there was to see,
Starting as a check on the condition of things,
His mind took him away from the present.
He saw acts using the now silent equipment, the best of the best —
From Ben to Wrinkles and on to today.
Friends from now and friends from the past
Filled the tent with activity; the music played,
Then all was in slow motion and they all paused at once.
Turning as one to their audience of one
They motioned for him to join them in the center ring
"Come join us. Let's do a show. Come on!"
Wrinkles smiled and waved back and started to rise.
He was buried that night in a cemetery nearby
Tears and laughter streamed from the crowd.
The next day, the apprentice took his place with the clowns,
Weeks before he had received permission to copy his mentor's make-up.
So Wrinkles was still there today and tomorrow and for years to come.

(9/11/16)

It Was

It was a June night
It was a June night in so many ways
It was a June night for the young
It was a June night for love

It was for the end of school
It was for the beginning of summer
It was for proms and dances
It was for dreams of the future

Stuff

It was for first dates
It was for a teenager knocking on the door
It was for a corsage and a cummerbund
It was for awkward moments with her parents

It was for a stuttered promise of their return
It was for the heart-stopping moment she came down the stairs
It was almost disaster
It was her little sister, the unknown saboteur

But her mother fixed her dress
But he forgot all the words he had planned
But her parents knew the feelings and smiled
But they still made them pose for pictures

It was time to be off
 It was his parents' car
It was his first time as a gentleman
It was time to close the door

It was small talk with her friends
It was all giggles and laughter
It was like time never moved
It was sitting and waiting, not knowing what to do

It was finally time for the music
It was crazy for a while
It was like a peacock's courting dance
It was almost going too far

But the music finally slowed
But now he was back to awkward
But she smiled and didn't make it last
But where did he put his hands

It was she who melted in his arms
It was she who was patient with his steps
It was she who put her head on his shoulder
It was he who now felt alive

It was an evening with classmates
It was an evening with friends
It was an evening neither wanted to end
It was an evening for answering questions

It was time to leave, but not go home
It was they decided time to be alone
It was a nervous drive
It was the end of small talk

It was like so many generations gone by
It was a secluded spot, their special place
It was soft music playing on the radio
It was slow music of generations untold

But the music seemed so far away
But now where do they begin
But also where do they end
But then that is the question

It was a June night
It was a June night full of moonlight
It was a June night's explorations
It was a June night, for promises they wanted to keep

It was a night into morning
It was a night of slow smiles
It was a night ending
It was a night that was a beginning

(6/12/16)

Diner
(A story told in single lines)

"Two eggs over hard."
It is a smidge into daylight,
And a long way to go.
A mumbled appeal; "Coffee."
Another day to drive
Hundreds of straight miles
With no real destination,
Alone with morning smells,
The unseen cook,
The uniformed waitress who'd seen it all,
A small TV softly chewing air.
He lifts his eyes to what was around him:
Menus stained forever
Clipped to the counter in a metal holder
That also sheltered ketchup, salt and pepper.
Fruitlessly he searched for sugar.
The nametag arrives with coffee.
Studying the person in front of her
She reaches under the counter
And, as the Great Houdini,
Produces sugar, spoon and napkins.
Without much certainty she adds a smile.
Her reward is a nod and eyes
Eyes bringing her into focus.
"Good morning, You OK?"
This got a shrug and after a beat
A pleasantly sarcastic, "Sure."
She gave a slight nod and moved away
Down to the end of the counter
Where she prepped for the rest of the day,
Sorted things to fill and make ready.
Then she moved around the counter
And added things to each table and booth,
Moving back behind the counter.
Just as his order slid out from the kitchen
The hand quickly retreated
And she moved the plate in front of him.
"There you go, Hon." →

He glanced up at her then down
"Thanks." As he centered the meal
She watched as the automaton
Dug fork from plate to mouth
In a bored, slow rhythm.
He was now reading things —
Cereal boxes on the shelf across the counter,
Signs on the wall, Cash Only,
The first dollar, the Special Board.
The place was open twenty-four hours
But it was too early for the early birds
And too late for the sobering set.
Suddenly he stopped eating and sought her.
She moved off her elbow back toward him.
"Excuse me, what day is this?
And where are we?"
"It's Sunday morning in Oak Bluff."
"Oak Bluff?"
"Oak Bluff, South Dakota. And no, there
Isn't one oak tree in town and
The land is totally flat."
She had his attention now
And with that she saw the inspection.
It wasn't obvious, but it was in progress.
So she started one of her own
He saw a woman caught in early middle age
Filling her uniform quite well;
The uniform wasn't flattering
But still there was evidence of curves,
Maybe an extra pound or two,
Hair done up in working mode,
Little or no make-up —
But gorgeous eyes, smooth features.
The fingers were clean of jewelry;
The hands seemed delicate yet strong.
The "Hon" bothered him, how much substance?
She saw a could be handsome soul,
Jeans, shirt, jacket clean and wrinkled,
Baseball cap on the counter
Strong but a little out of shape
Interesting face with some life worn on it
But something was definitely wrong.
The weariness was not just from long travel hours

Hair a bit ruffled, carelessly shaven
"Just passing through?" Might as well ask.
Again the little self-deprecating shrug,
"Yeah , I guess so." A pause then
"Did you grow up here?"
"No. I just ended up here."
"Sounds like a story, wanna share?"
Now she gave the shrug and caught his eyes,
"It's early yet. I'll swap stories with ya."
Another pause. "Deal" came with a grin.
'OK." She grabbed the coffee pot and refilled his cup;
She took another cup off the shelf and poured some for herself
Cuddling the cup in both hands she began.
"Been here a few years now
Can't really afford to be anywhere else.
Came west with the love of my life.
He didn't like the east and had plans —
Lots of plans - lots of dreams.
We had a little money when we stopped here.
Here is where he came from
We managed to buy a fixer-upper.
Funny thing is it never got fixed.
He was working on different angles,
But his main plan was to drink Budweiser.
I still thought things would work.
I got the graveyard shift here.
I thought a little money would be better than none.
This made the love of my life angry,
It wasn't part of his plans.
Then one morning I came home
And he had moved on.
Moved on with an old acquaintance,
One who appreciated his plans,
And could better help him reach them.
She was the daughter of a rich farmer.
Together they moved on to a better world
Away from daddy and away from me.
I can't afford to go anywhere
So I joke with the locals
And smile with the travelers —."
Through this her focus had been drifting
From her hands to out the window,
Out the window to the long thin road. →

Slowly she came back inside.
Gathering herself back to Sunday
She shrugged, finally looked at him
"OK. Your turn."
He traveled from her story and frowned.
"I'm Ben" he said as he stared at her.
"Jenny" she replied, a little taken aback.
"Not a very exciting story, I suspect,
I work in computers, - software design.
I'm good at what I do and enjoy it
I was married to a woman and the job.
My wife liked the idea of marriage,
Liked all the money coming in,
But wanted me to do what she wanted,
Was jealous of all the time at work.
And it was a lot of time.
And most of the stuff she found important,
I either didn't like, or hated.
I made a few efforts to be what she wanted.
It was all so phony, so many have-to-haves,
The fanciest clothes, jewelry, lots of jewelry,
Friends as synthetic as she would want us to be.
I wanted kids; she wanted to go to the spa.
I liked motels, she liked resorts.
You'd have thought we would have seen this coming.
Before the marriage it was all different.
And I truly loved her.
Finally she got a good lawyer.
After a short while I didn't fight it.
She got a big settlement
And relocated and quickly remarried,
An older gentleman I believe,
More it tune with what was important in life.
So I was left with my second love
And dove into it more than ever.
Flash forward a few years.
I was slowly coming up for air
And even found myself smiling on occasion.
Then a competitor made me an offer,
An offer that even I couldn't pass up.
Part of the deal was about me.
If I take the deal, I have to stop working —
For at least three years I can't work in the field.

Stuff

So here I am in Oak Bluff, South Dakota.
It's Sunday morning, and I have no place to go —
Nowhere except somewhere,
And maybe something will break through
And I'll see where I am."
This had all come rushing out,
Jenny was still absorbing it all.
Ben looked at her carefully.
"Sorry, not your problem."
He moved a bit on the stool —
Maybe it was time to move on.
Impulsively Jenny reached out.
She touched his hand
And gently pinned it to the counter.
Just then the door flew open.
"Hi Jenny, I'm here!"
Enter another uniform with well-worn features.
Sandy, the day shift, had arrived.
"Hi," Jenny acknowledged, but didn't move her hand
She looked at Ben then away.
She lifted her hand and asked
"How would you like to see the sights of Oak Bluff?"
Ben made eye contact again and kept it.
There was a silent dialogue.
It didn't stop when he spoke —
"I'd love to."

(2/16 & 17/13)

Cemetery

As I drove by, I noticed the four brothers and sisters gathered at the cemetery just outside the town they had grown up in. Ralph still lived here and though old enough to retire, he was a farmer and that meant to him, being one with the land until he was buried in it. He lived on the family spread, having long ago paid his brother and sisters their share of the property when their folks had passed away.

Emma, the oldest, lived in Charlottetown on the other side of the island. She had gone away to school, the first in her family, and had for all intent and purposes stayed away. Emma had never married and built her life around books, the books that carried all the adventures in her head that her feet were afraid to take. Being apart from her family had been a fearful thing and though she had excelled in her studies, her social life had failed miserably. An almost-beau, who she loved but who did not return the favor, had gone on in the world, leaving her with imagined memories to carry her through life.

Emma worked in the public library and did research for other people. She continued to take courses at the local college; to widen her knowledge and even had a dream, a pipedream really. She hoped someday to open a little bookstore and decorate it and live upstairs or in the back. But Emma knew in this day and age, such a store would be lucky to survive.

Emma saw Ralph a couple of times a year, mostly when he had to come across the island to handle some farm related business in town. Questions on taxes or new regulations he didn't understand, picking up supplies that were not available where he lived, would conspire to bring him to Charlottetown, but generally it was too big, too busy, and too full of concrete for his comfort.

Ralph and Emma would meet at a restaurant and ask polite questions and nod at the answers. They were mostly the same questions, safe questions, they never pried.

Ralph's wife had died several years ago and Emma listened to the sound of Ralph's voice, not his words, to learn how he was really doing.
The other siblings, Roy and Elizabeth had married and left the island. Their communications were seasonal and contact minimal with the two islanders.

Elizabeth had married a young man from the mainland who owned a business totally unrelated to farming. It was a successful business; he Over the years they had made a few obligatory visits with the entire family, but only Elizabeth returned annually to take part in the family custom.

Roy had married a local farm girl and the two of them couldn't wait to escape. They went to the mainland and thrived in an urban environment. Both worked in a large factory, had union jobs, had union wages, and didn't want kids and traveled their two weeks of vacation.
Both were retiring next year with a good pension, a house paid for and a little vacation lodge on a lake about a four-hour drive from home.

Roy represented his family at the annual family ritual not wanting to even suggest his wife come with him.

And so it was, year after year since their mom died and a decade after their dad had passed. It was an odd sort of obligation, unspoken but certainly the last thread of their youth.

It was an unusual gathering, the closest thing to a reunion they would ever have. They all met at Ralph's, but none stayed with him. Come late August, on an agreed upon date, they would appear.

Long gone were the "Remember when…" Their youth had been hard work and they were dutiful children. There hadn't been any serious mischievous adventures to look back on and laugh.

This day would be solemn with smiles with questions and well wishes passed on between brothers and sisters, about wives and lives and nephews and nieces and finally a common silence would come. Ralph would stand and mumble something about heading out.

All four would get in Ralph's car, dressed in Sunday's best for the short drive down the road to the cemetery. Ralph would pull in and they would all exit the car and head for the family plot.

This cemetery was on the edge of a wide-open field near the road, and the stones looked like an odd crop to be growing.

Emma, Roy, Ralph and Elizabeth, now, not so many years from a similar residence, circled their mother and father and mumbled awkwardly, for their own hearts. Sincere or insincere, no one would judge. Elizabeth would leave almost immediately when they got back to Ralph's. Roy might stay a day or two and visit, and then all would be done for another year.

Four neatly dressed people, gray-haired or balding stood near the road as I drove by.

(8/29/13)

Country Song ("Beans, Corn & Alfalfa")

An old red pickup ran over my dog, poor Blue
Ma ran off with the Fuller Brush man, that's true
My best friend married my girl on our wedding day
But the sun will come up and it'll stay
And I'll have another really fine day.

My crops are diein', everyone's cryin'
The wind's blowin' the topsoil away
And the bank man's tryin' to take what's left
But the sun will come up and it'll stay
And I'll have another really fine day.

Beans, corn and alfalfa, hitch up the tractor.
Take it any way it comes for now,
God will take care of everybody's hereafter.

Now it was Saturday night at Nellie's Bar
I was nursin' beer number three
My paycheck hovered at no grocery level
But the sun will come up and it'll stay
And I'll have another really fine day.

The entertainment had just begun
A pretty young girl a strummin' and singin'
Wearin' a big ol' cowboy hat and a smile
But the sun will come up and it'll stay
And I'll have another really fine day.

Beans, corn and alfalfa, hitch up the tractor
Take it any way it comes for now,
God will take care of everybody's hereafter.

I couldn't move and my face looked silly
My heart smiled and I tipped my bottle at her
She kept singin' and dipped the head of her guitar
But the sun will come up and it'll stay
And I'll have another really fine day.

When she was done, I offered her a beer
Well it was declined, but before my heart sank down
She said she'd like a late night walk with me
But the sun will come up and it'll stay
And I'll have another fine day.

Beans, corn and alfalfa, hitch up the tractor
Take it any way it comes for now,
God will take care of everybody's hereafter.

We started out talkin' too much about everythin'
Then we stopped talkin' and kept on walkin'
And let the moonbeams warm our shoulders
But the sun will come up and it'll stay
And I'll have another fine day.

Movin' in circles and curves, that way and this
The deep dark night turned into a brand-new day
We leaned against our cars happy and nudgin'
But the sun will come up and it'll stay
And I'll have another fine day.

Beans, corn and alfalfa, hitch up the tractor
Take it any way it comes for now,
God will take care of everybody's hereafter.

The next night we met and talked deep into the hours
It was all about plannin' and such
The next day, the next week, the forever
But the sun will come up and it'll stay
And I'll have another fine day.

Soon we were married and happy still
The rains came and the crops grew
Along came a baby and a puppy, Little Blue
But the sun will come up and it'll stay
And I'll have another fine day.

Beans, corn and alfalfa, hitch up the tractor
Take it any way it comes for now,
God will take care of everybody's hereafter.

(9/1/13)

The Field

Daisy smiles and Black-eyed Susans
Waggle on top of a happy summer day.
The field spreads toward the sunset,
With Golden Rod and Queen Anne's Lace
Filling the gaps in the blanket.
The breeze is warm with anticipation.
Insects fly their missions above the color
Dipping to attack a blossom
Rising again grinning, full of pollen.
On the ground, out of sight
Others hop, slither and move about.
It seems that the pace has increased.
No longer a lazy day,
The temperature has decreased
And things have to be done.
Birds now dip to catch a snack
Then move on with no hesitation.
Just then they appear, almost on cue
He from the far end bordered by trees
She nearby from the just forded stream.
Their eyes sweep the scenery briefly.
Blue sky with a menagerie of clouds
Look down as the lovers spot one another.
As one they move into the rainbow
Legs lifting high, the man crashes through,
Muscles tight against his shirt.
Single-mindedly he bursts forward.
She spins her summer dress, lightly
Her youthful body bending stems.
Their paths are aimlessly direct,

His stride is steady, his pace now calculated.
Her smile grows to include the world,
She now fills her life and dreams.
Midway the pace has slowed slightly.
Hidden furrows and tangled roots
Have them staggering but still moving.
Now within the sound of each other
They cry out of love and futures
Straining from the exertion.
Each protests and proclaims uninhibitedly,
A stumble and concern
A rising and reassurance.
The sun travels low
As they slow a few steps from one another.
He is bent and limping.
She is plump and breathless.
He steps forward seeing her beauty.
She steps forward seeing his beauty.
He listens to her words and wisdom.
She listens to his words and wisdom.
They carefully embrace, holding tight,
Squeezing all the years in before the night.
They swing wildly, he handsome, she beautiful.
They turn and turn and turn
'til they collapse in a bundle of love and laughter.
They love, they touch, they hold.
They are swallowed by
Daisy smiles and Black-eyed Susans.

(8/19/10)

Everybody Wants A Laugh

Everybody wants a laugh.
It's been a long hard day.
"Mike! Give me one."
That first long pull
Lets everything fall away. →

My back is hurtin'.
I can't rub the hours,
The weary hours from my eyes.
Give me the noise.
Drown out what's happened today.

Another long slow sip
To bring me to where I am.
Let me see who's here —
All the familiar faces.
"Mike, another beer."

Listen to the bullshit talk.
Sports echoes from the radio,
Trashing some guy
With another opinion,
The sentences already starting to slur.

From sports to politics
To bragging of the conquests.
Or maybe they haven't conquered yet.
Ho, that fellow feels disrespected.
Shit man, do I want a part of this?

I see a guy in the corner
On a stool, just starin',
His head leanin' on the wall,
Just lookin' through the air
Nestlin', caressin' his drink.

I don't know this face;
It's got a life spelled on it.
I wonder where he is,
Did he come here for a laugh,
To soak away his day?

Funny, watching him
I can ignore all around me.
Clothes and hair slightly ruffled —

But he's never been here.
I don't think he's ever been here.

Turning away for a minute,
Wondering if he's noticed my stare.
My eyes drift over the skyline of bottles
And catch the guy in the long dirty mirror.
He's still traveling – he's not here.

Finishing the first beer,
And, ha, savoring the second.
I try not to think of my night.
I want that laugh, that numbness
Before I stagger to my empty place.

The guy dips his head
And looks at his hands.
He seems surprised to find his drink.
Raising it slowly, he takes a sip
Gently it returns to the bar.

Then his head slowly lifts,
Lost above us once more.
I notice his eyes brown I guess —
But they seem to sparkle.
Then one tear slips.

Almost before it starts its journey
One hand moves quickly up
And clumsily swats it away.
He makes a small smile
And shakes his head to lose it.

I wonder what the kids are doing.
Hell, I wonder what she's doing.
Do they even think of me?
They seem so distant
Tolerating our little time together.

I try to do all the things
I never had time to do
But I never know when their games are.
My questions are answered.
The hugs are patient and empty.

Damn, how could it go wrong?
And it seemed so quickly.
But she was never satisfied
And angry that I was.
It's been so long now.

A bottle hits the floor.
I'm searching the mirror again
He's not there. Where?
I look quickly around
And catch him walking across the room.

He is watching no one
Keeping, trying to keep,
A straight line to the door
He bumps the side of the doorway
Pauses, fumbles with the handle

And he is gone —
Gone to his nowhere —
His problems – his memories
Driving him to his empty bed.
Will I follow in awhile?

"Mike, again, Thanks."
I see a few leaving
On they're way to their happy homes,
Maybe solving the day's mystery,
Maybe ready for an evening battle.

I swing back forward
Ready to read labels
And empty my head

Just above Captain Morgan
And to the right of Jack Daniels.

Wait, I almost missed it.
A pair of blue eyes
Nestled around a what? Pert nose?
And framed with a bunch of brown curls
Are watching me.

I shift on the stool
To look a little closer.
She has a quiet, almost - smile.
I must have asked a question
Because her nod is an answer.

(5/15/10)

Agnes the Angry Raindrop

Agnes sat on her cloud with a big frown on her face.
She was and is a very angry raindrop.
Originally she thought she would be a part of a spring shower
Helping the bulbs and seeds start to grow.
BUT, apparently her grades were not very good.
So she studied harder in hopes of becoming
A part of a gentle summer rain
To help flowers grow and the grasses stay green.
Not to be; she thought she was being punished.
As hard as she studied, nothing would go right.
Cousins and uncles jumped into the fray.
The yards and fields were lush,
Color was at its best, crops grew, fruit ripened,
And Agnes just got more frustrated and even angrier.
She blamed her parents, her teachers and her friends,
Everyone and everything but herself.
Well, this didn't help no not at all.
Now her parents, her teachers and her friends
Were mad and disappointed in her. →

Agnes didn't care what others thought,
She was ready to fall to earth.
Instead, because she was so bad,
Because she talked back to her parents,
Because she didn't do her homework,
And played nasty tricks on her friends —
She got to go to bed early without her supper,
Stand in the corner and have a time-out,
Do extra schoolwork and eat alone at lunchtime,
Write her name on the blackboard over and over,
Maybe a million, billion times, and promise
To never do this or that again. But she did.
This was wrong, very, very wrong.
But Agnes couldn't stop being mad.
She didn't know why or how to stop.
Late one night, feeling hopeless, she began to cry.
I didn't know raindrops could cry, did you?
Yup, little teeny-weeny mini-tears slid down her raindrop cheeks.
All the sadness of all the weeks leaked out.
Gulping sobs of not understanding
Things felt they were crashing in on her.
She wished she would just evaporate.
Her parents rushed into her bedroom and held her tight,
They loved her dearly, in spite of all Agnes had done.
Agnes tried to explain what feelings were inside her,
How sad and angry she had become being left behind.
She had tried to study more, but it all seemed to fall apart.
Her parents listened and worked to calm her down.
Finally her Dad said something very silly and made her smile.
Once she was listening to what her parents said
It sort of made sense… most of it.
Agnes asked some questions and all three found some answers.
The three of them talked to Agnes's teachers
And a plan was put in place. If Agnes behaved herself,
Behaved herself and worked extra, extra hard…
Agnes baked cookies and made little gifts for her friends.
Then, one by one, she visited them and apologized for being mean.
Most of them forgave her right away, happy to be friends again.
For others, it took a bit longer, but they forgave her too.
The teachers explained how Agnes could still be a happy raindrop.
She was told to start to gather all of autumn's color.
Just before a tree would let go of its' leaves
Agnes would sneak in and soak up the yellows —

Stuff

Then the oranges and the late showing reds.
Blending them along with steadier colors,
She put them in a special pouch that she always carried with her.
Next she started taking dancing lesson; 1,2,3, -1,2,3
And taking walks on cold mountaintops.
Finally, at last, just in time for winter,
Agnes joined her friends on some very dark clouds.
The clouds started moving on a northeast wind,
Heading north as life slid into winter.
The next day, the cloud hung over a cozy little village
And the people in the village stood around a tall green pine tree —
Yes, right in the center of town —
And smoke was curling up from all the chimneys.
The people were singing. It took a minute or two
But Agnes and all the others finally made out the words —
They were about a baby who was born.
You know who, don't you? It's His birthday
And this was a song to Him, a thanks-for-coming song.
The music was the most beautiful thing Agnes had heard.
She finally knew it was time, her time.
Off from the cloud, she pushed into the sky.
The others followed her and, because it was so cold,
They instantly turned into snowflakes, no two alike.
But, Agnes was something very special.
She had her special pouch with all the colors with her
And as she and the others danced across the sky
Agnes released some of that color, a little bit at a time.
It turns out, she was a very good dancer,
And as she spun and swirled, she blended the colors.
The snowflakes gently fell on the village
Covering the ground, the roofs, the tree,
And of course, one snowflake for the tip of everyone's nose.
Agnes kept floating up and around,
This way and that, and she was able
To make the most beautiful snowflake rainbow
Just above the tree with everyone around.
The rainbow slowly slid down the tree
Totally wrapping it in all those colors.
On the tips of all the branches, other special raindrops fell.
Glistening among the snowflakes, they reflected the colors
And each branch sparkled.
All this mixed into the hearts of all those around the tree.
Their voices became stronger, louder, clearer,→

And I know for a fact, somewhere in this world,
Agnes is still happily wrapping her rainbow around a special tree,
People still celebrate around them and their happiness is forever.

(10/24/17)

A TOWN AND ITS PEOPLE

Chapter 6

Most of these pieces could probably find their way into another chapter, but as I sorted through, they felt comfortable here. The people are real (with their names changed) or fictitious with memories tacked on. In all cases they moved warmly from head and heart to paper.

Lt. Page

Lt. Page did what was expected,
He was born in rural Maine
A son of a hard-working couple.
 Being the first born
It was expected that he would be a boy.

The family survived from year to year
And Lt. Page learned what was expected of him —
Chores, then work, long days, hard work.
In-between all this was his schooling.
Though his parents had little of it,
They expected him to study hard and do well.
Lt. Page always did what was expected.

His family never showed a great deal of affection.
There was hardly a "good night" at days end
Not a lot of hugs or "I love you"
Just a firm nod of satisfaction
And a quick crinkle that would Stuffice for a smile.

When years piled up, Lt. Page grew
Tall and strong and polite and hard working.
He fell in love with the neighbor's daughter,
A handsome girl of good qualities
And, as expected, they became engaged.
Then the War came to the countryside.
Being a good American he joined up, as expected.

He was loyal and trained hard
And, as expected, he went off to fight the war.
Lt. Page fought hard in a strange land.
He wasn't a Lt. then, but in war promotions come.
They come quicker at the front as the candidates thin —
A natural leader, he assumed command.

His troops were a small group of homespuns mostly.
There was a city slicker and a know-it-all or two
But they respected Lt. Page and fought bravely. →

At one point they walked into Hell.
The fighting was fierce and ugly.
This war was not a romantic romp.
Lt. Page saw his men falling around him
The enemy moved back momentarily
And Lt. Page gathered bodies of his comrades,
Living and dead, to safe cover.
Everyone who knew him would not have expected less.

As he made yet another trip to the scarred earth
He found two more of his men, one living, one dead.
Hoisting the dead to his shoulder, he helped the other to rise,
Giving that man support, the odd group moved for cover
Near the edge of the battlefield, so close to safety
Lt. Page felt several pricks in his back.
The noise of the gunfire seemed delayed.
On his face there appeared a moment of surprise.
For once in his life something was unexpected.

He helped his wounded buddy down the safe slope,
Then he laid the fallen gently to the ground.
Lt. Page then sat heavily and turned on his side.
His eyes were closed, his face peaceful.
He had begun his eternal nap.

As a boy he had held a little flag.
On the Fourth of July, watching the parade
He had waved it wildly, saluting all those who marched.
Now, in a small cemetery, in the center of town,
Not far from his childhood home
Lt. Page holds a small flag next to his stone.
Parades march by every year.
As expected, his siblings remember him,
Siblings he had hardly known.
His parents are gone.
Next to his little flag
As you might expect, a single red rose.

(11/19/13)

First Friend

Well, finally off the shelf.
Oh, not a plastic bag —
Ah, tissue paper, very nice.
Hey! What are you doing?
Hello! It's dark in here.
I don't know where you're taking me,
But do you think you could not bounce around so much?
Still in the dark here...
Catchy song, but somebody is off key.
Sunlight at last.
Thank you, thank you, please hold your applause.
 Hey, who's this? Wait a minute —
He's drooling on me!
Hmm, nice hug, what a laugh.
You know this kid's all right,
But, will you please wash his hands?
OK, frosting, peanut butter, who cares.
It's been a big day you go to sleep,
I'll keep guard; it's all right, its safe.
Monsters in the closet, dragons under the bed
All the loud noises outside, no fear.
What? OK, under the covers.
Another big hug, I must be off duty.
Good Morning! A brand-new day...
Nothing to do but play.
Go ahead, I'll sit here and watch.
Be careful. If you need me I'm right here.
Don't worry; I'm still here.
No, I don't want a bath —
Oh, I know it's pretend,
With this bandage my boo-boo will be all better.
What who else is coming to tea?
Decided your going to try? OK go on.
Hold on to Mom with one hand, me with the other.
Now let go of Mom's hand
And we're off – Watch out! Watch out!
Don't cry, just use the table and get up again.
There you go – Go, go, go – Watch out!
Turn, turn – No, no. Stop!
You don't have to go that fast →

And you don't have to sit down to stop.
Wow, you're getting big, no more crib.
What are we going to play today?
Are we playing grocery shopping?
Who's that? Oh, a new friend…
Glad to meet you don't be embarrassed.
He has a blankie. Come on in here.
Let's play trampoline on top of the bed.
Hey, where are you going? Don't forget me!
Well Blankie, it's you and me,
Then in awhile, I'm on the shelf again.
Wait, where am I going?
Oh no, in a box, in the dark again —
I guess I'll take a nap.
Wow! Hello sunshine stranger.
Hmm, where am I? Oh, the attic.
Who are you? You look kind of familiar.
Wait! I know that hug. Hi, friend.
Where are we going? Oh, down? OK.
Things look different. What? Who's that?
Wait he's a "frosting face" Ah! Oh, well…
Hey what's going on? Nice hug.
Rocking here, peanut butter lips isn't letting go.
All right. All right. I'll be your friend.
No, no, I'll never leave you.

(7/3&4/15)

Now When I Was a Boy

Now, when I was a boy,
It was my brother who played the fiddle.
Me, I wet my number two reeds on a licorice stick.
The neighbors never complained —
It wasn't a drum and one, two we were done.
I did my chores and my homework
Though weeds looked like grass to me.
I made sticky fingerprinted models
With decals sliding off tail and wing and then

Up on a shelf to collect its dust.
I was always in school; it was always summer.
I delivered papers on my bike —
The news reached the proper porches
But my mind was taking on a different adventure.
I fought wars with the boys.
Always wounded in the shoulder
Or, if I should rarely have to die,
It came with a fall fit for a ballet
And, like most wars, no one ever won.
With the girls, I rode invisible horses.
They were older, but I was Roy Rogers —
I had a red bandana that told me so.
Wiffle ball and baseball
I'm old enough for inkwells and fountain pens.
Yet the years back then seem to blend.
The world expanded with the "Weekly Reader"
Things were spotty and not easy to comprehend.
It was hard to envision the opening of the Suez Canal —
Much easier to build a sand castle
Or float a Popsicle-stick boat on a rainy day.
It was ice cream in the summer
And your imagination led the way.
Eventually girls would get as interesting as the Yankees —
But that's another story.
This was a time of Saturday matinees,
Of boats in the harbor being ocean liners
And cars on the road being tanks.
After all I was born in a war
And was growing up in another.
It was a time of innocence —
One that had heroes, white hats and black hats.
Common sense and logic
Were often not the best playmates.
This time would grow awkwardly
With a soundtrack of soft music into the evening
To bongo drums and Hi-Fi –
And grow still louder.
But it's nice to go back to that street,
To sit under the leaves of those trees
Or have the whole neighborhood playing "Hide and Seek"
'til it's dark and time to go in
To rock on the glider on the porch →

To see faces that have gone away or grown older
Leaves wiggling in the streetlight glow
Casting harmless shadows on the night.

(6/5/15)

Booths

I sometimes go out to dinner.
On my own it's often a diner
And because I have age on my bones
I often show up for the early bird.
The other day was such a day
And I was told to sit anywhere.
I didn't want to walk a mile.
First booth full, fourth booth full,
Second and third were empty,
I took booth number two.
Now, like children, old people can be loud.
Booth four appeared to have senior regulars,
Enjoying their night out together
And reassured because the waitress knew their order.
 The group in booth one was barely over middle-age,
Talking in a slightly lower volume.
I checked the menu and awaited the waitress's arrival.
I'm not trying to listen in, reading labels to pass the time.
Another elderly couple arrive just then,
Older than dirt and lucky to make it to booth number three.
Now, I've placed my order and am looking out the window.
A bug or bird hovers about, zips off and returns again.
This thing is the size of a hummingbird, with those kind of wings
But it has more of a bug's body, a big bug.
While I try to figure out Mother Nature,
I hear booth number one – this place is cozy,
So it does provide this unsolicited entertainment.
My guess is that this is a computer-generated blind date.
The guy had been alone on a bench out front
When I first drove into the parking lot.
 Now he was verbally traveling on a narrow trail,

And the lady, just behind me, was not helping out.
He would start in one direction, describing a part of him —
Getting a minimal response, he would then head off in a different direction,
It seemed a scary path to be taking
This early in the evening with maybe a movie to follow.
Without paying strict attention, he seemed to have hit on several subjects.
He talked briefly about his working career,
Complete with built in excuses,
Sports was covered with a recap of his coaching abilities,
Aha! He has a kid or kids and is therefore divorced or a widower.
I think, once he started on retirement and the stock market,
The conversation at the table picked-up.
My interest wanes and I got my soup.
Booth number three took center court with a jarring voice.
"You want a hamburger? You liked the hamburger the last time."
There came a mumbled reply from the Korean vet
He was wearing a Korean War vet baseball cap, no mystery.
To the waitress: "He'll have a hamburger, no lettuce, no tomato, no mayo."
Waitress as she writes; "One plain hamburger and for you?"
Slight pause; "I'll have a hamburger with everything."
Things calm down and I watch my bird/bug.
Someone coming into the restaurant encounters it at eye level
And there is an impromptu limbo dance.
My dinner comes and I am occupied.
Booth one is chattier, but I don't think they're a couple.
Still, I hope they both finish the evening and have a good time.
The food has arrived at booth number three.
In answer to a perhaps unspoken question —
"It's a pickle. You like them. You had it the last time."
Normally, I would rankle at this kind of talk,
But something in the tone tells me it is just volume.
The woman is not frustrated, nor is she angry.
She is in love with a man she has known for a lifetime.
This is love talking in a loud voice
For as long as she can, she is helping her man.
She is keeping his days as normal as she can.
Somewhere, a time ago they switched places.
Years ago they fell in love. He went to war.
He came home and worked and provided.
The home was there and the kids were raised. →

They were alone again, but the love was strong,
As strong as her voice and his helpless smile.
I had my dessert, included in the early bird,
And went home, jealous and sad about that love.

(5/11/15)

Or is that the Whiskey Talking?

Hey buddy, pull up a chair.
How's it going fella, why the stare?
So I'm a drink or two ahead of you.
It's been a rough day, to be fair.
Did I ever tell you about when I was young
How life was good and all the stars were out?
It was quite a while ago when smiles were there.
Or is that the whiskey talking?

I had gone to college and done quite well.
Party time sure, but still I got it done.
Got me a job right out of school —
Salesman, first class. I knew all the rules
The money poured in, the product went out —
New car, new threads, take the client to lunch.
It was fun and I was good at it.
Or is that the whiskey talking?

Fell in love, had to have her.
Right here in this bar,
We courted a minute or two,
Then we married. We knew it was right.
Got us a place. Got us a kid.
But I had to work late,
Then had to unwind.
Or is that the whiskey talking?

Years went after years,
I was at the top of my game.
My kid was growing. I was so proud.

Stuff

I missed the game. I missed the recital.
My wife was always angry,
But there were younger men now
And I must stay ahead of them.
Or is that the whiskey talking?

It happened before I knew it.
I came in one day, called to the boss's office —
New team leader, new direction, new products,
Thanks for all you've done,
Pick up your check and pick up your things.
There I was alone on the steps.
I needed some courage before heading home.
Or was that the whiskey talking?

Things continued sliding downhill.
The wife, she didn't want to hear it.
I'll get a new job, let me rest for awhile,
I came here to get some peace.
The bartender - he would understand.
Then I went home and it was empty —
The wife, the child gone, they didn't care.
Or is that the whiskey talking?

I got a new job. I'd show them.
But after all these years it was hard to start again.
I got another job, no special thing,
Never appreciated what experience I brought.
I sometimes spent the afternoon right here,
And so it went and nothing was fun.
No one would listen to my tales.
Or is that the whiskey talking?

I see it in your eyes, "so go on."
Just an old man sitting here —
No job, no life, nowhere to go.
I saw my kid's picture in the paper —
Quite successful standing there,
With her mother and her husband.
I wish them all the best
Or is that the whiskey talking?

(4/18/15)

Thunderbolt

"Come on Dad, Mom, come on!"
"Don't run off Buddy."
"Look, look, I'm tall enough!"
Buddy's head touched the clown's wooden arm.
"Let's go for a ride, please?"
"What do you think?"
"He's old enough. Tall enough. I'll go with him."
"Thanks dear. Wait, daddy's coming Buddy!"
"Pull the bar down, keep your hands inside."
This from the trained operator, all of sixteen,
And this is his seventy-fifth caution of the day.
"Here we go." dad comments needlessly.
Bumpada, bumpada.

The well-worn cars begin their journey
Bumpada, bumpada.

Dad's first ride was maybe twenty-five years ago
Bumpada, bumpada.

The car has started its first climb
Bumpada, bumpada.

A slow climb to the top of the first drop
Bumpada, bumpada.

Dad smiles at Buddy, who is now having second thoughts
Bumpada, bumpada.

Buddy begins to retaste the corn dog and the cotton candy
Bumpada, bumpada.

The silver and red string of cars has reached the top
Bumpada, bumpada, bumpada.

A quick angled turn and down it plunges
Bumpada, bumpada, bumpadaah, bumpada.

Down a little dip.
Father and son do a sharing gulp,
And up again, faster now
Bumpadaah dah. Bumpadaah, bumpada.

Another quick down and fast climb,
The sky, then the ground.
Someone behind starts to scream
Bumpadaah, daah, daah, bumpadah.

A plunge from heaven, stomach still intact
Buddy and Dad laugh.
"Woo, Woo!" is the sound they make
As the coaster banks and turns back on itself
Bumpadaah, bumpadaah, faster still.

It may not do loops, but it fits those that ride
Bumpadah, bumpadah, bumpadah.

And still it climbs to its highest point,
Then drops to the bowels of the earth,
And Dad and Buddy raise both arms,
A symbol of bonding, of bravery, of love
Bumpadah, bumpadah, bumpada.

Things are slowing down.
The few moments that seemed a lifetime
Are coming back to real time
And mother is waiting there
Bumpadah, bumpadah.

The breaks have been applied
Bumpadah, stop.

"Everybody please exit to the left."

(5/4/15)

Are We There Yet?

Here we go. I don't want to.
Yes, I did – I forgot.
Are we there yet?
That's my spot. Leave me alone.
Ate the snacks, played the games,
Are we there yet?
Dad is driving. Mom is on the phone.
Then there is my sister. I can't stand it.
Are we there yet?
It's so boring. I'm not tired.
Yes, I see it – A cow.
Are we there yet?
I'm hungry. I have to go to the bathroom.
Can we stop here? I don't like this.
Are we there yet?
Are we there yet?
Are we there yet?
Are we there yet?
Hi there. Can I go play?
I won't go far. When can we go home?
What's that? You made that, Grandpa?
Wow, that sounds like fun.
No, I never did that. Could I?
Aw, do we have to? All right.
Bye grandpa. I love you.
Can we come back soon?
Dad is driving. Mom is on the phone.
Then there is my sister. I can't stand it.
Are we there yet?

(4/4/15)

Mr. Crawford

Mr. Crawford came to church each week.
He sat about three quarters of the way back,
To the left, by the window.

Mr. Crawford dressed neatly,
With suit and vest and a big bow tie,
But his white shirt was frayed at neck and cuff.

Mr. Crawford had a droopy moustache,
As white as snow and his hair above
All neatly trimmed, everything in place.

Mr. Crawford rarely talked.
He would nod his greetings.
Most of his prayers were silent.

I first heard him, I sit nearby,
When he sang a familiar hymn.
The voice was soft as a tender reed.

I was in his company for several years.
Each week for an hour or so
He sat quietly and erect.

I happened to watch him one Sunday
During a sermon that was tinder dry.
Still, he listened undistracted.

I wondered what was behind the man.
What happened when he left?
Where did he work? What did he do?

Then, one week, I was taken ill.
In bed I stayed, and it got worse —
To the hospital, all fixed, recuperation.
→

As soon as I was able,
I returned to church,
An answer to their prayers.

The minister had visited.
I was listed in the program
As ill and in need of prayerful encouragement.

Now, feeling fine, a little weak,
I was picking up my routine
And felt a warmth inside.

Mr. Crawford smiled and nodded,
A twinkle in both his eyes
And during neighbor greetings

Mr. Crawford raised his thin voice,
Offered me his hand and said
"We missed you, glad to have you back."

I smiled at Mr. Crawford,
Took his hand and mumbled "Thanks."
He then turned back to the pulpit,

And that was apparently that.
I never saw him at church events,
He never said another word.

Mr. Crawford sang and prayed
For years and years
While lots of faces changed.

Sadly there came a day,
When Mr. Crawford wasn't there
And the program announced a special service.

I went that day and sat
About three quarters of the way back
To the left, toward the window.

(2/13/15)

Sammy B

My name is Sammy B.
Not the kind of guy you'd have to tea
Someone said I'd never see twenty-three.
I was deep into the neighborhood —
No cute little games with the other kids—
Survival first, reputation, and then power.

My parents didn't have a clue.
They worked hard for no money.
Maybe they cared a few kids ago.
When I came in line,
Duties were delegated
And I was left with unhappy teens.
Brothers and sisters, never close,
Trying to squeeze a life for themselves
Burdened with a toddler of two or three.

Parents became stationary shadows
And empty threats were soon discovered.
There was a minimum of supervision.
I was alone and never weak —
Always afraid, always strong —
Bluff and bluster, try not to be caught.

School was a joke, what need,
I lived in a prison of streets
And besides people said I'd never see twenty-three.

Love was a weakness, because it was unknown.
I take what I want
Even if I don't know what I want.
First I follow and imitate,
Going along with others, the strong others,
Till I was on top. →

By age, by being clever,
There was always room at the top —
Show no fear - feed on fear.
Prove yourself - always prove yourself.
Look for weakness in others,
Then tear into it.
Rip it open till they follow or die,
Insulated by death around you.

I am eighteen, twenty-one.
Hold the territory, stay in control,
Trust no one. I look out behind me.
There is always someone behind you.
Why take a job? Just take.
Aren't I owed something? Always angry —
Never a laugh, just a sneer.
Look out behind.
I have no friends.
Little yous, so many imitators.
Never relax; keep up your guard.

What was that, what did I do?
I'm dying in the street at twenty-two.

(3/30/15)

City Sounds

Sirens wail, scream, and warble.
Get out of the way! Get out of the way,
I'm trying to save a life,
Go to the scene, something that matters.
Variations of sounds going low to high
Trying to warn a way through,
Create a Moses path to resolve.
Wake up people this is life!
But it sometimes appears inconvenient
To clear a path, pull to the side,
Pause or hurry across against the light

Perhaps that isn't fair, maybe just the avenues.
Once you hit the streets, turn the corner.
When you're on my block
Up a little ways or maybe in my building —
Then it is suddenly real, quickly personal.
Maybe it will be on the news tonight,
After all the television truck was here.
What was that old lady's name?
I used to see her walking every day.
They've taken her away.
Is there family or is she alone?
Look up there at her window —
See the cat watching her life go away.

(1/1/15)

Rufus

Welcome to my town - any town —
Any town that is not in a race
With a natural, comfortable, sort of slow pace,
Big enough for a green and a gazebo,
Surrounded by farmland,
And populated with old family names
Added to some newcomers —
Those that have been here only a decade or two.

I wouldn't say everybody knows everybody
But everybody knows about everybody.
The roads that leave and enter town
Must connect to another road
And that leads to a main road.
News moves fast around town.
However news is slow to come into town.
Progress and change is almost never embraced.

Television and the Internet do intrude,
Only if it is actively pursued.
We have a church or three →

And they fill up pretty good on Sunday.
There are a few stores around the green,
As well as some big old houses.
There are seasons, holidays and ball games —
A library, a Volunteer Fire Department and summer concerts.

People come to town for special events
And of course to get supplies and groceries.
Two gas stations keep the cars running.
There is a mayor and a small government.
We also have a movie theater,
But it is safe to say we are behind the times.
Just off the green we have a restaurant
And two, if you're generous, bars.

Growing up here you have several options:
Be a part of "and son" business,
There are two small factories, well hidden,
That provide fall back employment,

Start a new business, not an easy task.
Go away to college; we have two grammars and one high school.
Stay away after graduation and join the rest of the world
Or come back to the town's womb.

So it was one day, as I headed past the far side of the green —
Headed to the newspaper office my grandfather had begun.
It was a well-worn rectangle of a building
And sat at the northwest corner of the green.
It had four full-time employees
Who looked out big windows, in the front.
They watched the world go by,
Past the backside of the gold lettering announcing "The Bugle."

It was a weekly, with local youngsters providing delivery.
My grandfather was gone - my dad a concerned visitor.
"The Bugle" was mine to run and I kept it simple.
We reported local news and ran local ads.
I wrote an editorial with dedication and concern.
The ball scores are there, with the names spelled right.
Society news is provided; births, deaths,
Even a police blotter listing of who had trouble getting home Saturday night.

Just before I got to the office
I saw Rufus sitting on his usual bench.
You took it for granted that he would be there
Any day it wasn't raining or snowing or bitterly cold,
Rufus would be neatly dressed, sitting on his bench.
He lived in a room or two, in a house a block from the green
And, for God knows how long, has populated the green.
I don't know why old Rufus passes his days on the bench.

I don't know how old Rufus is
But it is a safe to say he has out-lived his contemporaries.
I've seen him reading our paper or a book —
Still, mainly he watches the world go by.
He will nod greetings to a passerby —
Talk about the weather, if you engage him,
Yet I feel is most comfortable
Lost deep in his mysterious past.

It seems that he started sitting on the bench
When he came home from a war,
Or perhaps it was after, way after that.
All those years ago, other veterans joined him.
They were always old - perhaps because of the war.
On patriotic holidays they would wear a snatch of a uniform.
As parades marched by, they would stand and salute as flags passed
And they would smile and answer the salutes of younger soldiers.

I wonder why they were never asked to ride in the parades,
But they didn't seem to be bothered by the slight.
They would sit together and talk of past battles,
Their war and their different experiences.
I was never close enough to hear the stories,
So I'm not sure if they became fishermen's tales
Or old men reliving the most important time of their lives
And then coming back the next day to do it again.

Slowly the bench emptied as the seasons rolled over
Until Rufus sat alone watching the world.
I have thought off and on about doing a story about him
Not knowing if he would consent to an interview.
I have hesitated, not wanting to spoil a tradition.
His presence is an anchor to many people's day. →

We all know his name, my father told me,
But he knew, basically only that.

Had he grown up in town?
Was he ever married?
Did he have children?
What had happened to them?
What else had he done in his life?
How old is he?
Is he living on a pension?
What has he seen all these years?

Time again had passed
And I see Rufus rising to his routine
Waking, showering, shaving, dressing,
In shirt and trousers way out of fashion

A jacket, coat or shirtsleeves —
Depending of course on the season.
A slow walk. He uses a walking stick.
And there he is settling onto the bench –

Finally, one summer day at noontime,
I wandered out of the office with my brown bag.
I walked across the street to the green
And with some hesitation sat on the shaded bench.
Here I am next to Rufus.
"Hello," I mumble, "nice day."
"Yes it is Randal," answers a dry voice.
He knows my name and I am lost.

There is an awkward moment here
While I try to assemble my wits.
Rufus speaks; "I enjoyed your editorial last week."
He gives me no quarter, but does give me an opening.
"Thank you, can I offer you half a tuna sandwich?"
Rufus smiles at the world straight ahead of him.
"No thank you, but it was nice of you to offer."
"Rufus, can I ask you some questions?" I blurted out.

There was a pause; no there was a gaping hole.
Finally, he asked the air in front of him, "Why?"
My turn to collect my thoughts.

"Because, for no other reason, than I'm curious.
For years I've seen you here and
I'd love to get some background.
Frankly I'm just plain nosey,
Your life is a mystery I'd love to solve."

These pregnant pauses were now the way of things —
The conversation of one who is not used to conversation
And because I knew this I was not anxious.
"For the paper?" was his next concern.
"I don't know, maybe, but not without your permission."
He looked at me for a moment, giving no clue of his feelings,
Then back away to whatever he saw in front of him.
A car drove slowly by and he returned a wave.

"Ask your questions and then we'll decide."
Here I was with all those simple questions
About to begin an interview I hadn't planned on.
I had no notebook, no recording device,
But I didn't think I'd forget his answers
And if I did, I would know where he was.
If a follow-up was needed or a little bit of color,
I decided to keep it simple and see where that led.

"Did you grow up in town?"
Rufus measured his responses.
"Yes, just out of town, on a farm on Webster Road."
A farm boy who had come to town.
"Were you ever married?"
Somehow he didn't expect this question.
I can see his face telling me the answer
But what comes out is, "Yes."

I think it best to leave that alone.
"Did you have any children?"
This time he is expecting the natural follow-up.
Without emotion he answered; "Two, a boy and a girl."
Not giving me a break on this,
I was forced to ask the next logical question.
"What happened to them?"
There was an angry silence. →

I was waiting to be thrown off the bench,
To be told to mind my own business,
To not disrupt the orderly life Rufus led.
Instead I got a choked answer to my question.
"My wife and daughter were killed by a drunk driver,
Hit head-on by a man going the wrong way on a one-way street.
He survived, so drunk he was not aware of what he had done.
My son was killed in a park, in New York City for loose change."

It was time for me to watch whatever was in front of me.
Whatever it was I did not see it.
I saw Rufus standing alone in the world —
His life, all that mattered taken away from him.

I had instinctively reached out for his hand
When he shared the nakedness of his life.
I believe he was embarrassed by the gesture
But did not move his hand away.

When I had recovered enough to speak
I asked what he had done in life.
He sort of chuckled at our segue back to today.
"I left the farm, joined the army, and survived a war.
Then I started a business and it was successful.
I was offered a huge amount of money for it.
I sold it and returned home.
The farm was gone and the family too.

Well, that answered the money questions without asking,
So I combined the last two questions.
"Do you mind me asking how old you are
And what have you seen from this bench all these years?"
 Again, the wait as Rufus shuffled a bit on the bench.
He looked as if he was about to answer
But then thought he required a bit more time.
Putting weight on his arms, he lifted himself up in the air.

He swung his legs back and forth like a kid on a swing,
Then he settled down on the bench.
"I am older than a lifetime, certainly.
If you must attach a number, I'm in my nineties.
I have lived my life and, from this bench,
Seen others head in many directions.

I've seen people like you grow and mature
And fall into a full and comfortable life."

He paused a second and then continued.
"I have watched men and women in this town
Start a life or leave to begin somewhere else.
My life was gone on a highway and in a park,
But coming back here has meant a lot.
I was able to see others continue on to a full life —
A life of love, faith and friendship
And I felt all of that from this bench."

That was it; I had no more questions worth asking —
No questions that is, save one.
And Rufus gave me that answer straight out.
"I realize I'm sort of a town character,
But I think I would prefer you holding your story.
Would you mind not telling it until this bench is empty?"
I told him I would do as he wished and finished my lunch
And then went back to the office.

It is roughly three years since that interview
And as I came to work this fine summer day,
Rufus was not sitting on the bench.
I checked with the hospital and they confirmed my fears —
Rufus had been found dead in his rooms.
He had apparently died suddenly
As he was preparing to start his day
Walking slowly, to take his spot on his bench.

(5/24/16)

The Early Bird Special

The Early Bird Special," that's what we called it.
Around the bend and through the town
It was passing us by, but it slowed a little —
Four-thirty no matter what season.
Here it comes, all full of steam and whistle. →

Most of the town was still sleeping
But for a number of years, I was there.
The Engineer would wave to me
And I smiled and waved back to him.
The mailbag was extended on a hook.

It was caught and my newspaper bundle thrown.
The stationmaster grabbed the mail
Even before the train had passed.
I had my papers unwrapped
Before the train was out of sight.

Soon Mr. Jackson drove up.
He was the postmaster in town
And ran the general store
The two masters discussed the weather
While I folded the world, ready to deliver.

Into the bike basket went the sports news.
Pedaling down the hard-packed road
I carried all the factual gossip —
The notices of death around the world
And just over the hill —

My route took a curious pattern
Hitting outlying farms already busy,
Dipping close to town then away again,
The circle narrowing as the sun rose.
Sometimes a dog would run alongside.

I got plenty of "Good mornings"
And I knew all the faces
Sharing a few minutes of their lives,
Moving steadily with my youthful legs pumping
Spinning to the center of my world.

The houses and stores were tardy.
They were just stretching and yawning
And I was almost done.
All the seasons and all the weather
Wind and rain, sun and dust…

When I was done, I had school and chores.
Finally free to do as I wished,
I would play or read,
Hang around with the guys,
Play ball, or just wander down the street.

I brought the outside world to town
Courtesy of "The Early Bird Special"
But not much of the town listened.
The church social was more important
Because it was real to all of them.

Weekly, I would make the rounds
Collecting what was owed for my services.
I would hear all the local doings
And how things were a time ago.
Some of the old folks needed to talk.

There came a time when, I took notice
And timed my morning delivery
For a chance to see someone special.
It started by accident one day
But only took a smile to be on purpose.

Time passed and there were other special ones.
Eventually I outgrew the route
And had all the adventures of youth.
I did well in school and read the papers.
I got a scholarship to college.

My parents took me to the station.
It was early on a September morning
Here comes "The Early Bird Special,"
Right on time, all steam and whistles.
I waved to the Engineer and he waved back.

The train, on signal, came to a stop,
But it was panting, ready to move on.
I kissed my past good-bye for a while
And hefted my suitcase on board.
We were moving before I sat down. →

All these things would change.
All these things would be the same.
I pressed my face to the window
And watched a boy on a bike
With a basket full of the world to deliver.

(2/8/15)

Billy Buster Bean

Billy Buster Bean
Was the cutest baby you've ever seen
He smiled and gurgled
He pumped his arms and legs
He grew.
Billy Buster Bean
Was the smartest youngster you've ever seen
He laughed and talked
He walked and ran
He learned.
Billy Buster Bean
Was the handsomest teen you've ever seen
He studied and loved
He promised and planned
He dreamed.
Billy Buster Bean
Was the strongest young man you've ever seen
He listened and believed
He saluted and marched —
He died.
Billy Buster Bean.

(8/25/07)

*Previously published in "2007 High Tide" – Milford Writer's Group, Milford Fine Arts Council.

The Party

We're all set, doors locked, lights are on, let's go.
What, you want to be late? What's this?
You want to make a grand entrance?
That's us, being fashionably late – Ha.
Or maybe you want us to sneak in and not be noticed?
You got the damn invitation? I look O.K.?
Who's going to be at this party anyway? Do you know?
I know you said we had to go, but why?
To be seen, to make contacts, to impress others?
It wouldn't be to have a good time would it?
OK, here we are. All set? Check this place out.
What do you think of all these decorations?
Aren't they something else? Do you love it or what?
Hey, look who's here? Do you believe it?
I haven't seen George since he left Martha.
Is he with Abigail? Well I'll be damned. What?
Want a drink? Help you relax and feel calm.
Want an appetizer? I don't know, little fancy things.
Look, complete with toothpick and napkin, how nice.
Here comes more. Oh, just use your fingers?
I wonder why they were invited?
Could mean some angry words later on.
I'm just saying - I won't bring it up.
You can count on me. My lips are sealed.
Still, he deserves to hear a piece of my mind.
I'm OK. Sorry, lost it for a minute.
Where are we sitting at the table?
Wonder why they put us there?
Well they're nice people, I suppose its O.K.
Look at the fancy dishes and silver will you?
What? I'm just admiring, the place settings and linen.
Such fancy waiters. What kind of soup is this?
My soup is cold. What do you mean it's supposed to be?
Whoever heard of cold soup? Give me Campbell's Chicken Noodle.
Did you want some bread, rolls, whatever? Want some? →

What's this? Macaroni? Pretty small serving.
Hey, how ya doing? Me? I'm OK. How are your kids?
Oh, I'm sorry, really. When are they due for parole? Ah huh, I see.
I didn't know that. Why didn't you tell me?
I'm not surprised though. I remember them.
Rowdy little kids always getting into trouble.
Now what's the main course?
What do you mean I'm having chicken?
What are you having? What kind of fish?
How come no steak or prime rib? Oh.
Well, how did I end up with chicken?
You checked it for me when you sent in the RSVP?
Why didn't you ask me? Oh, you did?
What was I doing? Oh, who won?
This is OK, not great but OK.
Hey, you want to dance? Come on.
I don't know, I just feel like dancing.
No, I want to dance with you.
Don't worry; you'll get combat pay when it's over.
Kinda crowded on the floor, huh?
Remember when we went to the prom together?
That's a lot of years ago - lot of years.
You looked great that night. No, I didn't mean that.
You look great all the time - tonight too.
Not too much, not too little, not too high, not too low.
What, oh, you were teasing? I knew that.
Want to go out on the porch? Yeah?
Wow, look at this - big bucks, yeah, big bucks.
What? No, I'm not jealous. I was just noticing.
Look at that view will you? Really something.
What a location, right? Look at the big lawn and the fountain.
Then there's the water, something else, yeah.
No, I'm OK. You O.K.? You cold? Want my jacket?
How about my arm? Snuggle in. Hmm.
What? No, nothing. I was just thinking.
Well you know, I was just wondering.
I don't know. Are you happy?
Are you ever sorry we – um - got together?
Yeah, we have great kids - hmm.
At least they're not waiting for parole.
Ouch, I'm sorry. No. Are you ever sorry you married me?
Really? Not once in all these years?
Oh, me? No. Not once. Hell I'm so lucky.

Look at me, rough around the edges —
Thin on the top and thick around the middle.
Hey, that's funny. Get it; "thick around…"
OK. No but I forget to tell you I love you.
What? I do? Oh well, you're pretty to look at,
And you're smart and you know what to do,
And you have good taste. You love me too.
Are you getting tired? No. I'm not tired.
I thought you might be tired.
Hey, is there dessert? I could use dessert.

(8/12/16)

Joe Pepe

When I was growing up
I had a Joe Pepe.
You might have had one too —
He just had a different name.

Joe Pepe ran the hardware store,
Not a big box store
With a hardware department,
But his own wonderful dusty place.

He might have been your first contact —
First businessman you ever dealt with.
Your mom and dad had been his customer.
That's how you knew to go to him.

I see him almost always in flannel and suspenders,
Smiling and interested in solving your problem.
His store was a Saturday gathering place
Where projects and problems were discussed and resolved.

Mr. Pepe wanted your problem solved.
If it could be done without a purchase
That was fine with him, →

Because he knew you'd come back again.
Over my early years, I had been a tagalong
Watching quietly as projects and politics mixed,
Town news complimented family news,
And everyone left with a smile.

Mr. Pepe had that smile waiting for you.
I remember my first solo visit
My bike had a flat tire, what was I to do?
The answer was right there leaning on the counter.

I told Mr. Pepe what was wrong.
He looked at me, "You're the Gregory boy."
With a little swallow, I answered, "Yes."
Now he gave this some thought.

Finally he said, "I can sell you a patch."
"A patch" I repeated, clueless and concerned.
"Do you know how to get the tube out of your tire?"
I felt my shoulders droop as I shook my head.

"Can you walk your bike here?"
"Yeah, I can do that." I replied.
"Bring your bike in and I'll show you how to fix it."
"OK," I answered, with the slightest glimmer of hope.

Since it was summer, I had no school
So after I walked my paper route,
I walked the bike to Mr. Pepe's hardware store.
It was early in the day and he saw me coming.

He held the door open as I pushed the wounded bike in.
From behind the counter he produced a tire repair kit,
Showed me how to do it and then let me do it
We removed the inner tube from inside the tire.

Mr. Pepe filled a bucket with water
Then took out an air pump and had me pump up the inner tube.
He had me put the tube in the bucket and rotate it.
"Look for bubbles." And I saw them. "There!"

He marked the spot with a piece of chalk
Then had me dry off the inner tube.

Taking the special cover from the repair kit,
He showed me how to rough up the area.

Taking glue from the kit,
He showed me how to brush it on.
Next, he cut me a piece of patch material
And showed me how to hold it "in place tight."

After we let it dry, we replaced it in the tire.
We pumped it up again and I was good to go.
Suddenly, I panicked. How much would this cost?
The answer was simple and in my budget — twenty-five cents.

Over the years, I out grew my paper route
And Mr. Pepe, and then Joe gave me a job —
Part-time at first, after school
Longer hours during the summer.

He would teach by showing
Having me take part in the repairs,
Eventually quizzing me about how to do a project,
Guiding me to the right answers.

Joe made sure I did my homework
And had time to play.
He talked now and then with my parents.
This became a glorious routine.

Joe Pepe had a kind way of correcting,
But the mistakes were few because of his teaching.
I became part of those Saturday discussion groups
And Joe would watch and smile.

I was in my senior year of High School.
When my parents asked me what I was going to do,
Did I want to try for college, what was my future?
Frankly, I had no answer, I was happy now.

"How are you going to make a living?"
I had no concrete plan, but my dad did
"Go talk to Joe," he said. And I did.
It was Saturday, late in the afternoon. →

As I finished stocking the shelves
And moved some dust around
I asked Joe if he had a minute.
He almost laughed at my serious face.

I explained that I was a senior and had plans to make
Yes, he knew that and had talked to my family.
He asked if I liked it here.
"Oh, I love it. You know that."

"I do know that and I have a proposition for you,"
And he talked of full-time employment
With an eye to taking over the business
Somewhere down the line.

Well, I didn't ask any of the right questions.
I just said yes and secured my future
And Joe Pepe looked out for me.
He had no family and daily we were growing close.

I was and became his working hour son
And I stayed in town and worked in the hardware store,
Moving out of my house — but not too far.
I've married, and my love and I have two children.

Years have flown by and Joe lets me do the buying.
We survive in an era of unfair competition.
Because it's Saturday morning and everyone has a project.
Old Joe Pepe sits on a stool in flannel and suspenders and listens and nods.

(6/28/16)

Whisper at the Window

The young boy finally old enough to sleep on the porch,
Curled up on the glider covered with a blanket —
Eyes wide open — a stuffed animal at his chin.
All the night sounds — detached — out to get him.

It seemed like the night would never end.
Slowly his lips trembled and curled and he was ready to call out
When he hears a whisper at the window.
Just above his head, the voice soothes
And explains all the scary sounds.
Who's afraid of a cricket or a tree frog?
The porch screens will keep out animals
"What a brave boy, what a good boy
What a sleepy boy. I'm nearby,
Go to sleep now my brave and growing son."

And through life that boy, now grown, remembers
The first night away from home,
The night before he started the job.
You hear that whisper at the window
"Brave boy, smart boy, you can do that.
What you don't know, you'll learn.
You're right for the job. Stand tall boy.
Now sleep and be rested. Wear the blue tie."

Thousands of miles away, alone on patrol,
The young soldier hides among the reeds —
Silent and still till morning.
Somewhere over there is his buddy —
The one from Ohio, younger than he.
There is no breeze, and enemy everywhere.
Here it is again, that whisper at the window.
"It is all right to be afraid. Lie still. Lie still.
You may not sleep, but I'm right here with you."

It should be the happiest of times —
In love, so in love, newly married,
Job going well, things are going well.
But this is a hospital and there is a problem
A problem with the delivery, mother and child are in danger.
Leaning against the window in the waiting room...

How many hours have you been here?
They won't let me in; there is nothing I can do.
I must be dreaming. I hear that whisper at the window
"Be brave, be strong, hopefully all will be well.
Whatever happens you must be a rock.
And it's all right for rocks to cry. →

Here comes the doctor wearing a smile."
"Your wife and son are fine."

All that life gives you, you enjoy, and you give back.
The rewards of living your life grow daily —
Pride in your work, your family, in doing,
Playing and laughing, teaching and learning,
Running at a fast pace till finally you run in place.
Things slow down and the family grows strong.
It also grows thin as branches are formed and blossom.
Aches are introduced to pain, still hands hold tight.
Then, there is a moment, when the other hand lets go.
There is a whisper at the window — reassuring, calm.
"It's OK to let go. There's an end to pain —
Even to the pain you feel this minute inside you.
She will be fine. I already have her spirit with me
Laughing and telling me stories about you I already know.
Now it's all right to go to sleep my son,
 My brave man, and live your days.
Love and laugh and be happy.
And when it's time, come inside
And join us, don't be afraid — rest — shh..."

(6/22/16)

Joe

Joe lives in the city —
Fourth floor of an eight-story building,
Front apartment, two windows to the street.
Joe has lived here almost forever,
Really no one knows how long.
He was here before any of the current residents.
They don't know much about him
And really hardly notice him,
He is quiet and uncomplaining.
If they did poke their noses around,
Well, not much could be gained.
Joe only goes out once or twice a week.

Stuff

He shops two blocks over, with his wheeled wire cart
Filling it — not too full — to last a week —
And he goes out for dinner.
On Friday night, early on
He walks a few blocks to the "Blue Sky Diner."
He orders, basically, the same meal every week,
Sitting in approximately the same place.
Does he have family or friends?
There is no evidence of that.
He must be retired from something —
The rent and utilities are paid
And they are paid on time.
So, what does Joe do all day?
Well, it would seem that he has a recliner.
Some years ago, it was moved around
Away from the rest of the apartment.
The chair is angled to watch the TV in the corner
And the world passing by one of his tall windows.
Most days his world is a five-foot square.
In fair weather the window is open.
I guess you might get a nice breeze.
You would hear the busy traffic on the closest avenue,
The medley of sirens and horns that punctuate the day,
The trees bud and leaf, the rain puddles.
People and dogs walk by — below and across the street.
I suppose you can hear bits of conversations
Or, if not all the words, certainly the tone —
Three teenage girls gossiping with great excitement
An old lady praising her dog and greeting others,
Even a lone person talking with great spirit —
You hope to someone at the end of an invisible phone
Or perhaps God for how the world is treating him.
The recliner has molded itself to his body.
Rarely does he leave the chair, go to the bathroom,
 Fix a meal for consumption in the recliner,
And on a rare occasion to sleep in the bedroom.
He will smile at you, when passing in the hall, —
Perhaps a "Hello" or "Thank you" at the front door.
He does check his mail daily and tends to his garbage,
So even though no one knows him well,
Some do wonder how he can live like that.
I was one of those persons living in that building.
After a few years, curiosity got the best of me. →

So, as an amateur detective, I came up with some info.
Now, this is on the "QT," so don't tell anyone.
It would appear that Joe grew up near here.
Back then; the neighborhood was quite different —
Not the go to place for these new young up and comers.
It was one neighborhood among many,
Each separated by its ethnic background —
Irish, Italian, Russian Jew, a trail of immigration —
Safety in numbers and highly protective.
Later it would segue into Black and Puerto Rican.
Joe was born into this and he prospered in it.
He was strong and smart — street smart.
First protection, then numbers, a few robberies…
His stature and fortune grew rapidly.
Joe was able to "retire" early —
Retire a few steps ahead of some rivals and the police.
He settled here, but kept his business going.
A winning gambler, he had several bookies
And they deposited his winnings for him.
There were accounts spread all over town,
 As well as with several banks in the Caribbean and Europe.
One or more nights a week, Molly came to see him.
She was a waitress, who worked late, at the "Blue Sky."
At the end of her shift, she would walk to Joe's place.
Molly would let herself into the building with a key Joe had given her
Then she would let herself into Joe's apartment —
Again with a key that Joe had given her.
With her she brought leftovers from the diner
Or maybe some special desserts.
They would feast on the spread
And then they would feast on each other.
Molly would leave before the building awoke.
It was an arrangement they both enjoyed.
And so, more or less, that is Joe's story.
I have since moved out. I now have a wife.
I'm happy and we're happy.
Once in awhile, I'm in the old neighborhood,
And I can never resist looking up at my old building,
Just to make sure that Joe is sitting in the fourth-floor window.

(4/11/16)

T.T.

Tallulah Triscontorinni, "T.T." to her friends, was a spirited lady who gained some fame in the late 50s and early 60s. It was the end of vaudeville and burlesque, but a couple of "houses" hung on in Scully Square, Boston.

Tallulah was a headliner in a dying art form. What used to be daring and scandalous was now pretty tame, given what was available in the movies. T.T. had a unique act and that's what helped her keep the regulars and the curious coming back.

The regulars, some would slide over from an early morning barstool and others came in out of the cold or escaped from a cold and empty house and those that lived there. In the evening, you added the slummers and the college kids out to have fun and feel superior to the tired acts, the tired jokes and hollow entertainers.

T.T. came on in the middle of the show, it used to be later, but as the surrounding acts weakened, the manager had to move her to the middle or lose most of his audience.

This place was still using live music — one of the few. Four musicians playing several instruments each with a varying degree of success. Three of them had been playing for as many years as some of the bricks now crumbling from the outside walls. The exception was the piano player, barely past middle age, too talented to be here, but with sad stories haunting his waking hours.

The lights, never fully out, dim slightly and the band starts to play the "Russian Saber Dance." The spot wakes up on stage right. The music slows to an unidentifiable tune and T.T. steps out to applause — some real, some sarcastic. Dressed in glitter and plumes over a body that still has shape to it, perhaps a little wider and softer than a few years ago, but she is still compelling. The lighting helps hide her experience, as she moves to the center of the stage and then down toward the audience. The music ends with her final step, but the boys in the pit are poised, the audience is frozen, staring at T.T., when suddenly the spotlight goes out and a soft pink light envelops her.

The quiet continues as if everyone there was holding his or her breath. T.T. starts to look at her audience, at least the ones closest to her. She makes eye contact, where someone else might avoid it. From face to face, she takes a few seconds to read her audience, to have a silent dialogue with them. Some she welcomes with a quick smile, thank you for coming. To others she flashes an instant warning, this is my house — my stage — my act — don't act up. A few she reassures relax, don't worry, and don't be afraid. Yes, just let me have you for a few moments.

The survey done, as unspoken cue travels between T.T. and Mel (the piano player and default conductor), who nods a downbeat to the other three (Hank, Ben and Otto) and the music and T.T. begin. The music isn't brash or brassy; it is low down, slow down and sweet. It is Mel's composition, molded to T.T.'s every move.

T.T. slides one leg slightly to the side. It is a small move that causes the sequins and feathers to move ever so slightly. With just the slightest pause her body moves, what you might call organically. The moves are slow, syncopated with the music and beginning a conversation, one by one with everyone in the room. This is the beginning of a dance with only one person barely moving across the floor.

This is not a bump and grind, rather a hand leading a bonded group, ranging from dirty old men, losers, businessmen at lunch, preppies, and even a gal or two into her world for a few minutes.

If you were to ask this group at the end, what just happened? They wouldn't have an answer. A group so totally diverse who for an instant were equals, prisoners, willing prisoners of one T.T. Some might come back again or just hold the memory for a lifetime.

There came a point in the music when T.T. knew she had captured her audience. Yet her special act wasn't all that special. Slowly she removed her long, dress-matching gloves. Her eyes were riveted on each glove as she worked it over her elbow and then loosened the fingers and, only as she pulled them free, did you see that her eyes were running along the arm sighting an audience member. This hopeless happy victim reaped his reward recovered later by the usher or the stage manager.

T.T.'s cape or stole is in the hands of a great matador. The spaghetti straps traveled over each shoulder as if a man was crawling across the desert looking for an oasis. But this was an oasis, in the middle of a crappy day, in some man's crappy life.

There were no catcalls, no shouts from someone out of control. It was two people, T.T. and whoever else was enjoying themselves naturally. It was extremely sexy, but not dirty, not sordid, it was an experience.

At a certain moment, T.T. turned upstage. The music changed ever so slightly as she took a step or two away from her friends, new acquaintances and lovers. Moving on a certain trail, one pool of light gave way to another, embracing her once more.

This newly created space between the performer and her audience seemed to be needed. This is where she reached behind her back, took the zipper and with back still to the audience, she began what was anything but a traditional descent.

It was a story being told day after day, month after month, year after year. Beginning with a kind of innocence, then a learning curve and finally the summit — the goal. Thus the tantalizing journey from neck down the length of the spine, to where it ended or began.

Another step, another change of music, and another pool of light. She faced the audience; she confronted the audience; she teased the audience; and she took each person into her space. One on one, she faced each one and paused to make a decision. Everyone was in on it, everyone agreed; it was time for the contract to be honored.

It was her time, her moment and it happened so quickly, she just let go and as the sequins and feathers rained to the floor, the lights went black everywhere. It was so dark you wondered if you had seen anything.

Suddenly the audience lights came up slightly and the stage lights slowly warmed. By now the applause was surging upwards with the music. The oddball gathering sounded like an ovation at the Opera House.

T.T. stepped out from the middle of the stage curtain. Bowed, almost shyly, and vanished.

The music began for the next act.

(May 2016)

Noah

Noah loved to run
As a boy — for fun —
Not much else was,
Parents always fighting,
Schoolwork not coming easy,
Shy with no buddies,
But he could run.
Run away from a brutal father,
Not able to help a cowering mother.
No teacher went out of his or her way.
The kids just left him alone,
And alone didn't hurt, too much.
Running the neighborhood, the park,
No pattern, no direction, no smiles,
Run until tired, a wonderful prescription.
Run Noah run — all the time run.
In spring of his first high school year
The track coach taught Phys-Ed.
First hand he saw Noah run
Lap after lap with great ease.
He asked Noah to join the track team.
Dad still drank and mom made excuses —
Excuses for the brute and the bruises.
So Noah saw a different way to run
Why not? Sure, sign me up.
And so, in April rains, he ran with others.
Fast or paced, round and round,
Practice after school, Noah ran.
He ran with the others on the team.
Methodically his feet moved around the track.
Never tired, he beat some and lost to others.
It was always the same with Noah —
No special drive or feeling of competition,
One foot in front of the other,
Start to finish and done – no more sun.
Then the coach opened the gate,
Explained the cross-country course

Stuff

And sent Noah and some others off.
This was what he wanted, a freedom.
Back to running the neighborhood or the park.
He was his own competition. Get a better time
The coach explained, he was on a team,
But he was independent, stay on the course.
Noah flew, his legs already strong
Pushed and pulled him up hills and down.
He knew he passed others, but it was no matter
Warm or cold weather, muddy or dry footing
On and on he went until he saw the finish.
As steady at the finish as the start
He flew back onto the field and won.
And then he won, again and again,
Smiling weakly as teammates pounded his shoulders.
Embarrassed, he "Aw Shucks" the praise,
But for the first time in years, he smiles.
The coach helps him learn how to study.
By the end of four years, he has a scholarship.
His parents interrupt their war
Long enough to say good-bye.
They never noticed him before
And they would soon forget he existed.
Noah's world opened up — a rainbow.
It was hard, but he knew how to study now.
Noah runs, still runs,
Still runs alone, still wins.
He has learned to converse with classmates
Talk to teachers — even go on dates —
Awkward and inexperienced at first
But that got better and time passed.
In summary, he found someone to listen —
A lovely girl who challenged him
And at the same time protected him.
He ran the world over and studied.
When he was too old to race,
Noah still ran, slowing for a while
So his wife and then their children
Could keep pace and when they dropped back,
He continued running, running, running
But not away from his past —
No, he was running and embracing his future.
(10/26/15)

The Last Train

The population of a train station ebbs and flows.
As the time for a train nears, the platform becomes crowded.
I was waiting for the 8:34AM train to New York City.
Along the westbound stretch of platform, the people gathered.
Mostly they stood in small groups.
The experienced commuters waited in specific areas
Close to where they're favorite part of the train would stop.
They would enter, hoping for a seat there.
I was in position for a try for a seat in the first car —
This makes a shorter walk once we arrive at Grand Central Station.
It was a mild Friday toward the end of January
As four of us moved close to the painted yellow bar —
The bar that indicated where the first car doors would open —
There was no eye contact and no conversation.
Still, some would do a slow dance,
A shuffle to be closest to the door without being obvious.
A woman joined our little group and sat on the nearby bench.
She wished everyone a "Good Morning"
And got a few surprised mumbled responses.
She was a regular commuter I had seen here before.
She would sit on a stool inside the station
And carry on a rather one-sided conversation with the concessionaire.
As far as I could tell, this was her routine —
Moving to the platform just before the train was due.
She chain-smoked and sounded almost drunk
Or perhaps she was alone a lot and needed conversation.
I have known people who must have a sound track to their day,
Sharing family news or asking casual questions of strangers.
Such was the case this morning.
Calling a young man with knapsack and hard hat by name,
She asked what his plans were for the weekend.
Grudgingly he responded that he had to work on Saturday
But on Sunday he was going to a train show in Springfield.
I watched the woman as the young man spoke of his plans.
She had stopped listening early on and was staring at the platform,
Being polite, the man inquired about her plans.
Here we have what must have been the perfect dramatic pause.
Tapping the ash off the end of her ever-present cigarette

Stuff

She finally responded; "I don't know, this is my last day.
I've been laid off." The group reacted silently.
All heads had chanced a quick almost sympathetic look at the woman.
Details came out sporadically on the platform
And with another ear inside she continued as we sat on the train.
Apparently the place she worked was closing —
A small business where she had worked for years,
Dressed for office work, neat and comfortable.
This was a woman, who hadn't planned anything past today,
And today was her last day.
In a conversation, you wondered if she was listening
But she was following everything you said
And reacted to what was being said.
Her voice was slightly slurred, but she was sharp.
Most people seemed uncomfortable dealing with her.
Perhaps she had some early morning lubrication,
Or maybe it was just her speech pattern.
From her continued chatter, impossible not to hear,
I learned that her mother was living at her sister's house.
On her most recent visit, which seem close to daily,
She was banished to the backyard to have her smokes.
There she found a fruit basket and one of those edible arrangements.
They had come from her employer for her mother.
It would seem that mom is recuperating from something
And would otherwise live with our commuter or alone.
The mother claimed that nobody rang the bell
And appeared very defensive about the whole thing.
The simple conclusion is that our traveler
Is loved or respected by her employer —
My guess? A small family business that can no longer compete.
I don't know if there was a life beyond family and work
Or there was a chance once and now it is long lost.
Whatever the story, she had found a new listener.
Out of my earshot — the train moved on.
Finally, her stop was announced.
She stood and headed for the door.
The conductor was waiting at the door,
He gave her a hug and she left.
Tonight, she would catch the train back home
And it would be the last train.

(2/5/16)

Billy's Place

When "Billy's Place" had belonged to Billy, it had been a friendly neighborhood bar. But time had past, Billy long gone and years and generations had marched through, colors and nationalities rolled over and in the confusion, it's identity lost. No matter when you went to Billy's, you never had a suit or fancy dress on, and that was still true today, but conversations had gone away. There was no talk of the old country, no politics, no religion, no sports, not even a corny pick-up line; "Billy's Place" was sanitized by time and indifference.

What was left was a shell, a well-worn shell with faded pictures of people no one knew. The bar, the walls, the floor, were layered with dark wood soaked by long nights, booze, on top of dirt, on top of tears, on top of life. — A place that never welcomed the sun and had had early morning as a chaser — where you ordered a drink and stared at a TV screen. Then you ordered another drink or moved on. Those that stayed for the second drink said nothing more or less than during the first. They just delayed their trip to their hell, the house where love had left or the apartment with just four walls.

The owners rarely visited Billy's, three businessmen who needed an investment and who had hired a manager as a buffer. The manager in turn, hired a couple of tired bartenders. These men were long past working the counter. The drinks were served, money collected. You didn't pay enough for conversation. There was a menu, yes; well you went for a drink. A miniature sandwich board on each table and along the bar offered a selection of wines and exotic drinks, but this was a shot and beer, in your face place. The night was one of seven in a row that came week after week and fell from the calendar to the floor.

Beyond the glass wall with its wounded neon was the contents of Billy's Place. Through the door, a long bar with stools took up most of the right with a door to the kitchen in the back right corner. A variety of booths and tables lined the left side with a unisex bathroom halfway down. Some TV's mounted from the ceiling here and there, were flashing pictures that no one wanted to see — one was even making noise, but it was hard to say which one.

The hour was late into early and the contents of the bar included three people. Frank, the bartender, kept busy washing out and icing down glasses, restocking the beer from the storeroom in back and keeping busy and to himself.

He closed the bar down at 2AM and knew the time would go faster if he kept busy. That 2AM couldn't come fast enough and then he could resume his life.

At the back end of the bar, perched on a stool and holding up a wall, was Charlie. If this place ever developed a personality again, he was ready to be a regular. He was what stuff such men are made of. Charlie was old, very old, he had served in the Great War, sliding into the ranks at an early sixteen, lying about his age with the permission of a family who were happy not to have another mouth to feed. Charlie had been Chuck, C.C. (his last name was Connell), Charlie, and once, even Charles, then Chucky and finally Charlie again. He had come home from the war, having just finished the most important thing he would ever do in his life and still had a whole life to live.

He had stories; war stories after war stories, remember when stories and he was wedded to no shortage of opinions on anything he knew or didn't know.

Charlie had been married for many years and had almost been faithful. He had had a son and a daughter and they survived as a family unit for all those important years. Then his wife died and somehow the family was gone. The kids were already grown and he would forget to call them a lot and eventually they would forget to stay in touch with him a lot. It didn't matter they each had their stories and that was what became important. Everyone was happier and more loving as the stories were repeated over time.

Charlie would arrive and take his seat. His beer would appear, the money came down, the money disappeared and a nod here and there through the night would set the repetition in motion. He would glance at a TV screen for a moment or two. Then his eyes would move away and his head would give a little negative shake as if dismissing the whole medium as not worthy of the effort.

Sometimes, Charlie would have a conversation in a soft voice with a pause as he absorbed the response. There was, of course, no one near him and the responses were from a crony, a stranger, a son, a daughter — all long gone. He was reliving these moments and either repeating his thoughts or adding something he thought now maybe he should have said.

In the end, Charlie was maybe his own self-contained regular and when he decided his night was through, he would rise, make sure the proper tip was in place and that he was steady on his feet before moving out into his night.

The third person in Billy's tonight was Claire. She sat at a table against the wall halfway down on the left. Her back was to the bar, to the room, to the world outside. She wore a print blouse and gray slacks. If you could see her face, you would probably call her pretty and she was still pretty for her fiftyish age. Never beautiful, but then so few are, she held her glass filled with amber numbing stuff with two hands. Gently she swirled the liquid, eating away at the ice cubes and every once in awhile she would add some salty rain that rolled off her cheeks. →

Many years ago she had married Mike, the happiest day of her life. They had a small honeymoon and settled into their new life together. Both of them worked and their dreams were in full bloom. But within a few months, those dreams would melt and their happiness would end. She had returned from a doctor's check-up with news that would become an invasive weed in their marriage.

A routine test and blood work with some follow-up, revealed that she couldn't have children. The probable causes were varied and hard to pin down and her doctor would refer her to a specialist if she liked, but he was pretty sure that the findings were true and irreversible. Claire was first home that night and she sat at the kitchen counter staring out the window. There would be no dinner preparation that night; there would be a period of lost time, where nothing around Claire even registered in her head.

When Mike arrived home, he sensed his wife's mood but could not identify a cause. He came up next to her and lightly dropped his hand on her shoulder. An affectionate gesture that would usually bring her face into view and a smile or frown would welcome him and reach toward him for a kiss. Tonight the shoulder shuddered and he had to turn the tear-stained face toward him. He tried to pull her close, the head moved toward him for an instant then recoiled back and locked into focus on his face. The black news was delivered in halting sentences between sobs and gasping for air until the story was done.

There was the slightest pause before Mike drew her off the stool and pulled her into his arms. Then another gap of time — only a few seconds — before he comforted her with those protective everything is going to be all right lines that echoed falsely into the kitchen air.

Everything was *not* going to be all right and never would be again. For a while, nothing much was said. Then there was a brief discussion about adoption, but neither really warmed to the subject. And so, the walls slowly decayed and weakened with all the predictable estrangements until he finally moved out and virtually disappeared. Eventually divorce papers arrived in the mail and Claire signed them without a fight.

She was alone again for the first time. Going back to her family she decided was not an option. Claire decided she would move on. She got an extra job and eventually downsized to a smaller place in a good neighborhood, this neighborhood, Billy's neighborhood.

Over the years, Claire had become stable again with a few friends, mostly girl friends. She lived day to day and with some urging, would date once in a while. The dates were few and far between and would never last more than a few times before they ended. She would usually end them before they got too serious and before she would have a chance to be hurt.

This philosophy had changed a few weeks ago. It wasn't clear if this new relationship was something special or whether she was feeling her age and some impending loneliness. He was a nice guy and treated her well. They had some good times and she had let things develop deeper. It was past the time when having kids would be an issue. It was just about love and a lengthening time together. That had been until tonight. Tonight things had come to a screeching halt. Several hours ago they had been out to dinner and both had had a few drinks. She has been relaxed and they were talking about nothing special. At least to her it wasn't a big deal, but she noticed that he had grown angry; a storm was painted on his face.

Claire stopped talking, as through clenched teeth he started to call her names, — names with no foundation, no grounds, something from his past that had hurt him and he felt obliged to hurt her. Seemingly, out of nowhere, his hand flew across her face, striking her so hard that she was now facing away from him. He ordered her to the car and she followed in a daze. A silent ride back to her place and she finally looked at him. His eyes were fixed forward, as if straining to see through a fog and stay safely on the road. His jaw was slightly elevated and a frown deepened his mouth. Claire said
nothing, but exited the car. Immediately he sped off, darting out in traffic to the consternation of the driver that was now behind him.

Claire looked at the stairs that led to her place, but did not move toward them. Instead she walked, slightly stiff-legged toward Billy's Place. She sat at the table facing the wall and stared. It was too far for Frank to ask what she wanted; he would have to move from behind the bar to take her order. He did that with a customary frown and made the U-turn, made the drink and returned to the table, setting the drink down with absolutely no fanfare. He waited a moment and she offered a bill and indicated for him to keep the change. Like a boxer at the end of the round, he returned behind the bar with no indication of who had won the round.

Claire didn't feel the bruise on her cheek; that was just a surface wound. The real hurt was deep inside her and was bleeding profusely — a wound to the heart that was beyond explanation. Sporadically she would raise the glass to her lips and sip the liquid without really tasting it. Then she would lower the glass and stare at it, as if it were a cup of tea and an explanation of what just happened would appear in some tealeaves that had settled in the bottom of the cup. But no answers appeared and soon it was time to raise the glass again and try for more, — try for more answers.

And so the time passed at Billy's Place, Frank in his housekeeping routine, Charlie quietly addressing one of his ghosts and Claire exploring the depths of her cocktail. The ambient TV noise seemed distant; there was a kind of hush that surrounded the bar, a quietness that would soon dissolve in the early morning air.

Charlie dropped to his feet and touched the small pile of one-dollar bills on the bar. His other hand still gripped the stool. Next, Charlie rose a few inches in height, as if to impress a pretty girl at the other end of the counter. He then sighed back to his normal aged stature and struck out for the door.

Three steps later, he collapsed to the floor in all his flannels and suspenders, not moving.

Frank looked up for a second when Charlie had risen, one step closer to closing he thought, and had turned back to polish an imaginary spot from one of the back shelves. He heard the noise and turned again, but it was a moment before he identified the sound and saw Charlie crumpled there. He immediately headed for Charlie.

Claire heard a noise, but with her back toward the room, she made no connection until the lift up part of the bar slammed against the wall. She saw Frank, then the pile of Charlie, and she too rose and headed in that direction. Together, they gently rolled Charlie on his back and supported his head. Charlie was breathing, shallow quick breaths it seemed; Frank took the towel still in his hand and bunched it under Charlie's head and moved for the phone. "No early night tonight," flashed through his head.

Claire grabbed a napkin off the nearest table and started to wipe Charlie's brow and began to talk to him quietly. She didn't know his name, but he didn't look like a drunk.

Charlie's lips began to move; his face became animated and soft incoherent words began to flow. Claire leaned close to try to hear what he was saying, but couldn't make them out. Then Charlie stopped his conversation; Claire sat back next to him on the floor and saw the smile on his face. Frank was giving directions on the phone to Billy's Place.

(6/29/14)

William's Window

Through the window there is a newly decorated room —
All yellows and pale blues, where ducks and rabbits abound.
Soon there is activity; little William has come home.
It's a while before he moves in permanently
But that's OK; there are plenty of years to come.
And he does move in with stuffed animals watching.
Time is passing and the ducks and rabbits scatter.
Enter cowboys, football players and super heroes.
If we look in, we see spaceships on the shelves.
Then there is a rainy day, a long day, and a sad day.
Something is wrong with young Master William —
Fever and pain and the doctor is called.
Days and weeks go by and William's window is dark.
The family returns home with manufactured happiness.
Goals and dreams dip into sadness and are readjusted.
Blame is pushed around for a while, — with William alone.
Yes, William is alone in his room looking out his window.
He doesn't understand; he doesn't know what he sees.
His body grows to be a man. His eyes stare out, — empty
The glass holds him in; his mind takes only a few steps.
William leaves the room for schooling and therapy.
And so it will be, until everyone loses hope.
But for most of the time, through most of the years,
William sits by the window and stares out.
The sun warms him; the cold chills him, until the shade is drawn.

(11/30/14)

Bill

When my city was a small town,
I remember Bill on Daniel Street.
Bill, if I remember right, had lost his legs below the knees.
He had a cart and crutches
And was usually neatly dressed.
This was a time before wholesale homelessness. →

Bill was ever present during the hundreds of years of my youth.
Any day my Mom took me through downtown,
Or once I had my license, there he was.
This was the 50s and part of the 60s.
I assume, everyday, Bill set up shop on Daniel Street.
"The Crook" as it is called today and then
Was and is a short crescent-shaped street.
Back then it offered you a way to circumvent downtown.
In those days it contained a fish market, two bars,
Tony's Barber Shop, The Moose Lodge and other small businesses.
And the main attraction was the Capital Movie Theater.
Bill sold pencils from a cup every day.
As I think about Bill, I see him at one point suddenly seeming older,
I never thought much about him back then.
He was a fixture, part of the sights on the way into the center of town.
I don't know if he was a war veteran,
Whether he had a birth defect
Or if he was mentally challenged.
He was certainly a town character.
Usually his spot was in front of Jake's Bar.
I don't know if, when he was flush,
He made his way into the closest door
And there had himself a wee bit of refreshment.
There is a lot I don't know about Bill.
Was he bitter and nasty because of his predicament?
Maybe he was happy to be alive.
Did he interact with the citizens?
I don't know his story, I just remember him,
And I'm not sure when I noticed he was gone,
Maybe I had gone away to college.
Was he a Vet, maybe a hero of sorts?
What put him on Daniel Street?
And why is he different to me?

(8/9/16)

Frank

In the cycle of neighborhoods, it was an old neighborhood. The white house, with the dark green shutters, sat at the end of Maple Street buried in shade that no one would develop.

Most of the life had left the house; the kids had their own places, their own families and their own lives. Frank was the breath of the house having lost his wife more than a decade ago.

The house was in pretty good shape. The kids touched base and touched up the paint. It was a touchstone for all of them and Frank kept it neat and probably kept a little too much of the past.

Frank's neighbors, were for the most part, old-timers, though a few younger folk were edging in at the top of the street. There were signs of change on the horizon, but nothing that Frank couldn't handle.

Frank sat alone on his back porch and surveyed his little patch of view. Feeling his age and perhaps looking a year or two older, he rocked in his wicker rocker. It was autumn and he pulled his cardigan sweater closely over his ample belly. Of all the things he and his brothers had gotten from their father, their barrel-shape was the most unwanted inheritance.

Some squirrels were chasing each other up one tree and then swinging from one branch to another, without the benefit of a Tarzan yell. He smiled and his mind drifted back. Was he asleep? Dozing? Dreaming? Yes — all those things. The years peeled away; faces drifted on the wind, the sound of emptying branches fought each other — back over the years, over times he never visited when he was awake.

In front of him he saw a wall — brick, wood or concrete, he couldn't tell. He just kept walking into it. He would switch directions like some sort of robot, but after moving in that direction, the wall would block his way once more. Again he bounced off; he had no direction and frustration was setting in. Finally he heard a voice calling to him.

He tried to climb the wall; it was too tall, too slippery. An end-around move didn't work because the wall had no end, but he heard the voice beyond the wall. He knew the voice but could not place it. He made out his name, Frank. Yes, it was calling to him. Who? Why?

And this continued for as long as he let it, his name being called, it held him at the wall. What else was being said, he couldn't make it out. Besides his name, — that voice, — it is a sad voice, a calm but persistent voice.

"Frank, Frank show me that again." →

Is he still nodding, still sleeping? The wall has cracked, the wall is quietly crumbling, and slowly the other side is appearing. Summer, hot summer. Wait he knows this place. It is the backyard he grew up in.

He is ten or twelve; his brothers are at the far end of the yard horsing around on the swing set.

"Hi Penny!"

The dog wags her tail; the sky is that once-in-awhile pure deep blue, with white puffy animals charging across it. Sounds flow into his head willy-nilly and he hears his mom banging on something in the kitchen.

"Frank. Do it once more,"

He is sitting at the picnic table and his dad is talking to him; he is smiling. Frank follows his gaze down to where his dad is looking. It is Frank's hand and he is rolling a quarter gingerly through his fingers, first one way and then back the other. It is one of the magic tricks he has secretly been learning and practicing for hours and hours. He has borrowed and renewed the magic book from the library so many times; he might as well just made it his own property. He has mastered several sleight of hand tricks and develops his "patter" till the bedroom mirror approves. Now, he saw his Dad leaning back with a proud smile.

"That's a good trick," he boasts.

"How long have been able to do that?" he asks. He looks around to try and find someone to brag to about his son the magician.

Dad. I hadn't thought about him in years. Why was I so uncomfortable when I remembered him?

It was a happy time, a nothing-special summer family time. Come on Frank be honest. It was the last time you remember your dad being happy.

In a few short months, this simple, hard working man, loving man would come home after a hard day at work. He would complain of being tired. He almost never complained. Then he rose from his chair and a surprised look would appear on his face and he would raise his hand to his chest and fall forward.

Frank snapped his eyes open and jerked forward and the quarter fell from his hand.

(7/22/16)

I Was There at the Beginning

They came in the 50s and never went away
I was there at the beginning and still carry it on –
In summer we were called into dinner
By yells, by bells, and even whistles
Each child knew their call and stopped what they were doing
Hasty good-byes or "See ya later"
And all the adventures came to an end –
In other seasons the calls were self- contained
"Dinner's ready!" the pen, the book, the toys went down
And the migration toward the kitchen began –
The dining room area of the living room,
Well that was for Thanksgiving and special guests
Like when Aunt Clara came to visit from Worcester –
Dinner generally happened in that cozy kitchen
The maple table with four chairs
Glass-faced cabinets with a background painted Chinese Red
And doors, lots of doors and windows surrounded you –
There the meal was consumed and my brother and I did the dishes
So it was most days, and the rest of the night proceeded –
Until the day the blond Zenith arrived and life changed
I was the one home when it was delivered
Heavy and bulky, it sat on a blond swivel table
And without an antenna hooked up, not even bunny ears
I could make out a war movie on channel five –
Uncle Carl, the one who owned a Piper Cub and gave us a ride once,
Sent us a special TV lamp to sit on top of the set.
This coupled with warnings not to sit too close, would save our eyesight –
Taking residence in a corner of the living room
These floral wonders appeared one day with their own rack –
I was there at the beginning and followed Mother's orders –
"Set up the TV trays, dinner is ready."
Having mastered the art early on, I sprang to the job
Unfolding and snapping the tray securely into place –
Bring on the grub, regular or the new TV dinner.

4/18/15

Click-a-Mile

In the car heading somewhere
Click-a-mile
The night has taken over
I'm on my way home
Checking off landmarks
Fighting the ever present fatigue
Click-a-mile closer
It was just this morning that I left –
I haven't been this way for so long –
Dashboard illumination hides my emotions
And the road goes forever
Click-a-mile
Who will be waiting there?
Is there anyone left?
I've dreamed and dreaded this moment
What do they say it seems quicker going home?
Click-a-mile
After a long hard day on the road
After all these years, it's strange
How we parted and said good-bye
On the way to success, to run away
Click-a-mile closer
Off the highway, slowing down
Local roads, scenery changing
Remembering how it was
Turn here, quick turn here!
Click no more miles
Slow, slow way down
Neighborhood memories flash in the headlights
Faces race at the window
Into the driveway, stop
Well what do you do now?
Click

(7/10/15)

Nelly

Nelly spends her days in another world.
She wanders her neighborhood
Keeping track of her belongings
And is always ready to add to them.
Her treasures travel in a shopping cart.
The cart was "adopted" from a local grocery store,
But for reasons other than a missing cart, the store closed.
Well organized, the cart is Nelly's walker.
Never ask a woman her age.
And even then, I don't think Nelly could tell you.
She is resourceful and talkative.
What she is talking about is sometimes a question.
Her clothes are layered in chaos,
But her mobile closet has everything in its proper place.
Plastic bags serve as drawers hanging from it
And Nelly knows where everything is kept.
She accepts charity silently and cautiously.
Nelly wants her independence.
There is a routine to be followed.
Comfort comes from repetition.
When bad weather hits she Stuffers —
Not from what's falling from the sky,
But because her pattern is broken,
And she will get angry and have a conversation with God.
Staying warm or cool is fairly easy.
There are several bars and stores she frequents.
They will tolerate Nelly's visits if they are not long
And if she keeps a low profile.
She understands this and knows people look at her.
It is hard to be invisible when one of your cart wheels squeaks.
For income, she gathers bottles and cans
And returns them for the deposit money.
The store clerks give her looks as they cash her out.
Nelly doesn't make eye contact.
Rather, she stares at her own extended open hand
Ready to make sure she gets the right amount of money.
It is hard to know how much she understands →

Or how much she remembers about her own history.
When and where was she a little girl?
What kind of childhood did she have? –
Schooling — relationships — family— all a mystery.
How old is she and does she have any friends?
Hard to tell because she is a loner
And watches out for her own safety.
Sitting on a bench, she inspects her sleeve cuff.
Picking at it as if there was a piece of lint
Not noticing the wool unraveling from the sea green sweater
And seeming not caring about the world around her.
She is not a sweet old grandmother feeding pigeons.
In fact she may, on occasion, steal from the monument sitters.
Most people give her wide birth.
She is probably harmless they think —still…
Some people have tried to talk to her.
Nelly will turn away from them and move quickly off.
Sometimes she is cornered, but rarely talks.
Once she was forced to go to a shelter for a night.
That was a prison sentence and she fled as soon as possible.
Her routine does include a food kitchen.
Nelly likes that because they ask no questions.
She does appreciate their kindness.
So how did Nelly get to be Nelly?
Was she married? Does she have children?
Does she do drugs or alcohol?
That is not how she spends her money.
What brings her here?
Why do her words come out as nonsense?
She watches her world in quick glances —
A multi-colored bird looking nervously about to survive.

(12/11/16)

3:30 PM

It's all planned.
Check up the street.
A few minutes more.
They just turned the corner, —

The Wonder and her friend
Slide into sight.
Walking along laughing and talking —
"See ya tomorrow."
Now she's getting close.
What do I do?
"Oh, hi… how's it going?"
"Fine."
"I'm just working here in the garden."
"That's nice."
Oh God, she's still walking,
She'll pass me by.
"Did you get your homework done?"
"I haven't even gotten home yet."
"Right. I meant yesterday's."
"Yeah, I did yesterday's homework."
"Um, did you understand it all?"
"Well no, not really, not all of it."
A smile!
"Not much of it."
"Yeah it was hard, but I finally got it."
"You did?"
"Uh-huh, took a while."
"Um, maybe you could help me sometime?"
"Sure, anytime – um, got time later?"
"Yeah, let me go home and change."
"OK – um, meet you by the fence?"
"In a half hour — thanks."
She touched my arm.
Oh God, is this really happening?
Um — got to change — clean up —
Get my books — got to think of things to say.
Don't be stupid.
Don't say something dumb.
Wow, her hair is so long.
What a pretty smile.
She knows how to act — so cool.
Me — I'm all thumbs – Oh God.

---- (Time Passes)----

"Oh, I get it now – Wow, I would
have never figured that out – thanks."→

"That's OK – uh – wanna work on today's homework?"
"Sure, that'd be great."

---- (Time Passes) ----

"Great, all done, that didn't take long."
"No – um pretty easy huh?"
"Yeah, hey you wanna go for a walk?"
"Sure —um oops — here let me pick those up. I'll carry them."
"Thanks…nice day."
"Yeah…um… sky is pretty."
"It is…so blue and all those clouds."
"I see a horse."
"What?"
"In the clouds, over there, it looks like a horse."
"Oh, I see it…yes it does."
"There's a camel."
"Where?"
"There."
"No, that's a dog…running"
"Fine, but from here, it's a camel."
"Is not."
"Is too," she smiled.
"Camel."
"Dog."
"Camel."
"Dog."
"Hippopotamus."
She laughed, "You're silly."
"No. I'm Bill."
"How come we didn't talk before?"
"I don't know, I'm not very good at this."
"What do you mean?"
"Talking… girls… that sort of thing."
"Oh don't be silly. You're not a jerk like some of those other guys."
"Um…thanks."
(The longest silence that ever existed)
"Ah, you're pretty you know."
"No I'm not. Don't be silly."
"Yes you are; your hair, your smile…your laugh."
"My laugh, that makes me pretty?"

"Well yeah, I mean it's light, breezy, it can push those clouds around."
"Oh, stop."
"No, no...I mean it, you laughed and the clouds changed from a camel to a dog."
"Ha, Fine. My laugh's pretty."
"Not just that, but... well your eyes."
"What about my eyes?"
"Well...they sort of sparkle. I mean
I never really looked hard at them, but they're dark
and when they look at you... you're sort of frozen
by them and then they kinda sparkle."
"Stop now...that's enough...but thanks."
"That's OK..."
"Listen, I got to get home for dinner."
"Oh, right um..."
"You wanna work on our homework tomorrow?"
"Sure, sure...that'd be great."
She leans over and takes her books and gives him a quick kiss
and walks away toward her house. He stands there, he doesn't
know if he'll ever walk again. He almost reaches for his cheek,
but stops mid way, still feeling her lips there. Now feeling returns
to his legs and his mind comes back into focus. He turns toward his
house and tries to keep from skipping. It *was* a camel.

(1/19/12)

Ring-a-leave-e-o

I'm sure I could Goggle "ring-a-leave-e-o"
And give you a factual description
Of a neighborhood game from a few years ago.
The same with "Statue", "Red Light", "SPUD"
"Hide-n-go seek" — games of my youth —
Games of— well maybe more than a few years ago.
They were part of a universal summer night
Where a dozen kids put ages aside
And played together in total happiness.
They played so well, that it was dark
And their parents hadn't called them in. →

Dinner was over; the streetlights were on.
The only sounds you heard
Was a blind count to one hundred —
A breathless gasp "Home Free"
Or "I see you so and so. You're caught,"
And there is muted laughter.
Brothers and sisters don't argue
But as grudging teammates, help each other.
Rules are known and accepted.
You hear the night full of crickets.
You see shadows that don't scare you —
A breeze pushes some leaves into the light —
And those shadows dance on the road.
A figure emerges from the bushes — racing for the pole,
Racing for home. Finally the games end.
"Red Rover, Red Rover, anyone with red come over."
One or two head home, home with some grumbling.
Finally it's "See ya' tomorrow,"
And the night is left alone.
We can hear the freight train rumbling so far away.
The next set of night creatures emerge
While winners and losers head for pillows
Protesting weakly about cleaning up.
There was no homework.
There was no school tomorrow.
It was summer; it was summer a while ago.

(10/31/12)

Nellie's Kitchen

The day was concealing its intentions,
but then this was New England.
By late morning the sun had disappeared
only to smile out through the clouds an hour later.

 Rita and Charlie were slow to wake
and even slower to move into the day.
It had been a long and happy night

and because of the holiday,
work for both didn't happen until tomorrow.

So their tiny bedroom was filled
with love making, teasing, pillow talk
as well as deep dark secrets,
little stories and important dreams.
It was a most comfortable beginning and
slowly it shaped into a real vacation day.

To start with — there were no plans,
but suggestions started popping from each of them
"Want to go for a walk?"
"Want to go out for lunch?"
Yes and yes and still more.
They fumbled around, laughing as they organized
What to wear — where to go — no sign of snow.

Out the door, arm in arm, smile over smile,
down the steps, down the street, around the corner and
half way down the block they stopped.
Nellie's Kitchen. Why not, neither had ever been.
They walked past it everyday but had never stopped.
A quick glance through the window
and then they ducked in the door.

It certainly wasn't fancy
but it also wasn't dirty; Comfortable said the baby bear —
Booths and tables, the light from the windows
and deeper in a soft yellowish glow…
As they entered, everyone looked up —
customers and servers curious about the intruders.

The place was sparsely populated.
Probably everyone was a regular.
A waitress motioned for them to sit anywhere.
Without gawking it looked like there were eight or so patrons,
groups of two and solos all in their routines,
one or two in the kitchen and two waitresses.
There was a counter with seats manned by one waitress,
the other handled the rest of the floor.
→

Rita and Charlie picked a booth half way in and as they unbundled,
menus and coffee mugs appeared.
As they settled in and picked up the menus,
two glasses of water and a bright smile stood before them.
Coffee pot lifted off her tray,
the wordless universal question was asked. "Coffee?"
"Sure."
"Thank you."
"Need a few minutes?"
"Please."
And the waitress was off to clear some dirty dishes
from some tables, evidence of an earlier rush.

The menus showed wear and a primo list of comfort food.
Rita wanted breakfast and Charlie was ready for lunch.
Breakfast was all day so ordering would be no problem.
Charlie leaned over the table and Rita closed the gap.
He was fascinated by the place and wanted her take on it.
Together, they decided their waitress was not Nellie.
She was a veteran, a seasoned professional for sure,
but there was no sense of ownership in her manner.
The same held true for the woman behind the counter.
More like she handled things back there, because of years on the floor,
that had caused her legs to give out.
Back of the window was a crusty fellow
and another who was not visible to the diners.

"What can I get for youze?"
The question came from the returning waitress.
She was probably past middle age but sort of ageless.
Her voice reflected the neighborhood she was raised in —
a protective vibrato and a false intimacy.

After establishing how the eggs would be twisted
and what color the meat would be,
she put the order in, brought extra napkins,
along with the coffee pot for a refill.
The brevity and lack of wasted steps spoke of her experience.

"Her name is Vicky, May's behind the counter.
Victor shoves stuff through the window
and cooks with Little Nell.

This flood of information came from a man sitting alone at a table nearby.
His shirt was well worn, but clean
and only slightly out of season.
"My name is John. You folks live in the neighborhood?"
"Yes, we do."
"Thought I've seen you around. Haven't seen you in here before."
"First time." Rita answered.

 John was older, the couple thought,
retired from something with enough money to live on —
just enough. There were no trips to be taken
and he was alone, very much alone.
As if to confirm this, John said,
"I guess most of this bunch here are regulars.
Loneliness can start pretty early in the morning.
Little Nell owns the place and is fine with us nursing a cup of coffee for a few hours.
We talk to each other about nothing too important.
You know — weather and such or some little neighborhood gossip —
never mention religion or politics.
Around here when you ask someone how they are,
you expect to get a detailed answer and
there is no shortage of second opinions."

 Rita was warming to the conversation.
"Has Little Nell owned the place for a long time?"
John's posture had improved and his face had
certainly brightened. This was turning into the highlight of his day.
"Little Nell is Nellie's daughter. When her mom passed,
she kept it going, pretty much as it was.
Nellie and her husband, Bill, rented the place after the war
and it's always made a decent profit.

They worked hard and lucked out.
At one point, the owners of the building wanted to move on
and sold it to Bill and Nellie for a song.
But Bill died a few years after that and Nellie just kept running the place
and Little Nell — well, she grew up in here and their apartment on the second floor.
I think they rent the upper floors."
 By now, Charlie was resigned to the fact that→

the day's plans were changing right before his eyes
and that he better get over his little ego snit
and join in the adventure.
"John, do they really make this thing work?"
"Sure, it gets busy in here and we'll move on
so they have room for the paying customers."
He smiled.

 Just then Vicky returned with their orders.
"Anything more I can get youze right now?"
"I don't think so." Rita answered.
Vicky gave John a little bit of a look.
He responded to the look. "It's alright Vicky, they're from the neighborhood."
Vicky turned back to the booth and let down her guard a little.
"I guess you know, I'm Vicky
Welcome to Nellie's Kitchen.

Sometimes I forget to shift gears.
Anyway let me know if you need anything
and don't let John bother you too much."
Charlie sprang to John's defense.
"No, no, we're interested and have been asking him questions."
Vicky smiled, and then gave John a quick look.
It would appear it is a game they play and moved back to the counter.

 Rita and Charlie started working on their food,
while John studied the smooth rim of his coffee mug and drifted.
"How long have you been coming here?" Charlie asked.
"Oh, a long time, never met Bill, but came here most mornings
on the way to work and when I retired,

I just kept coming, I've seen Little Nell grow from child to woman."
"It feels so comfortable here," Rita added.
"Yeah Nellie decorated it and Little Nell has kept it pretty much the same.
There is a little story behind each thing,
but I only know a few of them."

 All of a sudden, there was a loud crash in the kitchen,
followed by two voices in a harmony of swearing,
that turned quickly to laughter.
Everyone in the place had turned to the source of the loud noise.

Now most were back to where they had been.

Just then the kitchen door swung open and Little Nell emerged.
A bit flushed and obviously making an effort to calm down,
she grabbed a pot of decaf coffee in one hand and
a pot of regular coffee in the other and started to make the rounds.
She chatted easily as she went table to booth
knowing their names by heart. Jokes were made
or an ear was given and smiles crossed every face, as she moved by.
Nell was playing around with middle age,
but some parts of her would always be young.
Her eyes were forever youthful and her smile a bit impish.
Her height topped off at about five feet
and her body was not slender,
but there were some very nice curves to it.
As for attitude, Nell would qualify as watchfully pleasant.
She was outgoing and caring, that was obvious,
But she was always in control —
This probably from her upbringing and running the business.

She came up to John with a sweetness
that would carry him through the day.
He was one of her unofficial uncles and was treated like family.
All she did was ask him how he was as she filled his coffee mug.
But she wanted to know and made eye contact with him
until John broke out his smile.
He also made introductions of sorts,
"Nell, these are folks from the neighborhood,
trying us out for the first time."

"Welcome!" she offered as well as her hand.
"I'm Charlie. This is Rita, and we live around the corner."
"Hi Nell, nice to meet you." Rita joined in
rather quietly as she too received the extended hand.
"I hope you'll be back now that you found us.
How was everything?"
Charlie glanced at Rita, who nodded, and said
"Everything was fine."
Nell continued, "It's not fancy, but we try to make it good.
Sometimes we'll have a few specials so the customers don't get bored
and we don't take things for granted.
We open at five in the morning and close around eight→

Tuesday through Saturday. Open till five on Sunday and closed Mondays.
Oh, as you might have heard, the soup of the day is no longer chicken noodle — but nobody was hurt and we'll come up with something else."

"John was telling us your mom and dad started the business in the forties."
Charlie offered.
"Yeah, they worked hard and after dad died, mom worked even harder.
It was an interesting childhood.
After school I had a lot of people keeping an eye on me
and helping me with my homework.
Actually it was more interesting and more fun than going out to play."
She reached over and gave John's arm a squeeze.
"Many of these people and others were and are an important part of me.
Sorry, I didn't mean to rattle on."

"No, no," Both Charlie and Rita put in spontaneously and simultaneously.
"We don't want to hold you up, but…"
"You're not holding me up.
Victor won't want me in the kitchen until he gets the soup cleaned up.
He swears like a sailor, but his heart is as big as a battleship.
He won't admit that, but it's true."

Rita asked about the decorations and Nell warmed to the subject.
"Most of them are mom's, she decorated the place when they first opened
and added other things that caught her eye over the years.
Nothing fancy, you know, comfortable stuff, like the food.
That teapot over there was one of her wedding gifts.
I've added a few things, but most are hers.

They meant a lot to her and dad, so they mean a lot to me.
That kitchen gadget, on the top shelf over there,
was all the rage when dad gave it to mom."
They caught John smiling. He knew this story.
Little Nell continued. "It is obsolete now, but back then no kitchen should be without one. The mistake was that he gave it to her on Valentine's Day.
She gave him grief then and continued even after he passed.

If only he had attached a rose to it or something romantic."

Mom missed dad terribly, but not during business hours.
She had a business to run and a child to raise.
Maybe late at night, a teardrop would fall on a stack of paperwork,
but in a while, it was back to work.
She made sure I dated and knew how to read the good and bad in people,
but I love this life and don't want much more."

Charlie asked, "Doesn't it get too much for you sometimes?"
Nell gave that a little thought and answered,
"No, not really, I love the people here, the staff — the customers."
She made a vague gesture encompassing the whole place.
"I take a few days off once in a while and have traveled some.
But it's like I'm gathering stories to tell my friends here."

There was a natural pause in the conversation —
Certainly a time when she could have moved on in her rounds
or found something that would pull her away from the small group.
Instead, she called Vicky over and whispered something to her.
Then she returned to smoothing an imaginary wrinkle in the table covering.

Little Nell asked, "So tell us a little about you folks?"
This time, Charlie was the spokesman for the pair,
though he would check his partner's face
to make sure his revelations were not
giving up more than they wished to share.
He gave a brief account of their meeting and falling in love,
what they did and how they found the place where they lived.
This was their first place together and they both thought,
that except for a few rocky spots, they were doing OK living together.
Both loved their jobs and, at this point, neither would be a millionaire.
They were content.

"Do you plan to marry, if you don't mind me asking?" Nell inquired.
There was a pregnant pause.
The two young people looked at each other,
This was not a new discussion to them.

Finally Rita volunteered, "We haven't decided yet
And we're not sure if we want children." →

Nell took this in and weighed it in her mind briefly.
Finally she said "I had a steady fellow at one time,
Even moved in with him, nearby."
This was obviously something John didn't know
and he was tempted to say something,
but was wise enough to sit back in his chair
and keep his mouth shut.

Nell went on, "Mom had no objections out loud,
but I think she was worried that this guy was not
my knight in shining armor.
What she did do was keep things as much business as usual as she could
and only offered carefully worded advice when asked."
A brief hesitation, "And she was right,
the guy was a user and may have become an abuser.
All the signs were there. So after a few months,
I came back here and jumped right back into the routine.
Mom said nothing about it, never mentioned it,
but I noticed she started to give me more responsibility."

At this point, Vicky returned with a tray
and on it four pieces of apple pie-a-la-mode.
With minimal protestations, John, the newcomers and Nell
dug into the impromptu dessert.

A few minutes later, after the pie was gone,
Nell and John made their excuses.
Nell headed back to the kitchen while John started for the door,
but paused to talk to an older couple at a table near the exit.
Charlie and Rita remained in their booth a bit longer,
ideally holding hands or touching fingers
while their minds finished digesting all that had come with lunch.

They paid their check and started for the door.
Vicky thanked them as they moved out of the booth,
John turned, smiled and nodded
as did the couple he was in conversation with.
Finally they reached the door and looked back.
A hand was waving through the order window of the kitchen.

They waved back, smiled at each other and headed for the rest of their day.
That smile said we are the newest regulars.

(12/27/16)

Miss Emma Flag

Almost everybody in my town
Knew Miss Emma Flag –
To almost everyone in my town,
Miss Emma Flag was their fourth-grade teacher.
Miss Emma could take credit
For every document or letter signed in my town.
She was the one, who taught us handwriting,
The "Palmer Method" all neat on lined paper,
Much like the staff lines on music paper
Instead of notes, A would lead off with B soon after.
There would be capital letters and small letters
All tumbling from young minds to the point of a thick lead pencil,
Or after a while, a fountain pen.
Generation after generation grew under Miss Flag's steady eye.
In my case I sat at a connected desk, with a hole for the ink well
But the inkwells were gone and ponytails were safe.
Our desktops opened and there we kept our Schaefer's Ink.
 I even had a cartridge fountain pen when they first came out.
The next generation had individual desks and ballpoint pens.
But Miss Emma Flag was our guide and teacher.
If you sneezed, you were warned to "cover-up"
While she flew to the window and threw up the sash.
There were reports to do, morning vitamins to take
And time walked by and students moved on,
But she would remember you.
She grew up in town and spent her life there.
Related to some of the town's original settlers
And to my generation, she was already old.
Age was something we had no concept of
Last year, last week, and last fad was old.
Why was she still Miss Flag. No one knew. →

Was there a love interest at one time?
No one knew her contemporaries — therefore no one knew.
She did retire to her home on Maple Street
And remained active in the community.
When something displeased her, like higher taxes,
It wasn't beyond her to make her way down to the Town Hall,
Not a long walk from Maple Street,
And let her former student, the mayor; know what was on her mind.
As she was downsizing and moving to an assisted living facility,
She mailed parents of her students' reports she had saved.
My mom got one of my reports with fresh notations,
A compliment on my understanding of the subject.
I was, I do believe, just about out the door to college.
Thank goodness I didn't have to stay after school.
Miss Emma Flag lived to be one hundred and four,
Outliving many of her students
And being loved by all the rest.

(7/2/16)

I Step Away and Around and Move on

A man lies on the sidewalk
His piece of cardboard a mattress
Possessions bundled behind him.
I step away and around and move on.

In my town we don't have these things
Well maybe I just don't see these things
I'm going here to there so,
I step away and around and move on.

I see the man asleep in the daylight
I'm not comfortable, somewhat frightened
He hasn't threatened me, still,
I step away and around and move on.

Do I want to know his history?
What blows life and society have struck?
What wars has he fought? Forget it.
I step away and around and move on.

Has he been cast on the street?
Released from somewhere or down on luck?
Or has he chosen this? I don't know.
I step away and around and move on.

If he were awake, would he speak?
Would he tell me his tale or lie for a buck?
Is he drunk? Is he crazy?
I step away and around and move on.

What battles are inside his head?
Why am I more suspicious than compassionate?
If he asked me, what would I say?
I step away and around and move on.

Does he sleep the day to survive the night?
Is he really tough or really scared?
If I reached to him would I be hurt?
I step away and around and move on.

Do I thank God I am not him
And yet ignore God by passing him?
I am disappointed in me.
I step away and around and move on.

(10/22/10)

*Previously published in "Our Journey" (Holiday 2010 edition). A Publication of Commonsense Media Group.

OTHER STUFF

Chapter 7

Well aren't we clever? It is just another way of saying "miscellaneous" and yet easier to spell.

This Silence Is So Loud

This silence is so loud and it is so early —
The cats come down once in a while and complain,
Missing a belly to snuggle in and the noise and
Taunts and love.

This silence is so loud and it is so early —
The sudden cold makes staying busy hard,
And I see a little boy in blue and white
Waving from the window.

This silence is so loud and it is so early –
The wind whips west or whatever and
The frost threatens what little spring
Has found its way.

This silence is so loud and it is so early —
No friends have yet climbed through
The door and so I will go and dream
Even if it is so early.

The silence is so loud and it is so early —
Maybe I'll conjure love and bring them closer —
Or bring home that current fantasy —
Old, old memory.

This quiet is so empty and the words
Are well rehearsed – the actions well constructed —
But the chapter's always
Left unfinished.

Spring night of winter reminiscences —
Crawls slowly to sleep, and soon the
Noise will stop and I'll fall asleep
And it will be another day.

(4/28/77)

Long Night

Now I lay me down to sleep
But my back is hurting
And I'm worrying about what I have to do tomorrow.

The sheet is all knotted.
The blanket has fallen to the floor.
I can't get to sleep.

Moonlight shines through the blinds on one side
The neighbor's security lights leak through the other
Squeezing my eyes together doesn't work.

I try turning on the TV
Hoping this will distract my mind,
At least long enough for me to drop off.

Nope. So I turn off the TV,
Roll to another position.
Being invisible doesn't seem to be an option.

Maybe if I add a pillow
Or take one away
Maybe I'll sit up for a minute.

OK, I'm tired, really, really tired.
I rub something soothing on my back
And straighten out my enemy.

I check the temperature of the room,
Open the window a little more
Slide back under the covers.

I settle in this way and that,
Hoping my body finds a notch
That breeds no discomfort.

Did I set the alarm?
What time do I have to be there?
How important is this?

Stuff

Wait! Wait! I never set my alarm.
What was I thinking of?
I'm only going out to lunch.

What time is it now?
I don't want to know.
It will be fun to visit over lunch.

What's the weather supposed to be like?
What shall I wear?
Does the ceiling need a fresh coat of paint?

I wonder — no, it couldn't work.
Where's my flock?
One sheep jumped over the fence.

Two sheep jumped over the fence.
What's the fence made of?
Three sheep jumped over the fence.

Are these fluffy sheep?
Four sheep jumped over the fence.
Split rail, and yes, they're fluffy.

Five sheep jumped over the fence.
Sure it's not a stonewall?
We have a lot of stonewalls in New England.

Six sheep jumped over the fence!
When do you shear sheep?
Seven sheep jumped over the fence.

In the Spring I think,
Eight sheep jumped over the fence
Near a stonewall and some juniper bushes.

Nine sheep jumped over the fence.
I've never shorn sheep. Does it hurt?
Ten sheep jumped over the fence. →

No silly, it doesn't hurt.
Eleven sheep jumped over the fence.
OK, I'll pretend the sheep are shorn.

Twelve naked sheep jumped over the fence.
Near a babbling brook —
What's the difference between a brook and a stream?

I don't know — but the naked sheep are shivering.
Thirteen shivering sheep jumped over the fence.
What do I do with all this wool?

Knit with it nitwit.
Fourteen silly looking thin sheep jumped over the fence.
How many sheep make a herd of sheep?

Or is it a flock of sheep? No, that's birds, isn't it?
Fifteen emaciated sheep struggle over the fence.
Where does the water in the brook come from?

The mountains, and it flows into the lake.
Sixteen sheep boost each other over the fence.
What's the name of the lake?

What does it matter which lake? Emerald Lake.
Seventeen sheep, male and female jumped over the fence.
Why is it called Emerald Lake?

Because the water looks like the color of an emerald.
Eighteen sheep jumped over the fence with poison ivy growing on it.
What's the difference between a sheep and a goat?

I don't know — two different species of animals.
Nineteen sheep jumped over the broken fence.
Do we get lamb chops from sheep?

I think so — and mutton too, I think.
Twenty sheep stepped on the broken fence.
Do they make mutton burgers?

Never heard of that.
Twenty-one sheep ran through the gap in the fence,
Across the brook, through the mulberry bushes and

One sheep jumped over the wall
And when I woke up this morning
I was wearing a brand-new sweater.

(6/16/16)

Driving

Gray and white clouds stretch over a sky blue sky
Casting moving shadows on the mountains —
A new wandering road with pine needles
Pushed in bunches by the Spartan traffic flow.
How easy to lock into reverie —
A different road, a different time.
Your driving becomes almost automatic.
You see the signs and hazards
But you're able to find another zone —
Compelled to form your daydream —
Putting all the characters in place —
Now moving them about
Like a life-sized chess board,
You reenact a passed time —
Or a never-was time.
And you smile and cry.
And now you must watch the road.

(10/12 & 10/16/07)

Quiet, Laughing You

The night is hollow and without voice.
The noise that surrounds is extra loud.
The stream of thoughts never stops→

And they all circle back to —
Quiet, laughing you.

The morning comes before I'm ready,
The kids head for school in rain.
The mind never quite says hello
And then it's round again to —

Quiet, laughing you.

The afternoon drags on forever.
The record player is no comfort.
The sleep I've missed catches up
And all I dream of is —

Quiet, laughing you.

The hours are days for me.
The sounds about me are nothing.
The only thing that really counts
Is that I'm in love with —

Quiet, laughing you.

(Date Unknown)

Travelin' To the Cape

My ribbon's cut out of the land;
Hills have been halved,
Valleys have been filled
So that I may spin right by
And not notice what used to be.
The color is just past prime
But then, so am I.
I've gone through these towns —
Seen these trees for years and years.
But it's been a year
So the leaves are new

And some are turning up
Or running to hide from me.
The day has gone beyond brisk
And the sun is a pinhole in gray.
"I've been coming here man and boy,"
Since before I remember when —
Three, I'm told — to visit Uncle Charlie
Who I never knew, but who
Threw me to the heavens
And spoke loudly of Goliath.
Little man, young man, married man,
Family man, now old man.
To see what's here new and old —
To walk the trails and remember times —
To wander still and discover things
And in a few days, home again.

(10/19/08)

Church Bells

There are a variety of bells
Hidden in the steeples of the world.
Some are automated — programmed
To ring out the hours
And perhaps give us a tune — a hymn.
Others still depend on strong arms
To fulfill their daily duties.
Church bells sound loudly —
The hour of the day —
A call to worship —
A post-worship serenade
Here is the day.
God go with you.
It rings feverishly in celebration
And tolls mournfully
To recognize a loss.
God take them home,
We will miss them →

But they are safe with you.
There are no instructions with this —
This is my interpretation.
For so many, the church bell rings
Counting the hours of our life
Celebrating our unions
Welcoming us each Sunday
Sending us home with God's word
And wishing us well
On our journey from this earth.

(12/28/12)

Winter's End

Winter's end is in full swing —
Barren branches passing through pinpoint pastels
On the way to the leafy, fruitful season.
And the energy of life seems renewed.
The return of the sun's warmth
Draws up the corners of our lips.
The hammering and mowing heralds
The invasion of the contractor army
As well as the skilled and unskilled amateur.
Well-intentioned projects
Are accomplished or eventually abandon.
Already some arms are bared and more –
Figures hidden in wool
Are exposed in cotton and spandex —
Some with pride and exposition,
Others with total disregard to taste and exhibition.
We waiver from fantasy to disgust.
Kites and daffodils are moving toward
Iris and roses and diminishing winds.
Weathermen search for fault —
As daylight hangs onto the hours.
The evenings, still cool bring hesitation
To an all-out summer celebration.
The calendar says, "a month and more."

The sunrise says, "I'm here."
Rain welcomes new growth —
Our eyes catch nature in all directions.
Reality, of course, is there,
Checking on life and making us face it.
We share the fate and frustration
Of friends that hurt despite the awakening.
Our faith, our heart, our compassion
Greet each fear with resolve and attempted resolution.
We do what we can,
And we are insulated somewhat.
In the fact that day follows day,
We hope to comfort, we pray for life.
We help when we can
With words, with deeds, with what we've got.

(5/6/06)

My Song

My song lifts from a quiet face
The words start as a jumble
Little thoughts strung together
Stumbling along to find direction

My song starts softly searching.
Is it worth giving voice?
There is both sincerity and conceit
As the focus finally clears

My song and its ideas
Probably not new or earth shaking
Try to find an audience
And just explain things my way

My song is best spoken
For except in my head
It is likely out of tune
The music is clear to me →

My song comes from the past
Usually wrapped in nature
It lives deep inside
And is masked in clever phrases

To sing my song
You must know why I shiver
And be willing to take the time

To sing my song
Join in the silly games
And follow where I'm going

There are faces to touch and trace
Snappy comebacks and hearty laughter
Just a beat away from tears
Everything is trumpets and clarinets
Timpani, marching bands, jazz bands
French horns and wind chimes
Bird songs and walk alongs.

The music rises in bubbles and pops
Some right away, the simplest bit of iridescence
Others smaller, more delicate
Fly high on the breeze
Or come to rest on the grass
Hesitating to release their notes
Those resting seem more fragile
Subject to little feet and cat paws
While those that climb
Seem strong and vivid in the sunlight
Drifting over the fence and out of sight
Surely they're still going
Ready to drop my song on newer ears

Are you ever surprised that someone's listening?
You'll be going along with a memory
Or God forbid a new tune
Stringing notes one after another
As much for yourself as anyone else
Then you'll look up
And there are eyes absorbing every word

Ah, but it's a rare face
And too often you embarrass someone or yourself
Trying to force the tune

Think of the notes of love and understanding
How many ways we try to sing that song
We struggle a lifetime, often without talent
Searching for the softness that fits in your hand
And puts a skip in your step

And yet here I sit, late at night
Drifting into my reverie
Wondering what magic is found in those notes
That we all have, to what use we've put…
What purpose, was the priority hitting right notes?
Were we afraid to hit a real clunker?
How much joy is in our song
Symphony or folk song
Silly song or love song

There I just went the easy way
My song is the simplest, most complicated
Thing you've ever heard
I'd love you to hear it.

(3/26/06)

Whiskers

I think everyone loves whiskers
On a dog, a cat, a grandfather's chin.
If we're wee ones we learn
"Pet the kitty gently. Nice Kitty."
"No, the dog is not a horse."
"Stop! Mom! Grandpa is tickling me!"
A little steeper in time
The cat nuzzles and purrs,
The dog chases sticks and pulls on his toy,
Grandpa reads a story with silly voices.
Up the age ladder we climb.
You feed the cat and it sleeps in the sun, →

You feed the dog and take it for walks,
Grandpa tells stories of when he was your age.
Life gets busy and you're on the run.
The cat meows, you pet it and it sleeps in the sun.
The dog moves slowly and plops at your feet.
Grandpa moves slowly and sleeps in the sun.
You've grown and gone and come back again.
The cat in the sun raises its head,
The dog wags its tail and puts his head in your lap.
You sit in Grandpa's chair and are comfortable.

(11/5/16)

Rose it up!

Feel a bit down
A little in the dumps?
Well hell man — Rose it up!

Crumbling thoughts
Unhappy streets you're traveling on
Days coming one after another
Drifting and spinning
With the compass in all directions.
Well damn it — Rose it up!

Had a long day
Feeling a bit alone even surrounded
Doesn't have to be a problem
Unless you enjoy wallowing
Just — Rose it up!

Put on those shades
They block the litter
And hide the reality of it all.

It's your favorite day
With your first love
Or your life's love.

Sun is shinning in an April shower.
It's snowing on Christmas Eve
Family and friends all gathered.
The happiest time, shuffling through leaves
And watching the flowers grow.
Rose it up till you're strong enough
To handle things when you put them away.
(1/25/08)

Water and Me

Water and me
We gets along.
I drinks it
Once in a while
No fancy stuff
Straight from the tap.
Well, maybe ice
And a squeeze of lemon,
But no bubbles.

Me and water
We grew up together.
We weren't always buddies
Saturday night baths
Lots of fights
But we made our peace
Sprinklers and pistols
Oceans and waves
And wonderful puddles.

Water and me
We've grown some.
Showers or baths
Almost everyday
Car washing
Lawns and gardens →

But it costs me now
Big bucks every three months.

Me and water
We've had our time.
Romantic walks
I hardly noticed

Lonely times
I traced the drops
Rivers rushing
Casting reflections
Freezing solid.

It's amazing
Holding up boats
Hiding fishes
Coming in and out

Flooding and waving
Separating and joining
Even evaporating
Right before my eyes
It's a big part of me.

(3/27/09)

Willows and Wishes

Willows and wishes
Talks and touches
Winds and breezes
Wandering mind

Giggles and laughter
Shuffles and staggers
Memories and smiles
Empty hands

Drifting in dreams
Dancing in clouds
Running from
Embracing something

Sounds and scenes
Next day's hopes
Rich colored flowers
Following streams

Not always understanding
What is perfectly clear
Making too much
Of little steps

Finding the path
To take into the night
Full of stars
Bathed in moonlight

Hearing the notes
That carry softly
On the backs of fireflies
From fence, to tree to sky

(6/30/07)

*Previously published in "High Tide - 2008" Publication of "Writer's Group" Milford Fine Arts Council, Milford, CT.

"Kite"

Build or buy — get ready
Run, run into the spring wind
Friend following — lift it high
Feel it catch — let it go
Jerk and pull — give it line
Pull it safe up above
The trees and wires. →

See it twist as the tail spins
Climbing out to chase the clouds.
What must the birds think
And Charlie Brown.

(6/28/06)

Two Little Versus

Words that spill out of your pen
Are easier to correct than words
That spill out of your mouth.

It's yellow time
Trumpet and coronet
And of course
The dandelion

(4/21/07)

I Lost My Hat

I lost my hat
I loved that hat
I have many hats
I loved that hat

Nothing special
Just comfortable
Macgregor plaid
Style "Golfer"
"Ivy League"

I had it a long time
Wore it fall to spring
It's no big deal
But I loved that hat

It was a cold day
I was walking
My twice weekly
Three-mile stroll
Behind some, ahead of others

I don't think
It made me dashing
It wasn't worth much
Just sentimental like me

The wind gusted at some corners
I reached up to hold it on
But my gloved hand
Felt only my curly locks
So I don't know where

I lost my hat
I loved my hat
That hat is gone
Sigh – I have many hats
Just no favorites

(Unknown)

He Left Her Seven Pounds

It was true love — not puppy love.
He loved her — cared for her.
He brought her gifts;
He told her how beautiful she was.
He was older than she was.
He didn't make her work.
He didn't make rules — like some —
He understood her — made her laugh.
They did things together.
They went to the movies.
They hung out with friends.
They went for rides in his car.→

They went out — out of her house.
They kissed and they made out —
They eventually did more
They did more and more, more often.
She didn't care about school.
She started to feel funny.
She tried talking to her friends.
She felt ill at different times.
To confirm her fears,
She took a drug store test.
She talked to him — told him —
He said everything would be OK.
He stopped calling — didn't take her calls.
He was never home.
He had no family.
He wasn't at his job
She heard he'd left town.

He left her seven pounds and it was crying.

(12/29/11)

Apples

If you like an apple
Then you must eat it to the core.
When you finish one
Ask politely for two more.
They are mostly green and red
And you buy them at the store.
Or you can ride out to an orchard
Climb a tree and pick three or four.

Apples are great to eat
Just as you find them —
Wash them off and take a bite
Or cut them up and share.
But people like to do much more.
They peel them and put them in a pie,

A cobbler, or hide some in a donut.
Maybe deep-fry them in a fritter.
You can give one to your baby sitter
Some will crush them into applesauce
And squeeze them into juice or cider.
Apples come in many flavors
And they have many, many names —
There's Macintosh, Cortland and Gala
Just to name a few.
Why there's even one called Delicious —
And it is.
Some are soft – some are hard
Some are best for baking
But most are ready for you
Ready for the taking.

(9/27/10)

So I Said

So I said to the room…
So I said to the dark…
So I said to the night…
And they all listened.

They said get busy
They said don't be afraid
They said morning is coming
And I listened.

So, I embraced my memories
So I embraced my plans
So I embraced my dreams
And was ready for dawn.

(10/26/10)

Phineous and Benjamin

Phineous and Benjamin were friends. They had been friends before they knew what being a friend meant. They were friends in the morning, and friends when the sun went down. They were friends before school. They were friends before they could leave the yard and remained friends till Phineous's mom rang a bell or Benjamin's dad gave a whistle and they had to go home.

Phineous and Benjamin played in the summer. They played in the winter and they played in those two seasons in between. They were the best of friends and shared all their knowledge and all their dreams that grew more and more each day. Once, they even talked about girls but neither had anything good to say about them.

One summer day, with no school to interrupt them and all their chores done, they wandered across the street, through the neighbor's yard and into their favorite world, the field. That was what they called it and it went on forever. It had a hill for sliding, a place cleared for baseball — something they couldn't do very well yet — and a little, excuse me, a huge forest of little sumac trees and blackberry bushes.

Life had gone on before in the field, there was a foundation of an old barn and evidence of an earlier generation of adventurers, but that didn't concern Phineous or Benjamin. Most days the boys had no trouble venturing into a world of their choosing, a world that blurred the ages from dinosaurs and knights, to sailing great ships and capturing pirates, or pirates capturing treasure and burying it in their field. Even on days when neither could think of anywhere to go or anyone to be, they would cover the field from edge to edge, tromping down high grass, picking wild flowers or, better yet, blackberries when they were in season.

Getting back to this one summer day, Phineous had an idea — or maybe it was Benjamin. Neither could remember and it really didn't matter. They were going to build a flying machine. They gathered their materials and thought of their design. Each had a different idea of what it should look like and didn't bother to share that idea. The important thing was to get it built.

Phineous wanted to go fast and dive down close to the ground and scare the cat and his older brother. Benjamin wanted to soar into the clouds and glide along with the birds.

And so the construction began. Phineous borrowed some nails from his father's workbench and Benjamin grabbed a hammer from his house. Carefully they nailed board to crate, this to that, and "don't forget that other thing." They were careful not to nail fingers or flatten thumbs and before you knew it, they were done. It had two wheels from a broken wagon, a crate empty of oranges, long boards, short boards and a broomstick out the back. There it stood and it was beautiful.

Before anything more could happen, a whistle came and a bell rang and their day of construction ended.

The next day was Sunday and Phineous had to go to church. His folks were saved and they went every Sunday to church to get saved some more, and Phineous went to Sunday school to learn how to be saved in the first place.

Benjamin's parents were not saved. His father sat reading the Sunday paper in his pajamas, while his mom cleared away breakfast and started making Sunday dinner. Sunday dinner was a big special meal that came in the middle of the day and not at the end like it did every other day. And there was more food and sometimes relatives came and pinched cheeks and asked dumb questions.

So, with his parents occupied, Benjamin went outside and wandered across the street and across the neighbor's yard and into the field. He wandered to the spot of the construction. It was, of course, hidden from any outsider's view and when he saw it, he marveled at the fine job he and Phineous had done.

He sat in the crate, the flying machine and felt like he was already high, high up in the sky, climbing over purple mountains and green valleys. Then he realized there was a problem. Assuming both he and Phineous would fit in the crate, how would they take off? They had talked about going fast off the hill where they went sledding, but how would they get enough speed?

Then Benjamin had an idea. It was a good idea he thought. Carefully he kicked out two of the three boards on the bottom of the crate, leaving the one in the middle to sit on. Then he hiked up the flying machine and rolled it toward the hill. Everything stayed together and nothing fell apart. And right then and there, he sort of got carried away. He thought Phineous wouldn't mind if he took the first ride, just to make sure it worked. So he made sure the broomstick in back was off the ground and he ran for the edge of the steep hill. He ran faster than he had ever run before, he ran faster than the wind, faster than the dog who chased him when he delivered papers, faster than anything anybody could think of.

When Phineous got home from church, he heard about how the ambulance had come and how his friend Benjamin had been found half way down the hill with lumber, and crates and broomsticks and wagon wheels spread all over the place.

Once he found out there wasn't much blood and that his friend would be all right, he got mad. He should have waited for him, it was *their* flying machine, but before long he was sort of glad he didn't get hurt.

He had to wait 'til Monday afternoon to go visit Benjamin. When he was let in the house, Phineous was told he could only visit a little while, because his friend needed his rest. He had broken his arm and he had a neat, no, a big white cast on it with just his fingers peeking through.→

Neither boy spoke of "you shouldn't have" or "sorry," there were just questions about how the cast felt and did Phineous want to sign it. Benjamin's mom said it was OK, so Phineous wrote his name in black ink on the white plaster and made a little picture of their flying machine.

Once Phineous was sure Benjamin was all right, and Benjamin was sure that Phineous was not mad at him, they started making plans. They started making plans for a pirate ship. It would be a ship that would sail all over the world and would be steady in a storm. It would have a pirate flag and would be able to go under water and swim with the fishes if there was any trouble above.

Of course, neither told the other what the ship looked like, but each could see it as plain as plain could be. Then it was time for Phineous to go home and they were both left with their thoughts of eye patches and swords and treasures.

Or maybe they could build an automobile!

(10/20/10)

The Lady and the Moon

The lady and the moon
She watches it in daylight
As it pulls in the night.

She drifts in memories
Repeating some often
And pulling others from deep within.

She is clear and peaceful
Her friend once said and she believes
"When it's your time."

But all her friends are gone
And the cat won't talk —
So it takes a while to find her voice.

Sometimes she is frightened
Sometimes she doesn't understand
She assigns someone for reassurance.

Today she cracks a joke
And watches things around her
She is happy and can see.

There is nothing that needs attending
No "one, one, one" for concentration
'til she can speak her mind.

She opens her bag
And brings out October flowers
They may mean love and "thank you."

The lady and the moon
Heads home in daylight
Because the night closes her in.

A "bright night" she predicts
And "thank you but…"
She gets her religion from the tube. →

Today, because she's relaxed,
She hears most of the questions
And will write someone of her adventure.

The lady and the moon —
"Imagine, somebody walked on it..."
"And the news is never good."

Her flowers, her garden —
Summer nights on the porch —
Resting within her space.

The lady and the moon —
Climb under the afghan.
You are safe and through another day.

(1/25/01)

Gas Station Rose

A horrible fight in the middle of the night.
It started small and just grew and grew —
The screaming, the pot thrown to the floor,
What was said or probably not said.
The words were wrong, nothing right.
All this built up from somewhere.
I need to think, I need to get away
I can't think, leave me alone
I'll be back, slam the door.
Walk. No get in the car.
It's dark and late — shit, the kids.
They must have heard it all.
Park down at the beach
Look out across the shore
What am I looking at, I really can't see?
These tears, where were they?
It doesn't matter, right or wrong.
If we calm down, we can talk it through.
Will she believe me, will she even listen?

Let me go back. That's the answer.
Just one stop, the gas station and then…
Finally home, the lights still on —
Enter softly and close the front door.
The light is from the kitchen
So I make my way.
She's sitting at the kitchen table
Coffee cup between both hands.
She doesn't look up.
I hand it to her before I speak,
That frail and tired gas station rose.
It replaces the coffee cup
And the words start from my heart
Nothing rehearsed and it comes easily.
Those words that are anchored in my soul.
Then her words start overlapping
And they are of a common theme.
She stands and meets me in the center of the room.
As she undoes the plastic wrapper
The petals fall to the floor one by one —
An empty stem in hand — we stare.
Then the two of us start laughing
And we hug and hold and squeeze.
I hope the kids can hear.

(12/11&12/11)

Davy Crockett

Davy Crockett died the other day —
Oh, I know the Alamo —
But mine died the other day.
Roy and Dale long gone now
My coonskin hat worn thin
The red kerchief chewed, lost.
My baseball heroes gone
Or barely able to reach the foul line
All except Yogi.
My youth is black and white reruns
Not often watched →

All the sweet memories
Softened by years into gold
The world of family and friends.
The real world is separate
This was the age, what six to twelve.
Just outside the front door —
The innocent time when war was a game
And no one ever died.
Hide and Seek, Red Light, Statue and SPUD
Neighborhoods of kids not in gangs
But in groups or teams
Rolling down the street or across the field.
Generation sliding into generation
Adults were lost to this world
They only came into focus
When the whistle blew.
Home to homework
Staying up late for "I Love Lucy."
Guys or girls it didn't really matter
It was about play and imagination
Worlds were contained in streets and blocks
The summer lasted forever
It never came.
Fall was Halloween and wrestling leaves
Getting through school
'til the next walking home adventure.
Movies surrounded you
You were the hero – you were Lancelot.
Winter was Christmas and small explorations.
Spring was rain and facing the never-ending school year.
Then it was summer AGAIN!
Ball games — discoveries — a different education —
We must have raced through them
For they are all gone
Flipping baseball cards — doing chores —
All those old real people gone
Or almost gone.
All our believing and make believing
"Born on a mountain top in Tennessee
Kilt him a bar' when he was only three."

(3/19/10)

(On the passing of Fess Parker)

Pedestrian Travel

The echoing footsteps on a midnight city walk
The shuffling through the fallen leaves of autumn
The quick steps across summer beach sand
The high stepping trudge through a field of snow
The slapping hop-slide of a boy through a puddle
The happy dance step after a goodnight kiss
The purposeful march from here to there
The aimless wandering of two lover's walk
The military "Sound off – one, - two, – three, - four…"
The precision of a dance two, three, four
The baby's stuttering first steps
The senior's doddering, supported hobble
The hopscotch prance of a little girl
The nice day, beautiful scenery stroll
The firm and steady steps of a hiker
The jarring repetition of a long distant runner
The blur of the sprinter
The varied gates of the walker and jogger
The feints, cuts and squeaks of the athlete
The pause step in a wedding march
The "you don't see me" race of the embarrassed flower girl
The stagger at the end of a long, long day
The stagger after the elbow's bending
The haphazard pace of a little explorer
The measured step of outlining boundaries
The stumble through a darkened room
Jackson's "Moon Walk"
Gleason's "And away we go!"
Snagglepuss's "Exit stage left"

(2/11/11)

70's Scraps

To fall in love is very easy.
To say "I love you" is a good deal harder
To be in love and admit it is hardest of all.

Night speaking to day at sunrise,
Lifts the light and warms the air.

9/23/70
It is now when the summer is Indian
A giver of the first breath
Of colored wondrous cold coming
And a final moment of sun
The last dance of heat.
Waiting for the next morning
Wondering what waking will find
The wind blowing winter's way.
Rhythms are changed and found.
Where is the lazy line in the river
Or barefoot silly melodies?
Locked in frost and broken
To rush back into grinding
Days following one another.

Squares

I was born in a square
I was raised in a square
I married a square with a squiggle
We had two kids who are squares with squiggles
I even learned to have a little squiggle
We live in a square
A little square.
Some others live in big squares
And own little vacation squares
They spend a few summer weeks
In their vacation squares in sunny places →

And travel far and wide the whole year round
To fancy squares to play croquet
And other dangerous sports.
I like to vacation in triangles
To wander far and wide to rectangles
And travel in circles all wrapped in string.
I'm still a square about those things.

(8/21/13)

7/26/11

Sun splattered days
Sticky twisted nights
Exhaustion without movement
Finishing the day a celebration
The night is challenging
To find a position
A comfortable condition
Just to leave the day behind
Finding the solution
For the clearing of the mind
Which then leads the body
To start to relax
A pealing away of aches
Twisting the body this way and that
Focusing on sounds
Making them faint and distant
Until you think never mind
And the door of darkness closes
And its several hours later
And the challenge begins again

When I See You

Sometime in the winter of '69

Poem that Craig Carnelia added music to – I was working at Center Stage in Baltimore – he was part of the acting company – the song was sung by his friend Diane Keaton on the Merv Griffin Show – she performed it between guests Jack E. Leonard and Little Egypt. As a result of this performance, I became a member of **ASCAP** (American Society of Composers, Authors and Publishers) and received approximately $236 in royalties that first year and 10 years of residuals of $2.36.

When I see you
The world becomes very small
Your eyes light the path I walk
Your hair frames my whole day
When I see you
My life becomes warm and tall
Your smile is all you have to say
When I see you

The sun begins the day
She lights the path and guides the day
Climb birds, sing along
The trees are giving out with song
My heart moves forward uncertain
My hand touches unknowing
You have my love
When I see you

Dewdrop, Raindrop – Little Tear Instead

Dewdrop, raindrop — little tear instead
Then the sun is up — see it shining.
Sleepy little eyes no longer afraid →

Hear all the morning noises — safe,
Oh, hungry. Let me out of bed.
Bathroom, open closet, open drawers —
Today I'll be a cowboy, maybe an Indian too —
Underwear, socks, plaid shirt and dungarees,
"Roy Rogers" kerchief, holster and gun,
Cowboy hat with tie under the chin.
Wait! Practice your draw in the mirror
"Take that you low down…!" Click, click.
Load the gun with a fresh roll of caps —
Now draw – Bang, bang, "Ow!"
"I'm OK partner, he just winged me in the shoulder.
Come on, let's mosey out to the kitchen for some grub.
Hi Mom, what's for breakfast?"
"Sit down dear and drink your juice"
"Where's Dad?"
"He went into work early."
"What's this? Oh no. — Give me rattlesnakes instead!"
"Sit back down and eat."
"Wheatina, yuck."
The cowpoke sinks into his chair.
His day is already a disaster.

(9/10/16)

You Are My Friend

Because you have whiskers
That does not make you Santa Claus.
Because you are popular
That does not mean you are loved.
Friends come in all shapes and sizes
And they are appreciated at different levels.
Friendships, like any relationship, must be worked at.

You are my friend at three or four
Because your square is next to mine
And you don't hit me.

Stuff

You are my friend at five or six or seven
Because you have great toys
And you let me play with them.
You also think the opposite sex is icky.

You are my friend at twelve or thirteen
Because we can talk about things →
And try and figure out what is going on
And the opposite sex is dumb but…

You are my friend at teendom
Because we share our discoveries.
We become brave and ask them out,
Then try to figure what is going on.

You are my friend in high school —
The world is slowly about more than us
And every once in a while we talk about it.
We also have found our true love forever and ever —
Or until next Saturday night.

You are my friend when we leave high school:
 Work or college we are separated,
We reunite for a summer or two,
And talk of our futures and listen.

You are my friend as a young adult
Knowing everything there is to know
And realizing there is so much more.

You are my friend as we begin our ladders.
They may be pointed in different directions,
But I'll hold yours steady and you'll hold mine.

You are my friend. When different families begin
We share news but remain in the background
Until the boat is steady and we can find the common ground.

You are my friend in dribs and drabs.
We were closer then but we are still friends —
Life and years take us to different circles
And yet we have enough to reminisce about.
We have enough to offer help if things get rocky. →

You are my friend as years pile on years.
We wish each other happiness once a year
Or we stay involved and close.

You are my friend when tragedy hits —
When all is wrong and life has gone.
You are my friend in all the different stages.
Sometimes I said the right things, sometimes the wrong,
Or worse perhaps, when I said nothing.
That can't be undone — perhaps a trace of guilt.

But you are my friend and you will be my friend
And I will remember you with laughter and corny jokes,
I will remember you happy and proud of family,
And I will remember you having me as your friend too.

(10/17/16)

Quiet Time of Night

Are we walking in the night
Filling out the days —
Keeping this time for our dreams
And resting from the world?

Wind rushing, looking for the leaves —
Stars climbing out of sight —
Smiles with the memories —
Footsteps in the moonlight —

Idle silence with sleep.
No one is here with us
And yet the faces
Are outlined in a cloud.

Chattering small talk
Our minds miles away —
We touch hands and
Our worlds awake —

The two of us walking
Steps light with laughter —
Eyes bright, faces alive —
We kiss and embrace.

This quiet time of night.
(Undated)

First Steps

"I'm up! I'm up!
Hey, anybody watching me?
That's better.
OK I'm up, now what do I do?
I was up the other day.
I liked the shiny thing on the table.
I tried to reach it.
But I tipped over, went bonk with my head on the table.
I needed those kisses and hugs.
So here I am, taller than the kitty cat.
What's the big deal?
What? Huh?
You want me to walk to daddy?
Walk? What's walk?
When I get down, I'll do my new snake crawl.
Neat huh?
Faster than before and my knees don't hurt.
Oh, you want me to move my feet.
Well OK, but I can crawl faster.
Yeah, I got your hands ma.
I'll let go of the table.
Wait, wait, wobbly knees, wobbly knees!
OK, I'm OK let go.
Well Mister, I'll give you my John Wayne 'Pilgrim' walk.
STEP, STEP – step, step, step step –
Catch me, catch me, I can't stop!
PLOP – Yeah, yeah big deal. →

That's not why I'm smiling.
Something besides my diaper cushioned that landing.
Wanna change me?
Then I'll do my, 'I'm a ballerina walk.'"

(3/11/11)

Tarnished

To live a good life —
A simple goal, universal.
Earn money, Fall in love,
Children to make you proud,
Years cluttered with laughter
And now, working done,
Ready to enjoy your goldens.

Then one morning you wake.
You stare at your bathroom mirror.
Something has slipped away.
Still, it couldn't have been important.
Time to start a brand-new day.
"Its Tuesday… grocery store time.
What was it I needed here?"

Time passes with little faults.
"We already have two of those,
Why did I buy another?
Another — what do you call it?
What's the name of that guy?
The one I was talking to?
He seemed to know all about me."

"My daughter stopped by today.
I'm very proud of her and…
She brought me a great lunch.
Why is it dark out?
Is it time for my program?
I never miss the guessing thing —
What's his name — and she spins the wheel.

Stuff

"Of course I ate breakfast.
I had a...cereal...juice...
What day is this? What...?
I've never liked a big breakfast.
Really? Are you sure? ... Well...
You haven't been by lately.
Oh that's right...that's a pretty...

"Why do they tell me these stories?
I don't remember any of them
Who are these people anyway?
I feel warm here. What...
What — I don't understand...
Um...no...um...
One...one...one."

These last lines are empty.
As he is helped through the day,
There is no meaning.
Finally, there is no dignity —
A piece of furniture
That must be moved daily
Kept quiet and settled.

If his life was a silver ball
Containing a lifetime of memories,
The ball slowly tarnished.
The past and the present have slipped to the floor.
Piece by piece he is stripped.
What is left is not even a child —
A shell alone in the world.

And all that attend him,
Loved ones and caregivers,
Fight a losing battle daily.
Pictures, names, hugs have lost their meaning.
They visit the empty eyes,
The stares looking past them,
Until one day they just close.

(9/30/13)

The Last Seat in the Last Car of the Train

I sat in the last seat in the last car of the train.
The 6:04 left on time, but seemed a slow traveler.
It was taking me away from you —
Through the tunnels to the remaining light.
Right away I saw the daylight moon
As it chased the sun toward the horizon.
After the 125th Street station I searched for the wisteria —
A lone shot of lavender brightening the ugly buildings,
Squeezing beauty out of hopelessness.
Now I could see all sides, all directions:
To the front the conversations,
To the rear the tracks, thinning to perspective,
Understanding the loss and committing
Memories of smiles and touches and adventures —
Saturday walks in the rain
Punctured by the fragrance of lilacs
And the beauty of all that surrounded us —
Fading blossoms of tulip and cherry.
The pending blossoms, the touch of your hand —
Watching the spring in concentration,
The quick smile, the quick kiss and move on.
Out the side window, the back of the world
Seen only by train riders, graffiti makers and time —
The back of neighborhoods, the glimpses of nature,
A voyager for a second's worth of life.
In an apartment, in a city, a lonely flower pot in a window —
Then gone to the back end of a cul-de-sac.
Urban, suburban, almost rural — repetitions, —
Saving memories of our time together.
Who gets off at the next stop?
The backs of little businesses,
The skeleton of industries gone by,
The house and dock on the river.
The miles pile on out the back window —
The time, the awful time until reunion —

The local of locals, — stop after stop.
Gone the voice, the smile, the touch.
Unpack the bag and start the wait.
The train pulls out, the noise has changed.
Early darkness frames the fading light
That surrounds the last seat in the last car.
Clickity-clack is replaced by emptiness.

(5/12/14)

The Night

The Sea Monster carried me through the night,
Gliding with little outward motion
It challenged the dark and endless ocean.
I traveled to sleep embracing my love
And guided by a moonlit path to the horizon.
We lay staring through the glass
Until we were released to dreams.
Around the time a swinging day ends
And an ambitious night pushes morning,
Our eyes were pried open by beauty.
Venus must have wanted us to see
The moon, now full, and directly in sight,
Her trail to us an open hand
Holding us in her palm till daylight.
A few mumbled words, another kiss,
And again we settled in, free.
We had nowhere to be and we had each other.

(9/26/14)

The Shortest Day

The tide pushed against the sunrise;
A warm horizon was defeated by a fast-moving sea.
When the sun finally came into view,
It was already at a summer noontime position
Except it barely climbed the sky.
Bright sunshine lit the day
But almost - winter's winds drove the warmth away.
Stepping out of my decorated cocoon
I pulled my jacket tight — moving quickly.
More time was spent securing the place,
Fastening down and covering over,
To offer some measure of protection.
The world was tying and bowing
Taping and mailing and last minuting.
Delivery trucks paced restlessly along the streets
And mailmen were bringing the greetings.
People were smiling and wishing —
Except the worriers and grinches.
Workers coming home; a human advent —
One less day to go.
While it is still light we have candy canes and inflations,
Wreathes and sleds, with decorations.
As the sun sets, I return inside.
The timers click and lights blink on with varied illuminations —
Each family's conception of the celebration.
Some put spotlights on Jesus' birth.
Manger, wise men, choir, and animals,
Surround the infant, Mary, and Joseph —
While others have icicles dripping and hanging.
A solar spotlight hits the snowman Master of Ceremonies.

With a wave of his twigs, "On with the show!" —
Lights on bushes and outlining houses —
Santa and reindeer prancing and flying over the roof,
Burst to life, from tried and true to this year's projections —
Simple statements to way overdone —
Steady to blinking to chasing lights brighten the night.
Inside children are restless and questioning.
Outside the moon and the stars compete for attention.
Clock hands spin and little ones yawn.
Finally, their parents win.
The eyes close with a bit of a struggle.
Outside, the timers shut off
And the solar batteries run low.
What's left is the natural beauty —
God's light from above.

(12/19/15)

Confusion Time

Autumn is here and that is confusion time —
Temperature racing up and down the thermometer
Dipping deeper and rising not quite as high.
The winds seem to have come home
And they are unpacking, opening their drawers,
Bullying the branches and ripping at the leaves.
Leaves seeming to be in a dither, go and let go,
Change into more colorful duds for the party,
Or stay green to make the winter Irish.
Children back to school, veterans now,
Have the routine down pat, both grinning and groaning.
The beginners start to look beyond one day.
Soon their lives will be guided by holidays —
Halloween, a chance for dress-up and candy.
At home, at school, "What will you be?"
"Witches, goblins, cider, Trick or Treat?"
Then, about a month later — not as much fun —
Pilgrims and Indians and families together,
Lots of food and Uncle Al asleep in the chair. →

Starting in October, now the build up —
Decorating from bushes to tree,
Shopping lists made and checked off.
Closer comes the singing, the wrapping,
Thinking about and caring about the baby Jesus,
Holding that moment, helping, loving, celebrating.
Then, enjoying and wishing, with tales from the past —
Giving and sharing, continuing traditions —
All reflected in the eyes of the children.

(10/2/15)

They All Tumble Out

Random rhymes to pass the time
Or words to serve a purpose —
Whiskey thoughts set for eternity —
Morning's natural revelations —
They all tumble out.

Risk of stuff sticky and sentimental,
Keen observations of my fellow man,
Whatever is stirred up or discovered,
It sits in my head for a while then
 They all tumble out.

A drop of rain poised on a rose
Or wandering down a window.
Brain alert, brain alert —
Get me to pen and paper before
My ideas all tumble out.

That little wetness is a sure sign
Of love or sadness or both —
Maybe a love lost and reflections —
Memories of all those dreams. Well
They all tumble out.

→

Stuff

We're at the circus, under a tent;
We are thrilled by all the acts.
Then, in the middle ring,
An ugah horn, a little car pulls up and the clowns
All tumble out and out.

The thoughts of a learning child
Fresh from some new discovery
Corners the parent — the friend.
He takes a deep breath and his observations
All come tumbling out.

The bell rings on the final day.
June is here and the brain shuts off.
Excitement of vacations dance about
And all the children squeeze toward the door
Soon they all tumble out.

The sly cat moves forward.
It slinks across the floor.
With ease, it springs to the counter.
It attacks, pushing over the open bag of treats
And they all tumble out.

Down the hill the toboggan races.
Cold winter air rushes past the passengers.
There is screaming and laughing
As the wooden carpet tips
And they all tumble out.

Words of love, sometimes in a jumble —
Expressions of sadness for someone's loss —
Explanations and excuses when caught red-handed —
Reasons and rationale all the same,
Until they burst and all tumble out.

(8/26/16)

"Snap – Snap"

"Snap — Snap"
The intensity of youth
Dressed in black,
Sitting in deep dark cellars
Void of wine.
"Snap — Snap, Snap — Snap"
Bongo drums and guitars,
Voices blended or quivering
Telling stories of love,
Often touched by tragedy.
"Snap – Snap, Snap – Snap"
Folk songs and fables
Build the unions, end the wars
Borrowed from the past
Or created for the day.
"Snap – Snap, Snap – Snap"
Bad coffee, berets and goatees,
Insights that aren't there,
Convictions carried up the stairs,
Smoke encircling the speaker.
"Snap – Snap, Snap – Snap"
Words reaching the crossover,
Working to enrich some
While tearing others apart
And slowly reaching morning.
"Snap – Snap, Snap – Snap"

(3/1/12)

Pets

Pets are things kids ask for
Not knowing the attached responsibility.
They are instantly loved —
A floppy-eared dog licking a boy's face,

Stuff

A puddle of purr in a little girl's hands.
Even the most hardened adult, Mr. Grumpy,
Will take on the tasks that the little ones forget —
Changing the litter, walking the dog —
Just blend into the daily routine.
The reward comes when the kids go to bed.
You are joined on the couch by a head with a cold wet nose hat,
After a circle or two, flops on your lap,
Or that little bundle of fur that scales the furniture
And ends up curled by your neck purring loudly.

I'm a dog and cat pet person.
I know there are fish, assorted birds, hamsters,
Gerbils, snakes, rabbits, frogs, turtles and baby chicks.
Maybe on a farm you add a horse, a cow, and a pig —
But many of those don't really interact.
Dogs and cats are immediately part of the family.
They chew on the stairs, shred the furniture,
Chase Frisbees and balls, fetch sticks,
Tangle themselves in yarn and make "puddies,"
And both dogs and cats like flashlight beams.
There are negatives; you have a schedule to keep —
Feeding them, caring for them, training them (?),
Finding a solution when you go away —
And you can't take them with you.

Life goes on; children grow, animals age.
I remember, with dogs, one year equals seven.
Big dogs live shorter lives than smaller ones.
Cats live longer, but slow down as they age.
Children grow and go off to life,
But rarely do the pets go with them.
The kids will start their own lives
And add pets if they want them.
What stays home is not forgotten
But somehow is a left-behind piece of fur —
Like a favorite doll or toy truck in the attic —
Something left behind that can be visited
But must remain as a security blanket —
A connection to the past. →

The pets are aging and the folks are too.
They age together in a wonderful routine —
Comfort for each other, as the kids are gone.
The walks are shorter and the naps are longer,
Both for the animal and the person.
It's harder to get on the couch, or get up after.
Still, the cold wet nose appears, "Here I am."
The cat nuzzles your head. "Here I am."
You pet the head and scratch under the chin.
The dog sighs, the cat purrs and you smile,
All caught in contentment and, maybe memories.

Years pass together and problems can arise.
The person, the pet, time, aging, sickness —
Doctors and vets help smooth the path;
They nurse you into the ending time.
Never a happy scene — finally — achingly —
Where is that nose? Where is that lap?
Remember running in the field —
Throwing the stick and the dog would fly
And bring it back to you, its friend.
Remember chasing the stick, grabbing it,
And bringing it back to your friend.

(3/11/14)

The Light

(Start Softly)
The light
Do you see the light?
The light shining down there
From the star
That so bright star
The light shining down
In the night
Moving light, leading light
Shining down there
Searching — no guiding —

Pulling shepherds from the field.
They hear a song on the wind
Through the hills
Soft singing
Angel's songs, calming them
As they sing to their sheep at night.
See the light – follow the light
Don't be afraid.
The King is born — go see him
Worship him — praise him.

The light
Do you see the light?
Moving across the night sky
Calling, calling those who seek him
Wise men — kings are coming —
(Build Slowly)
Follow the star
Follow the light
Do you see them?
Resting by day – following by night
They have heard – they have heard.
The chorus guides them
They follow the star
They follow the light throughout the night

The light
Do you see all the people?
Moving, moving through the town
Quietly moving, moving with the light
Drawn with hope
Believing, believing.
This is their hope
Their hope for freedom
There hope for love and understanding
Their hope for a future.
The road is lit into Bethlehem
The voices — hear the voices
Singing softly — carrying them
Pulling them through the streets.
See the boy there —
The little boy with the drum there
The boy who stands on the corner
On the corner all day banging his drum →

Hoping for coins, for food, for a smile.
Feel the pull as he falls into step
Falls into step — Following
(Keep Building)
The Light
Do you see the light?
Shining bright — Brighter now
Finally standing still
Standing still above them all
Above a manger — a barn in Bethlehem.
See the light, so close, so close
It blinds out all the night sky
Still the music calms the visitors
(Slower/Softer)
The kings and shepherds, even the drummer —
Everything comes to a stop
All are standing — watching

The light — the light
Do you see the light?
(Start Up)
Beams of light climb down
From the sky — the night sky
The light weaves its way down
Finding cracks and holes in the roof on the manger
Surrounding the building
And pushing through the roof — fragmented —
(Slower) Little pin spots of light break through
Do you see? Do you see?
Look there — look there —

The light on the mother's face
See the light soft on that youthful face
Mary's face — Mary's face
So calm and peaceful, gentle —
(Quick Build and Keep Going)
Looking down — Looking down
The light has found it
Her child — her child — God's child
His only son, lying there
Alive, swaddled from the cool night air.
Joseph stands calmly behind his wife
The light shows the way

The chorus of angels is close by now
(Faster)
From our hearts they sing now
They sing in celebration
God's son is born
Here among us
Do you see?
(Faster)
Do you see?

The light in the night surrounds us all
Our fears are gone for the moment
(Be Amazed)
There is hope tonight
There is peace tonight
There is love tonight
Mary knows – she understands
She and Joseph have made the journey
Now all these people have made the journey
And we here today have made the journey.
We have followed the light
Do you see it?
Do you see it?
Do you see the light?

(1/25/16)

Dreamin' Road

I'm headin' down the Dreamin' Road
Turnin' ribbons into bows.
Its all country roads and sailin',
Roundin' bends to different vistas —
Pastel cities made of cardboard dreams,
Fields and farmhouses and fences.

→

The road winds left and right
All smiles and laughs and sunlight.
Clouds crossin' in the blue
Sendin' signals to the raindrops —
The animal watchin' my every move
As I close my eyes on the Dreamin' Road.

Moonlight rolls out across the water
Soft noise walks through the night
Voices hushed in lazy tones
Magic melodies play in my head.
Words and faces wander by
Wishes are passed along the Dreamin' Road.

Naked women and dollar bills
Turn to gingham and flannel.
Seasons win out over days
Rivers smooth their stones.
Movin' easy tonight, it's all right
You're at the end of my Dreamin' Road.

(8/26/15)

Rust and Residue

That old car sittin' out back —
Can't hardly tell what make and model —
It's sportin' weeds and nighttime animals.
Why that thing is nothin' but rust and residue.

But I know that car from way back when.
I never knew her new. Still,
She was the sturdy family car
Before her parts stopped movin', that pile of rust and residue.

That old metal lady dates back before chrome,
Before fins and hundreds of horses.
She wasn't fancy — black, four doors —
Hard to find any paint under the rust and residue.

Stuff

This lady was born before WW II
Yet she was sweet sixteen when I met her —
I was still just a passenger
In this sensible heap of rust and residue.

But this lady taught me things —
From shifting, stopping on a hill, parallel parking...
Then it was the car to borrow,
Wheels at least, this bucket of rust and residue.

It contained my anger
When I was too old to be young,
Too young to be old,
Slam the door on all the rust and residue.

It made it to the drive-in,
Why it even went to a prom.
It parked in darkness, — patient,
Waiting to take someone home, good old rust and residue.

Nothing was completely clear in the front seat —
Skirts covered, but there were explorations.
Sadly in the back seat sat another couple
And the car never broke down, faithful rust and residue.

The summer before I went away
It became my first car
I was the third and last owner —
Twenty-two years, now just rust and residue.

Suddenly I could shift without the clutch
And things started to go wrong
And there was no money
To fix this car starting to look like rust and residue.

She's really not out back, except to me —
Long ago she was crushed or melted down.
Not very fast, but sturdy as a rock —
My freedom-giving piece of rust and residue.

(1/27/14)

Your Eyes Open

Your eyes open to the day,
The same day as yesterday.
The cell door opened years ago
And you were ushered in.

Concern on the doctor's face had been the key.
You and your family had been slapped in the face.
Without total understanding life pushed you in.
This is your life — accept it.

There is something wrong — something hard to explain.
Your child has ADD, MS, MD, Cystic Fibrosis or something else.
What will happen is presented.
The choice is accept it and make it your life —

There are explanations and causes are listed,
Some gene from distant family years ago.
   If not genetic, then certainly not like catching a cold —
Reactions twist as an autumn leaf
This way and that, ready to break free.
And so, what's to be?

For the sake of the child, I'm going to say there is a rock.
My thought is that the mom is the most trusted rock.
The fertility cry shifts to the mother's protection —
She learns what has to be done
And what is going to happen.

With luck dad is at her side,
Either sharing what needs to be done
Or expanding his role to allow the caring to continue.
Responsibility becomes the out front word.
In some cases things fail, the chain is broken.
Someone eventually cannot handle the 24/7.

The sibling must cope with his/her picture gathering dust on the mantle.
They can jump in by taking on adult responsibilities early,
To sharpen the protective skills needed with their peers.
Understanding as well as they're able and maturing quicker.
Still the years carry a heavier burden.

Mom is prouder of smaller things.
Dad realizes "the catch" will never come.
The brother or sister cannot tease.
Time pulls heavily on a family's life.
Friction on some days has no end
It is beyond understanding; it is there, always there.

The child really does understand, not just mimic.
The encumbered step is taken.
Things didn't fall back today.
With any disease or affliction "Hope" has many definitions.
Bluntly, there is <u>hope</u> for survival, <u>hope</u> for lessened pain,
The more simple <u>hope</u> for a decent day.

What was learned, how something was handled.
But it's everyday, every minute, how to handle the next emergency,
How to provide a quality of life,
How to face the wall, the fear, and the fatigue.
How far will they develop, what is their future?
What is the normal? HOW – WHAT – WHY?
Why, why, why! Oh, God — Why?
What did they do?
Each day they struggle, to find their normal —
To understand as best they can.

As they are helped into bed,
As they are made as comfortable as possible,
Their eyes look up and your reward is here.
"I love you Mommy."

(8/23/17)

This Page Is Empty

Hey! This page is empty!
It needs some words on it —
Something to break up the blank.
Pristine paper calls for description —
It calls for emotion, great observations. →

Characters must now come charging forward,
Castles and porches must appear
Drawn vividly for the reader —
Truths put forth, souls bared.
Gardens must show their beauty.
Heartless, dastardly black-hatted villains
Must force themselves upon us —
Their views must be aired
Then defeated by white-stallioned heroes.
 Cute little kids, like you were,
Must peek around the edges,
Work up their courage, and dance into view
Telling of childhoods and dreams.
Old folk must get comfortable.
They must scrunch up their pillows
And arrange themselves in their chairs.
From there they must take us away
On journeys real and mystical,
So well told, if perhaps too often,
That truth and fiction become blended.
There must be smiles on the page
And little bumps caused by teardrops.
The adventure must be exotic.
It must be what we recognize everyday —
Form and language don't matter —
Perhaps a few lines will fill the page.
Their wisdom is enough to fill our heads
Or, maybe we have so many thoughts
So many genuine ideas,
That we must move on

To Page Two

(11/19/13)

A Night Out

I sat at a back table in the small cabaret. It was a Friday night, after a hard week, and I was treating myself to a night on the town. The reason I was here sat at a beat-up baby grand. She was doing a final sound check before *Showtime*. To say things were informal would be an understatement. The club was the bottom step of the nightclub world. The next step down being a dive or a bar with a piano player.

I watched her with hesitation, years ago, when at the top of her game, this singer, this entertainer Madeline Rogers by name, had brought a night alive for my wife and me. She the complete entertainer; piano player, singer, joke teller, and storyteller. She took over a room and yet she refused to fit in.

There was no set list of songs; she matched the night to those in the room. She was not background entertainment, she demanded the spotlight, but she kept it low. She would talk to those near her and pull requests from those conversations.

Years had passed, my wife had passed, and I wondered if this woman shared my fear of getting old. When I saw her as the advertised entertainer, I was surprised she was still around and I hesitated, but then curiosity won out.

She was not introduced, a light was switched on and she began to play. Keys were firmly struck on the intro to a jazz standard and I picked up my drink and moved closer. As she played and then began to sing, she studied the audience.

Her voice was a little huskier and not quite as strong, but the feeling she gave to lyrics and the piano arrangement quickly reeled you into her circle. Her face was lined with age and nights and whatever was in the glass on the edge of the piano. The first song ended to polite applause, but she didn't stop playing.

Once in awhile she watched her fingers on the keyboard as if detached and wondering how they remembered what notes to play. The songs were independent, there was no theme and the tempos varied, some were touched with humor, and others brought people to a moving silence.

Couples moved closer to each other and the applause grew louder or was sometimes forgotten.

It was about a half-hour into the set when I looked up from my second drink and saw her looking at me, staring at me. There was a quick smile and then a shadow crossed her face. She quietly began the next tune and then the words began soft and building and my hand began to shake. I set the glass on the table and steadied it with my other hand.

Her voice, now full and strong, belying her years with emotion and strength. The words and music tore across the room and took my heart. Tears fell from my eyes; it was the song my wife and I had requested all those years ago. How could she know, how could she remember? I looked up, holding back sobs, she nodded to me, I felt her sympathy and then the warmth of the memory of the last time I had heard her sing.

(Sat around for months and finally finished on 8/25/17)

About the Author

Dave Gregory holds a BFA from Boston University's School of Fine and Applied Arts. (Its in the attic somewhere.)

He began writing in the 4th grade, though Miss Platt was never pleased with the quality of his penmanship.

He has written poetry and essays over the years, for his sanity and others' enjoyment. Published in several newspapers and poetry collections, he also had a poem published in a Christian publication that was distributed free in fourteen counties in Tennessee.

As for jobs, he has been, in no particular order, a light designer, built sets, acted, was a tour stage manager, assistant stage manager, production stage manager and a newspaper boy. He has also been an accounts receivable clerk, accounts payable clerk, and office manager, flipped hamburgers, managed the Bernhard Center (Fine Ats Center) at the University of Bridgeport, managed a hardware store, worked in a electrical supply store, sold fertilizer, flowers, bushes and Christmas trees (real and artificial), helped build mechanical indicators for airplanes and shutters for assorted uses, including one that is part of the Mars Rover.

Life changes in a few years. Father of two and grandfather of three, Dave now reads to daycare children through the Literacy Volunteers of SW Connecticut, works with the Milford Historical Society, and pulls an occasional weed

www.ingramcontent.com/pod-product-compliance
Lightning Source LLC
Chambersburg PA
CBHW051934290426
44110CB00015B/1970